Wills, Probate & Inheritance Tax

FOR

DUMMIES®

2ND EDITION

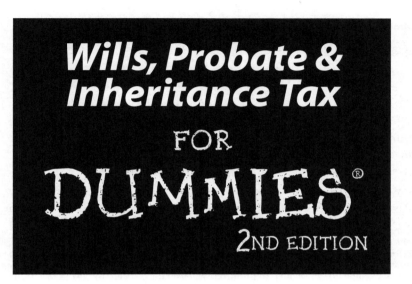

Wills, Probate & Inheritance Tax

FOR DUMMIES®

2ND EDITION

by Julian Knight

John Wiley & Sons, Ltd

Wills, Probate & Inheritance Tax For Dummies,® 2nd Edition

Published by
John Wiley & Sons, Ltd
The Atrium
Southern Gate
Chichester
West Sussex
PO19 8SQ
England

E-mail (for orders and customer service enquires): cs-books@wiley.co.uk

Visit our Home Page on www.wileyeurope.com

Copyright © 2008 John Wiley & Sons, Ltd, Chichester, West Sussex, England

Published by John Wiley & Sons, Ltd, Chichester, West Sussex

Wiley also publishes its books in a variety of electronic formats. Some content that appears in print may not be available in electronic books.

British Library Cataloguing in Publication Data: A catalogue record for this book is available from the British Library.

ISBN: 978-0-470-75629-4

Printed and bound in Great Britain by TJ International Ltd, Padstow, Cornwall

10 9 8 7 6 5 4 3 2

About the Author

Julian Knight was born in 1972 in Chester. He was educated at Chester Catholic High School and later Hull University, where he obtained a degree in history.

He is currently the Personal Finance Editor for the *Independent on Sunday*. He was the BBC News Personal Finance and Consumer Affairs Reporter for five years and wrote for the BBC News Web site. Before joining the BBC, Julian worked at *Moneywise* magazine and contributed to the *Guardian* as well as many other publications.

Julian Knight is the author of *Retiring Wealthy For Dummies*, *The British Citizenship Test For Dummies*, and *Cricket For Dummies*.

Dedication

To Val, my mother, for her love, support, and working so hard to give me the best.

And to Charlotte de Veras (1973-1999) for always being right.

Author's Acknowledgements

Great thanks to Francis Klonowski, one of the UK's leading financial planners, for all his help and advice on the inheritance tax passages of this book.

Publisher's Acknowledgements

We're proud of this book; please send us your comments through our Dummies online registration form located at www.dummies.com/register/.

Some of the people who helped bring this book to market include the following:

Acquisitions, Editorial, and Media Development

Project Editor: Rachael Chilvers

Commissioning Editor: Samantha Spickernell

Proofreader: Christine Lea

Publisher: Jason Dunne

Executive Project Editor: Daniel Mersey

Cover Photo: © Blend Images / Alamy

Cartoons: Ed McLachlan

Composition Services

Project Coordinator: Erin Smith

Layout and Graphics: Claudia Bell, Reuben W. Davis, Alissa D. Ellet, Melissa K. Jester, Stephanie D. Jumper, Christine Williams

Proofreader: David Faust

Indexer: Christine Karpeles

Contents at a Glance

Table of Contents

Introduction

We probably all know a story about wills and inheritance. From the recluse down the road who left millions so that Tiddles could enjoy the best cat food money can buy, to the 20-something glamour model who inherited a fortune when her octogenarian husband died of a heart attack but with a big smile on his face.

However, two-thirds of people haven't made a will yet and half of us never will. These people are missing out on a golden opportunity to look after their families and frustrate the tax-collector.

You've bought this book (and if you haven't, better hurry along to the checkout) and that means you're already thinking about putting a framework in place for your family's future for a time when you're no longer around.

About This Book

For Dummies books are all about giving you useful advice and information, in a light, easy-to-access format, and this book is no different. I go through the benefits of making a will, how to write your own will or get the help of a solicitor, and what tax-saving steps you can take to stop Her Majesty's Revenue & Customs (the snazzy new name for the Inland Revenue) indulging in a post-death tax grab. I include hints and tips on reducing your liability for inheritance tax, how to use trusts to help your family, and what to do if you want to pass on your family business. Just as importantly, this book helps you maintain your sense of humour as you jump those inheritance-planning hurdles before you.

Conventions Used in This Book

To help you navigate through this book, I've set up a few conventions:

- *Italic* is used for emphasis and to highlight new words or terms that are defined.
- **Boldfaced** text is used to indicate the action part of numbered steps.
- `Monofont` is used for Web addresses.

What You're Not to Read

I've written this book so that you can

1. Find information easily and

2. Easily understand what you find.

And although I'm sure you want to pore over every last word between the two yellow covers, I actually make it easy for you to identify 'skippable' material. This is the stuff that, although interesting and related to the topic at hand, isn't essential for you to know.

- ✔ **Text in sidebars.** The sidebars are the shaded boxes that are scattered through the book. They share observations and interesting snippets, but aren't necessary reading.

- ✔ **The stuff on the copyright page.** No kidding. There's nothing here of interest unless you are inexplicably enamoured by legal language and reprint information.

Foolish Assumptions

In this book, I make some general assumptions about who you are:

- ✔ You want to make plans so that your money and property is used to help your loved ones when you die but you don't know where to start. You probably have a vague idea about what you'd like to do, and have heard lots of stories and anecdotes about the strange laws governing wills. You feel a little intimidated by all the legal and accountant speak that surrounds wills and inheritance tax. Don't fear, this book is hell bent on busting the jargon and making things crystal clear.

- ✔ You want to copper-bottom your inheritance plans to reduce any tax liability and ensure that as much of your property as possible passes to your nearest and dearest but you don't want to be blinded by tax science. You want to know how to make the tax system work in your favour just for once!

- ✔ You want to know how to cope if someone close to you dies and you have to deal with their estate. From arranging a funeral to dealing with HM Revenue & Customs, the whole process is explained from top to bottom.

How This Book Is Organised

Wills, Probate & Inheritance Tax For Dummies, 2nd Edition is organised into five parts. The chapters within each part cover specific topic areas in more detail. So you can easily and quickly find the topic you need.

Part 1: Planning Your Will

The chapters in this part help you do the right preparation for making a will. This part helps you figure out your worth and what sort of professional help you need to set up for your inheritance strategy. I give handy hints and tips on how to prioritise the gifts you want to leave. I set out easy-to-use tactics to protect your family home from being sold from under your family's feet when you're gone. I also explain what happens if you adopt a 'sit on your hands' strategy and don't make a will.

Part 11: Writing Your Will

In this part I show you how to get your wishes down on paper. I look at the practical side of will-writing, including appointing executors, trustees, and guardians for your children, as well as how to make gifts to your loved ones through your will.

Making your will legal by signing it and getting it witnessed properly is essential – I steer you around the pitfalls. I also explain what life events should prompt you to review your will plans and change your will without running the risk of invalidating it.

Part 111: Managing Probate

This part takes you through the process of dealing with someone else's estate when they pass away. I take you step-by-step through all the people that you need to inform when someone close dies. The preliminaries of securing a death certificate, arranging a funeral, and following any donation requests are covered in depth. As for handling the financial affairs of the deceased – a process called *probate* – every angle is covered, from tracking down creditors, calculating and paying any tax due, and distributing the estate to the deceased's beneficiaries. If you find yourself in the sad position of losing someone close, this part shows you how to take the admin in your stride so that you can get on with the grieving process.

Part IV: Taxing Times: Inheritance Planning

More people than ever are being drawn into the inheritance tax net and you could be one of them. This part shows you how to secure your estate from a post-death tax grab. Remember, the earlier you start and the more thorough your tax plans, the greater the amount of money you can leave to your loved ones.

In this part I explain how inheritance works and how by doing relatively simple things you can reduce the tax bill on your estate. I also show you how you can use trusts to beat the tax-collector. I peek behind the myths and complex legal mumbo-jumbo of trusts and show you how you can use trusts to protect your home, property, and business.

Part V: The Part of Tens

Here, in a concise and lively set of condensed chapters, are tips on getting your estate into tax-saving shape, avoiding making mistakes in your will, ensuring that your beneficiaries really will benefit from your will, and the documents you need to keep with your will.

Icons Used In This Book

Scattered throughout the book are icons to guide you along your way and highlight some of the suggestions, solutions, and cautions to bear in mind when making your will.

Keep your sights on the target for important advice and critical insights into the best practices in writing your will.

Remember these important nuggets of information and you'll stand a better chance of achieving your aims.

This icon highlights the landmines that you need to steer clear of.

Beat the tax-collector by following the hints and guidance offered with this icon.

I sometimes go into more technical detail about a particular law or tax issue, so this icon prepares you for brain strain.

Where to Go From Here

This book is organised so that you can skip to wherever you want to go to find what you need. You don't have to read it from cover-to-cover. Want to know how to change a will? Head to Chapter 9. If you're interested in avoiding inheritance tax, go to Chapter 16. You can use the table of contents to find broad categories of information, or use the index to look up more specific things.

If you're not sure where you want to go, why not begin at the beginning?

Part I
Planning Your Will

'This is a fine time to remind me we haven't made a will.'

In this part . . .

Before putting pen to paper you have to put in the groundwork. First up you have to work out what your estate – everything you own – is worth. You then have to put together a clear picture in your own mind of who you want to inherit your pot of gold. As for your biggest asset – the family home – I show you the tactics you can use to make sure this passes intact to your loved ones when you die. If you want the reassurance of using a solicitor, accountant, or financial adviser to draw up your estate plans, check out this part because I show you how to spot duffers from the able and committed.

Whatever your will plans, you'll need the help of family and friends to make it happen. This part shows you what to look for in will executors, trustees, guardians, and witnesses.

If you're embarking on the estate planning journey and want to know how to prepare properly, this is the part for you.

Chapter 1

Preparing for the Inevitable

. . . .

In This Chapter

▶ Recognising the advantages of 'having a plan'

▶ Understanding the twin goals strategy

▶ Realising you have lots of people pulling for you

▶ Making sure you can adapt to changing circumstances

▶ Going for strategy launch

. . . .

*A*re you a wise owl or a head-burying ostrich when it comes to the dreaded d-word?

If you're an ostrich, you prefer not to think about the inevitable. Being an ostrich means trusting the fortunes of your loved ones to chance once you've gone, and having no control over what happens to your possessions and who should benefit from them. To an ostrich, death is five letters, one syllable, and a load of stigma.

If, however, you're a wise owl, you take the time to think, question, and act in order to write a will, and take tax-saving steps to protect your loved ones when you're gone.

I'm betting that as you've picked up this book you've had enough of the ostrich lifestyle and want to be a wise owl instead! So don't be squeamish – this book has lots of examples of things that can happen when you're no longer around, so grit your teeth and bear it! I'm going to be talking about your death – yes, yours – so no hiding behind the sofa; it's time to look the grim reaper squarely in the scythe and make proper plans for the inevitable.

In this chapter, I look at the basics of what should make up a bang-on strategy to protect your loved ones and frustrate the tax-collector.

Recognising the Advantages of Putting Your Estate in Order

A particular life event – a wedding, the birth of a child, or a health scare – can prompt you to start thinking about planning for the inevitable. Alternatively, you may just have a general feeling that it's time to stop putting off writing down your big plan.

Oddly, people spend days choosing everyday items such as cars, kitchens, or just the right colour scheme for the downstairs loo, but won't spend a few hours – and that's all it has to take – drawing up a will and getting their bits and pieces into tax-saving shape to save their loved ones a mountain of heartache.

Whether you're in your twenties and have just got your foot on the property ladder, or you're an octogenarian with a gaggle of grandchildren around you, making a will and tax planning have huge benefits. The benefits include:

- ✔ A will allows you to set out clearly who should get what from your *estate* (everything you own at the time of your death, from your home to your teapot).
- ✔ A will empowers you to appoint special people to deal with your estate and look after your loved ones when you've gone.
- ✔ A will enables you to give your property away in a tax-efficient way.
- ✔ Tax planning while alive can reduce inheritance tax when you die.

If your estate is worth more than £300,000 (2007/08 tax year) or £312,000 (2008/09 tax year) when you die, HM Revenue & Customs may impose an inheritance tax (IHT) charge (no, I don't know what the 'H' stands for either). Turn to Chapter 15 on ways around paying too much IHT.

If you do decide to make a will and have a spouse, ex-spouse, children, or other people who depend on you for their upkeep, you are required to look after them through your will. Failure to provide for these people could lead to your will being challenged in the courts. Chapter 4 has more.

Understanding what happens if you don't plan

Sorry to bring the tone down – this is a book about death and taxes, after all – but think about the situation if you were to die next week, tomorrow, or even right now! What state would your financial affairs be in? Most people would answer: A bit of a mess.

More than half the UK population dies without making a will, and an even higher percentage make no tax-saving plans during their lifetimes. The tax-collector loves these people because they leave their estates wide open for a tax grab. However, the family left behind is probably less pleased at the lack of forward planning.

What's more, the tax-collector doesn't hang around, but, in most cases, demands IHT before the deceased's assets can be sold. As a result, the deceased's nearest and dearest sometimes need to borrow money to pay the tax. Just a small planning step like buying a life insurance policy to cover any IHT bill can save loved ones a great deal of hassle and heartache at what is likely to be a very difficult time.

Making plans for the inevitable makes you, as Yogi Bear was fond of saying, 'smarter than the average bear'. Your plans may take the form of a full-blown will with lots of tax-saving steps built in, or you may simply decide to talk to those around you and sort out your paperwork, making it easier for those who have to cope when you're gone. The key is to do something!

If you die without making a will, you die *intestate*, which means your property is handed out to your nearest and dearest according to the strict laws of intestacy.

Intestacy laws are designed to ensure that the deceased's nearest relatives, the spouse in particular, receive the estate. These laws make a good backstop for most people, but by no means fit everyone's circumstances like a glove.

You'll find some sample wills at the back of this book that you can replicate when writing your own last will and testament. Now you have no excuses not to get cracking after you've read this book!

Although the tax system in all parts of the UK is nearly identical, Scotland has a very different legal system to England, Wales, and Northern Ireland. Laws governing making a will and the distribution of a deceased's assets can differ markedly in Scotland, particularly when someone dies intestate. Although I point out many of the differences, consult professional legal advice if you are in any doubt whatsoever.

Counting your pennies

Bet you're richer than you think you are! Although it may not feel like it when the credit card bill lands on the doormat with an ominous thud every month, most people are far wealthier than they realise.

Debts don't die with you!

When coming up with a figure for how much you're worth, don't forget to subtract any debts you have. Most people have some form of debt, often in the form of a mortgage. Your *creditors* (those you owe money to) have to be paid before any beneficiaries (those you want to give money to). Some people's debts outweigh their assets. If you find that you're in this position, consider taking out a life insurance policy to ensure that your nearest and dearest at least get something on your death.

Working out your debts and assets can be a lot more complex than simply sitting down and creating two columns on a sheet of paper. You may need to have your assets independently valued. As for debts, check out whether penalties exist if you were to die and the debt repaid early. Chapter 3 has more on valuing assets and debts.

For starters, more than two in three households are owner-occupied and a house is one big, big asset. Then look inside your four walls: Domestic appliances, TV, music centre, clothes, artwork, and, of course, a priceless copy of *Wills, Probate & Inheritance Tax For Dummies*. Insurers know from experience that people often underestimate their own worth.

Your home may only be the tip of the iceberg – don't forget your cars, cash held in savings accounts, shares, and pensions.

Also take into account that many employer pension schemes offer very generous 'death in service' benefits, and life insurance policy payouts can run into the hundreds of thousands of pounds!

To choose the right strategy for helping out your loved ones, you must first know what your estate is worth. Chapter 3 has more on working out your wealth.

How much you're worth in real money alters all the time, usually not by much but over time the changes can be quite major. Make monitoring your wealth an ongoing process, so you always have an idea of how much you have to give away to your loved ones.

You can use a will to achieve many different objectives or just one major goal, such as setting money aside for a child's university education. You'll probably find that as your knowledge grows during the reading of this book, you'll think of new and interesting ways to help your loved ones and beat HM Revenue & Customs (HMRC) at their own game. Go for it!

Plotting Your Estate Strategy

A good estate strategy – through a will or tax planning – means that your loved ones win on lots of fronts. Good strategies have two main objectives:

- ✔ Doing right by beneficiaries – being aware of the needs of loved ones and what you can do to help.
- ✔ Doing wrong by the tax-collector – taking steps during your life or through your will to ensure that HMRC gets as little as possible of your pot of gold. The less the tax authorities take, the more your loved ones get.

Essentially, having a strategy is all about two things: Protection and control of your estate.

Thinking about what your family needs

This is the central challenge of any will and estate strategy. Forget about saving tax for the moment and consider what each of your beneficiaries need now and in the future – and what you own that could help them.

Matching what's in your estate to your loved ones' needs is all about communication. As hard as it is to discuss your own demise, talk with your family about what will happen when you've gone and what help they may need.

The needs of your beneficiaries and your assets are unlikely to fit together perfectly. You need to appoint a good *executor* of your estate. Executors are the people you appoint in your will to make sure what you put down on paper makes it into reality by distributing your estate. Executors are usually close friends or family. Chapter 6 has the low-down on executors.

Knowing your enemy: The tax inspector

HM Revenue & Customs is a huge organisation with millions of pounds of funding, thousands of tax inspectors, and is lawyered up to the eyeballs. In a head-on fight, the odds are that you won't win!

But the tax inspector lives by rules and you can use these rules to shield your estate from a post-death tax grab.

The big inheritance tax trap

We Brits are far richer than we were a generation ago – we drive better cars, enjoy more exotic holidays, and, boy, can we shop. That's all very nice but a downside to being rich is inheritance tax.

Back in 1993 fewer than one in 25 estates were large enough to breach the IHT threshold (the magic figure above which IHT may be due), but experts estimate that this proportion has now risen to close to 1 in 12 estates. The main reason for this situation is a huge increase in the price of houses.

IHT, a tax that was once the scourge just of the rich, now has Mr and Mrs Normal in its sights!

At first glance, the rules aren't easy to understand – couched as they are in accountant and solicitor speak – but they boil down to a few simple winning moves you can make to cut tax. The chief ways you can save tax include:

- ✓ **Make gifts to a spouse.** Any assets or gifts passing between spouses are tax-free, regardless of whether the transfer is on death or during life.

- ✓ **Make limited but regular gifts to others.** You're allowed to give away some of your assets during life and on your deathbed, cutting the IHT bill in the process. See Chapter 15 for more.

- ✓ **Put assets into trust.** This is when you pluck an asset out of your estate and hand its control to a group of people called *trustees*, who look after it for a beneficiary. Under certain circumstances the asset in trust becomes free of IHT.

  Trusts have lots of other uses other than saving tax. Chapter 17 has more.

- ✓ **Own tax-exempt assets.** Some businesses, agriculture, and woodland come with very tasty tax breaks.

All these tax-saving strategies are covered in greater detail throughout this book.

The family home is likely to be your biggest asset and hence the tastiest morsel for the tax-collector. See Chapter 5 for more on special tactics you can adopt to protect your home from HMRC and other dangers.

Getting by with a little help from your friends (and family)

No one is an island. Your spouse, family, and friends can lend a helping hand with your big plans.

The main ways that your nearest and dearest can help include:

- ✔ Acting as executors or administrators of your estate
- ✔ Agreeing to be appointed guardians of your children
- ✔ Acting as trustees of any trust you set up
- ✔ Co-operating with your tax-saving steps such as gifting and putting assets into trust

When deciding which role a loved one should play in your estate planning, think hard about the skills they have. Some people are more suited to administrative work involved in being an executor or trustee; others have more experience of bringing up children. Talk to the friends and family you have in mind for particular tasks. Chapter 6 has more.

Calling in the pros

Professionals can help you when you're writing your will:

- ✔ Solicitors can answer most will-related and trust enquiries.
- ✔ Accountants are useful if you have very complex financial affairs. They can advise on saving tax today and in the future.
- ✔ Independent financial advisers can help you choose investments and savings that are tax efficient.

Professionals can also multitask – some independent financial advisers and accountants are very good on trusts, where some solicitors may be uncomfortable with complex trusts.

Question any professional you may employ about their expertise.

You can write a simple will with the help of this book. But use a professional when you're at the limits of your knowledge and to check over the plans you have in place. Circumstances when it's advisable to call on a professional include:

- ✔ Setting up a trust
- ✔ When the terms of a will are being challenged or a dispute between beneficiaries breaks out
- ✔ Setting up a joint, mutual, or mirror will (this is when two people – usually a married couple – legally tie their wills together; head to Chapter 2 for more on these types of will

---

Estate strategy: It's a time thing

Time is probably your biggest ally in estate strategy. Most people don't know when the grim reaper will come knocking, but generally the younger you start to make estate plans, the more effective they'll be.

For example, many tax-saving ploys require a gradual approach. Small financial moves made as life rolls by – such as making exempt gifts and transferring property to loved ones – can eventually lead to check-mating the tax-collector on death.

Agencies are springing up offering to write your will for you. Be aware that the legal background of the people who draw up the will may be negligible. Often these services are cheaper than using a solicitor – but in life you tend to get what you pay for!

Being adaptable

To be a true success in making sure that those closest to you are looked after when you're gone isn't just a matter of writing a will and leaving it gathering dust year in, year out. Life stands still for no one. Your circumstances change, as do those of the people around you.

Review your plans when any of the following circumstances occur:

- A beneficiary dies
- Your marital status changes
- Your financial circumstances alter substantially
- Someone enters your life who you want to make provision for – perhaps a grandchild or new partner

You can help prevent disruption to your plans by naming a substitute beneficiary who inherits the gift should the first beneficiary die.

Gearing Up for the Probate Challenge

Planning for the inevitable doesn't just mean putting in place a strategy for your own demise – it also means being prepared to cope with the death of someone close to you.

A loved one may name you as executor of their will, or, if they don't have a will, you may decide that you ought to act as their *estate administrator* (the person appointed by the courts when there is no will) on their death.

The process of dealing with someone else's estate is called *probate* or *administration* and the ins and outs of the process are examined in Part III.

Taking an estate through probate is no easy feat – even relatively simple estates can take months to wind up. If you act as an executor, be prepared to do some or all of the following:

- ✔ Obtain the death certificate and perhaps arrange the funeral.
- ✔ Calculate and pay any inheritance tax.
- ✔ Locate the deceased's assets and debts.
- ✔ Deal with financial and other institutions holding the deceased's assets, or to whom the deceased owed money.
- ✔ Sell the deceased's assets to pay bills, tax, or beneficiaries.
- ✔ Gather in the deceased's assets and distribute the estate to the beneficiaries.
- ✔ Go to a solicitor should you need legal advice on what you're doing.

The role of executor or administrator is not to be taken lightly. Make a mess of the job and you'll have to deal with dire consequences: The deceased's relatives can win legal damages from a negligent executor.

If you've been asked to act as executor, ask the person making the will where you'll find their will and other important documents in the event of their death.

Launching Your Strategy: The Checklist

Your best chance of making sure your loved ones are looked after and the tax-collector frustrated at every turn is to be systematic about your estate strategy. However small or large your fortune, or your estate strategy ambitions, you need to do the following:

1. **Decide on and be clear about your goals.** Think about what you want to achieve, who needs your help, and what scenarios you want your loved ones to avoid when you've gone.

2. **Work out what you have to offer.** What will you be worth to your loved ones? What financial problems and debts might you leave behind and how can you arrange for them to be solved on your death? Decide what your beneficiaries need to see them through life and, hopefully, ease the pain of your parting.

3. **Get advice when you need to.** If you have complex financial affairs, you may well need legal and financial advice. Even if you write your own will, you might want a solicitor to read it through for you.

4. **See your plans through.** *Thinking* about what you've got and what you want to achieve is all very well, but without making that will or drawing up that trust it's just one more brick in the road of good intentions. And we all know where that leads. Once you're kick-started into action, dot the i's and cross the t's.

5. **Keep an eye on your plans.** As a rule of thumb, review your will once a year. When you do review your plans, go through Steps 1 to 4 again.

Chapter 2

Recognising the Benefits of Making a Will

*T*he fact that you have picked up or, hopefully, purchased this book (build up those royalties please) means that you're thinking seriously about what you're going to leave behind. Whether you're Bill Gates or Albert Steptoe, there's always something for you to leave behind – even if it's just debts!

Your will is your big chance to make sure that your loved ones are looked after once you've gone. Through a properly drawn up will you can pass on your property to whoever you choose – with certain provisos. Even if you're not rich, your will can have a huge impact, even if you just leave an item to bring a smile to someone's face or jog a happy memory. Get your will right and you can ease the pain of your parting and help people to move on.

In this chapter, I look at what should prompt you to make a will, who can and who can't make a will, and what happens if you do nothing.

The Circle of Life: Events to Prompt You into Will-Writing

Life is eventful, and would be pretty dull if it wasn't. Many life-changing events prompt people into making a will, including the following:

✔ **Getting married.** When you get married or divorced this automatically impacts how your estate – all your property, money, and belongings – is distributed after your death. If you die without a will your spouse will inherit every penny – up to a set level. But you may not want your spouse to get absolutely everything, however lovey-dovey you are. For example, you may have an elderly parent or children from a previous marriage whom you want to support in the event of your death. Alternatively, you may want your spouse to be better provided for. The simple truth is, if you want to ensure that your wishes are followed, make a will.

✔ **Getting divorced.** If your marriage comes to an end and you die without a will, your ex-spouse usually has no right to any part of your estate. If you want your ex-spouse to get anything when you die, make a will and name them as a beneficiary. See Chapter 8 for more details.

✔ **Having children.** Dying without a will, or just leaving your money to your spouse, means that your little ones – or not-so-little ones – may go without. Your estate may be large enough to attract the interest of Her Majesty's Revenue & Customs (HMRC) – who impose inheritance tax at a whopping 40 per cent. Early transfers of property between parent and child reduce any eventual tax bill. For more details on how to sidestep inheritance tax, check out Chapter 16.

You can also use your will to give gifts to your grandchildren so that they inherit a family heirloom – or even a fat wad of cash.

Children younger than 18 can't inherit. The answer is to put what you would like them to have into trust. You can instruct the people running the trust to hand over the asset, such as shares or property, to the child when they reach a specific age. Chapters 17 and 18 cover using trusts to help your children.

✔ **Owning property.** You don't need me to tell you that buying your first home is a very expensive undertaking. Overnight, your financial affairs become many times more complex both for you and for whoever eventually sorts out your estate. A will can help make dealing with your home far easier and you might be able to do something with your home to benefit others. With house prices having more than doubled in the past five years, more people than ever own enough for their estates to incur inheritance tax (IHT). If your estate is worth more than £300,000 (2007/08 tax year) or £312,000 (2008/09 tax year) the taxman may cometh but you can avoid passing part of your inheritance on to him if you're clever with your will and financial planning. Go to Chapter 5 for more info.

✔ **Hitting the jackpot.** Wealth apparently doesn't bring automatic happiness, but wouldn't it be nice to check that theory out? A sudden injection of readies into your life through a bumper work bonus, prize win, or inheritance means that you can do more with your estate and, on the flipside, that the tax authorities may be able to get their claws in. Make a will to ensure your new-found wealth goes where you want it to go – assuming you don't blow it all in a weekend.

✔ **Counting crows' feet.** Becoming aware of your own mortality can either creep up on you or hit you all of a sudden. The death of someone close, experiencing serious illness, or reaching a major birthday can put everything into perspective. Realising you're not invulnerable and that the world will carry on when you're gone can prompt you into making a will.

✔ **Working on the edge.** People in high-risk occupations such as deep-sea divers, security specialists, and members of the armed services are wise to make a will. You're the best person to know whether your work is high-risk or not; an insurance company will tell you if you're unsure.

✔ **Feeling compassionate.** A family member or friend may fall on hard times. Naturally you'd like to help. You can help by breaking into your savings, selling shares, or even your home. Alternatively, you can make a will naming them as a beneficiary; if you're a fair bit older than the person then there's a good chance they'll benefit. You can also name a favourite charity in your will.

If you don't make a will you can't choose an executor to deal with your estate when you die. The burden of dealing with HMRC, creditors, and distributing your estate is likely to fall on your very nearest and dearest. If you want a particular person or group of people to tie up all the loose ends once you've gone, make a will and name executors.

Some people can make a claim from your estate if you don't leave them enough in your will. Individuals who can claim include your spouse, any children, anyone treated as a child of the deceased, a former spouse who has not remarried, a person being maintained by you (such as an infirm relative), or anyone you have been cohabiting with for two years prior to death. If any of these people make a claim, the courts decide whether they should get some or all of your estate.

If you die leaving money or an asset to someone who is bankrupt their creditors may grab it. If you want to gift an asset to someone who is in financial difficulties, think about putting it into a trust. See Chapters 17 and 18 for more on using trusts to help your loved ones.

Making a Will with Your Spouse

You share your life together so why not your will? For the sake of simplicity, and as long as you have similar goals and objectives, you can join forces with your spouse, partner, or same-sex partner and make your wills together.

There are three ways that you can do this:

✔ **Joint will.** This is a single document stating the wishes of two people. Joint wills are rare and can be very complex.

- ✔ **Mirror wills.** This is when two wills are made in identical terms, although these can be revoked at any time by the people making the will. These are the most common form of will written by a couple.

- ✔ **Mutual wills.** These are very similar to mirror wills, but each party agrees that the wills cannot be revoked at any time. Mutual wills can have complications and are therefore not common.

If you think that joining forces with someone close through a joint, mirror, or mutual will is a good idea, see a solicitor for advice.

Considering Who Can't Make a Will

If you're aged 18 or over and are in possession of all your mental faculties, you should be free to make your own will or sign one drawn up by a solicitor on your behalf. Here I cover those who are not allowed by law to make a will.

Checking the grey matter: Being of sound mind

Picture those will-reading scenes in period dramas – the sombre oak-panelled solicitor's office with a gaggle of relatives hanging on every word – and remember the will's opening gambit: 'I, Lord Farquar Dalrymple Bazelgette, being of sound mind hereby leave . . .'

But what does the phrase *being of sound mind* actually mean?

In simple terms, it is a declaration that the person making the will enjoys a sufficiently robust mental state to fully understand what they are doing through their will. The sound mind hurdle is designed to protect the person making the will – a vulnerable person can have undue pressure put on them by a dishonest person or avaricious relative.

Solicitors are duty-bound to turn away people who are clearly not of sound mind who wish to make a will. However, anyone can make their own will, but if the court decides that they were clearly not of sound mind when they drew it up, then it can be considered to carry no legal weight after their death. In such circumstances the law of intestacy (see 'Understanding the Consequences of Dying without a Will' later in this chapter) is invoked or a previous will may apply.

A person is deemed *not* to be of sound mind if they are an in-patient of a psychiatric hospital or have been declared criminally insane.

However, grey areas exist. Some wills may not be accepted by the courts. Possible problem areas include:

✔ People with degenerative brain conditions such as senile dementia, Alzheimer's disease, Creutzfeldt-Jakob Disease (CJD), or late-stage brain tumours.

✔ Wills drawn up for people with severe learning disabilities.

Seek the advice of your GP if you think that the will of a friend or relative, or even your own will, might be challenged on the grounds of mental capacity. This action can lead to the will being overturned in the courts. A GP can give a medical opinion on whether the prospective will-maker is of sound mind. However, a medical opinion isn't a get-out-of-jail-free card, as a court is able to disregard it if they wish and overturn the will anyway.

If you fail to jump the sound mind hurdle, then your previous will stands. If there is no previous will, then the estate is distributed according to the rules of intestacy, which are explained later in this chapter.

Unusual circumstances where the will is still valid

If someone suffers from one of the following conditions, their will is still valid:

✔ **Being illiterate.** Not being able to read or write isn't a bar to making a will. The law allows illiterates to dictate their will to a solicitor and then make their mark – usually a cross – at the bottom of the document.

✔ **Having a physical disability.** If someone has been paralysed and is unable to sign, they may still make a will. Likewise, blind people may make a will. The law allows blind people to appoint a person to sign their will on their behalf, but the signing must take place in their presence after the will is read to them and they have understood it.

✔ **Being eccentric.** You have probably heard of cases where a person spends their last years looking after a beloved pet, then leaves their fortune to fund its upkeep. If there are no near relatives, such a bequest should be fine. However, if there are close relatives they can challenge the will claiming they and not the pet should be provided for. The key point of their challenge is unlikely to be made on the grounds that the person making the will was mentally incapable, instead it will be made on the grounds that the relatives relied on the deceased for support.

✔ **Being terminally ill.** People diagnosed with a terminal illness no doubt suffer a great deal of stress and anxiety, but this fraught mental state does not bar them from making a will. After all, the person making the will doesn't have to be of sound body – just of sound mind.

✔ **Suffering from certain mental illnesses.** People suffering from a bout of a depressive illness or even schizophrenia, for which they are receiving medication, should be fine to make a will provided that the will is made during a lucid interval. Consult your GP for advice.

✔ **Being in prison.** Prisoners are allowed to make a will, unless sent to a secure psychiatric hospital by a court of law.

Minor inconvenience: Being too young to make a will

Your 18th birthday means that you're allowed – at long last – to legally drink in a pub. The birthday also marks the day when you can make a valid will. (But don't celebrate both at the same time.)

People in the armed services under the age of 18 and on active service are allowed to make a will. In the army and air force 'on active service' is defined as being in combat or on duty somewhere where there is terrorist activity. Taking part in a military exercise doesn't count as being on active service. Sailors under 18 have to be at sea to be allowed to make a will.

There is no upper-age limit for making a will, just as long as the person is clearly of *sound mind*.

In legal circles a man who makes a will is referred to as a *testator*. The female version of a will-maker is a *testratrix* – which sounds vaguely kinky to me!

The estate of a child who dies, including any assets held in trust, usually passes to the surviving parents under intestacy rules, which are explained below.

Understanding the Consequences of Dying without a Will

'Don't underestimate the value of doing nothing, of just going, listening to all the things you can hear, and not bothering.' Who said that? No, it wasn't the builders you paid to complete that extension in time for Christmas. It was that oh-so-lazy character Winnie-the-Pooh in conversation with Christopher Robin. Doing nothing can have its attractions in life, even when it comes to wills.

If you die having made a will, you're deemed to have died *testate*. To die without making a will is to die *intestate*. If you die intestate, your estate is distributed under the *law of intestacy*.

The law of intestacy is a serious business and there is no way around it for your family other than for them to unearth a valid will of yours and trump it. However, the law of intestacy is certainly not an ass: It places your nearest and dearest in a clear pecking order and distributes the goods to them accordingly.

You might find that the law of intestacy does a great job for you and your estate, and you don't need to make a will at all. Take a look at how your property will be divided up and see for yourself. Remember, though, if intestacy doesn't work for you then you need to make a will outlining your wishes.

The spouse gets it all (well, nearly!)

Your husband or wife is in pole position to benefit from your estate under intestacy. If you don't have any children or any other surviving relatives, then it's simple: Your spouse gets every penny – minus any administration costs. If you have a partner but are unmarried, they won't see a penny under intestacy. See 'Modern Life: Intestacy Isn't Geared Up for It!' later in the chapter for more details.

The order of priority in divvying up the estate goes like this:

1. **Your spouse.**

2. **Your children.**

3. **Your parents.**

4. **Your brothers and sisters.**

5. **Your half-brothers and half-sisters.**

6. **Your grandparents.**

7. **Your uncles and aunts (your parents' siblings).**

8. **Your uncles and aunts (your parents' half-siblings).**

9. **The Government.**

Where any of the relatives above die before you, their *issue* – this is legal speak for children or other descendants – automatically take their place in the order of priority. For example, if your adult child is dead, your grandchildren will inherit.

A kingdom for a spouse

Your spouse gets the lion's share of your estate if you die intestate. You can try and disinherit a spouse through a will, but that would leave it open to a likely successful legal challenge (see Chapter 8 for the ins and outs of will challenges). In order to inherit, your spouse must 'survive you' – that is, live – for 28 days after your death. Under the laws of intestacy, if your spouse dies within 28 days of your demise, your estate will be treated as if there was no spouse in the first place and passes on down the order of priority (see earlier in this chapter).

If you die without children but your parents are still living, then your spouse gets:

- ✔ All your personal items, often called *chattels*.
- ✔ The next £200,000 of the estate.
- ✔ Half of the remainder of the estate.

The other half of the residue goes to your parents. If your parents are dead, then your brothers and sisters inherit half the estate residue in equal shares, and so on down the line of priority.

As long as you own your home together – known as *joint tenancy* – then your spouse automatically inherits your share of the property. Legal eagles call this situation one of *beneficial joint tenants*.

But if the deceased spouse owned the property outright on a *sole tenancy* basis, then the home goes into the mix and is distributed according to the order of priority above.

If your estate is worth less than £200,000, and you die intestate, your spouse gets everything.

Don't forget that any gifts between spouses are free of inheritance tax (unless one spouse lives outside the UK).

Letting the kids in on the act

If your spouse is still living and you have children, then your estate is divided up as follows:

- ✔ Your spouse inherits all your personal items (chattels) and the first £125,000 of the estate. Your spouse also gets half of the remainder of the estate after the £125,000 has been deducted.

- ✔ Your children get the other half of the residue of the estate in equal shares and when your spouse dies they inherit the other half.

Living it up with life interest

From the half of the estate residue that your surviving spouse inherits, he or she receives a *life interest*. Their share is invested to produce an income, a maximum of 6 per cent a year, while at the same time keeping the capital intact.

The job of investing any money used to create a life interest for a spouse falls on the person administrating the deceased's estate (often called the *administrator* or *personal representative*). The administrator can employ a suitable professional such as an independent financial adviser to help choose the right investments. The administrator is likely to be your surviving spouse.

Here's an example: The case of husband and wife, Mark and Pauline, and grown-up son, Graham.

When Mark dies he is worth £400,000 after taxes, debts, and funeral expenses are paid. But Mark failed to make a will – boo, hiss! As a result his personal items (chattels) worth £25,000 and the first £125,000 of his estate go straight to Pauline. £250,000 is now left in Mark's estate. Of this £250,000, Graham inherits half (£125,000) immediately. The other half (£125,000) goes to Pauline on a life-interest basis.

Pauline's £125,000 is invested and used to produce a maximum income of 6 per cent a year – equivalent to £7,500 for Pauline – but the capital is left untouched. When Pauline dies ten years later, the £125,000 passes to Graham, who is free to spend it as he wishes!

Over the years, inflation will erode the value of the £125,000 that passed to Pauline on a life-interest basis. When Graham gets his hands on the £125,000 on Pauline's death it will buy a lot less than it would've done ten years earlier.

If your spouse dies before you and then you die, your estate goes to any surviving children. The children can get their hands on their inheritance when they are 18 or marry, whichever is soonest.

What is a child?

Easy, I hear you shout, a child is a little person who on arrival takes over your entire life. But for the purposes of intestacy the actual definition of what constitutes a child is a lot more complex.

A child can inherit if they fall into any of the following categories:

* They are from a current or former marriage.

* They have been legally adopted.

* They were born out of marriage.

* They were conceived but not yet born at the time of the father's death.

* They were conceived by artificial insemination or surrogacy.

However, stepchildren are not blood relatives and cannot inherit under intestacy.

No spouse, no children – if, if, and more ifs

You may notice a lot of ifs in this part of the chapter. Intestacy is full of ifs and if there is no spouse or children to leave your estate to, the ifs start multiplying.

If you die without any living children or a spouse, then the order of priority in dividing up the estate is as follows:

1. **Your parents.**

2. **Your brothers and sisters.**

3. **Your nieces and nephews.**

4. **Your half-brothers and half-sisters.**

5. **Your half-nephews and half-nieces (or their issue).**

6. **Your grandparents.**

7. **Your uncles and aunts (your parents' siblings).**

8. **Your uncles and aunts (your parents' half-siblings).**

If no relatives survive, the Crown – in other words, the Government – takes your estate, and spends it very wisely no doubt!

The Crown can claim your cash because it is deemed *ultimus haeres* – no, not the name of a hirsute wrestler. The phrase roughly translates into 'last or remaining relative'. Bet you never knew you were related to royalty!

Under intestacy rules, the spouse has to survive the deceased by 28 days to inherit their share of the estate.

Modern Life: Intestacy Isn't Geared Up for It!

The law of intestacy has developed over a long period of time and to some extent is a bit of a relic. There has been the odd nod made to modern living, such as including children born out of wedlock, but not nearly enough for many people's liking. The following are just some of 'modern life' circumstances to bear in mind if you haven't made a will yet:

- **Divorce.** A divorced person has no right to any part of the estate of a former spouse who has died following the granting of the decree absolute (that is, when the divorce is formally recognised by law). However, they can make a claim through the courts.

- **Separation.** If a Magistrates' Court Order rules that you're separated from your spouse, then your spouse still retains the right to inherit under intestacy. But if a separation order is granted as part of divorce proceedings, then your spouse loses his or her right to inherit.

- **Cohabitation.** If you're living with someone at the time of your death, that person doesn't get a bean through intestacy. However, a cohabiting partner can apply to a court to receive an income from the deceased's estate. Normally, they must have lived with the deceased for two years to stand a chance of receiving a penny.

- **Same-sex couples.** Up until recently same-sex couples haven't been recognised under intestacy. However, under the Civil Partnership Act, same-sex couples in the UK who've gone through a civil ceremony enjoy recognition under intestacy. In essence, same-sex civil partners have exactly the same rights under intestacy rules as married couples.

  Unmarried heterosexual couples are barred from benefiting under the Civil Partnership Act because the Government argues that they are always free to marry.

Pride and prejudice

Britain is recognised around the world as a liberal society. But same-sex couples still face prejudice. Gay rights groups report numerous cases of relatives of the deceased excluding same-sex partners from benefiting from the estate, keeping small items of sentimental value, or even from attending their loved one's funeral. Sadly, when money is at stake, niceties and common decency can fly out of the window. Even if your relatives are comfortable with your lifestyle, making a will that clearly outlines how your partner should be treated is a sensible step.

Ashes to ashes

You can use a letter attached to your will to indicate what you would like to happen to your remains. Just make sure that your loved ones and executors know that the letter exists so that they read it soon after your death and before

any possible funeral. If you made any prepaid funeral arrangements, make the details of this clear in the letter. This will save your loved ones a packet! See Chapter 10 for more details about prepaid funeral plans.

The order that your nearest and dearest inherit under intestacy is dictated by a sub-section of the Administration of Estates Act 1925 – no wonder it's not in tune with the way we live today!

There is something far worse than dying without a will and that is dying with one that's badly written. By badly written, I don't mean that the grammar's askew, although using proper English is important. The language used in a will needs to be precise and unambiguous: Avoid words like 'around', 'approximately', and 'about'. Be very specific about what you want people to inherit and who you're leaving stuff to. Otherwise family and friends may end up squabbling over who gets what. See Chapter 8 for more details.

Looking at the Different Rules in Scotland

The laws governing intestacy discussed so far apply to England and Wales only (the differences in Northern Ireland are infinitesimal). There are key differences in the laws governing intestacy in Scotland. If you're resident in Scotland, you need to take note.

Whichever set of intestacy laws apply to you depends on where you live rather than where you die.

The spouse does get it all!

Under Scottish law your spouse has *prior rights* to your estate. Prior rights mean that he or she has first call on your assets when you're dead.

The level of prior rights is often large enough for the spouse to end up with the entire estate. Only after the prior rights are satisfied do children get their share. If the value of the estate is larger than the prior rights, then the spouse has extra legal rights in the remaining estate.

The level of prior rights is set every five to seven years. At assessment time, the amount of prior rights normally goes up to keep pace with inflation. Law-makers in Scotland last adjusted the prior rights rules in 2006.

The spouse has prior rights on three distinct property areas:

- ✔ **Home.** The surviving spouse will inherit the house, farmhouse, or part of a shop up to a value of £300,000. If the family home is worth more than £300,000, the administrators or the court will almost certainly allow the spouse to remain in the home. See Chapter 5 for more on how to pass on the family home through a will.

- ✔ **Furnishings.** The spouse has the right to furniture and furnishings – known as _plenishings_ – up to a value of £24,000.

    Plenishings is a Scottish legal phrase to describe goods as diverse as linen, glass, books, pictures, televisions, washing machines, and other items of household use.

- ✔ **Moveable assets.** If the deceased spouse left children or grandchildren, the remaining spouse takes the first £42,000 of any money in bank accounts and shares. These are called _moveable assets_. If there are no children or grandchildren but there are other close relatives alive, such as parents, then the spouse can claim up to £75,000 worth of _moveable assets_.

Under Scottish law the spouse's rights don't stop there. If there are children or grandchildren, then the spouse has rights to one-third of the remaining moveable assets. If there are no children or grandchildren, but there are other relatives still alive, then the spouse scoops half the remaining moveable assets.

If there are no close relatives surviving – and the search stops by law at brothers and sisters and their descendants – then the spouse inherits the whole estate.

Even where you leave a valid will, in Scotland your surviving spouse or child can claim _legal rights_ to your estate. The surviving spouse is entitled to claim one-half of all moveable assets if there are no children, and one-third if there are children. However, by exercising any legal rights they forgo rights granted to them under the will. For example, if a woman leaves her husband £2,000, then the widower has the choice of accepting the £2,000 or taking one-third or one-half of the estate (the proportion depends on whether there are any children).

Letting the kids get a look in

If one of your children dies before you, then that child's share of your estate goes to any offspring they have produced – your grandchildren. The portion of your estate that would have gone to your child, if they were still alive, is shared equally between all the grandchildren. This prevents the surviving child inheriting all of the estate that doesn't go to the spouse.

For example, say that after a surviving spouse has been given his or her prior rights – and their share of the residual estate – £100,000 is left. The couple had two children, one of whom died before the deceased spouse but not before having produced two grandchildren. The first child will inherit £50,000, while the remaining £50,000 will be split equally between the two grandchildren.

Under the intestacy laws of Scotland, Northern Ireland, England, and Wales, your grandchild only has a right to a part of your estate if their parent – your son or daughter – dies before you. If you want your grandchildren to inherit anything, make a will.

In Scotland, if the deceased spouse had no children this share of the estate is still deemed to exist. Half of it goes to the parents of the deceased and the other half is shared out equally between the deceased's brothers and sisters.

Looking at who inherits when no spouse survives

If no spouse survives, or if the deceased was single, the estate goes to the nearest and dearest in the following order. Each group in the list only gets to inherit if the one above has died.

1. **Living children and the descendants of dead children.**

2. **Brothers and sisters (or their descendants) and the parents of the deceased get half each.**

3. **Aunts and uncles and their descendants.**

4. **Grandparents.**

5. **Great aunts and uncles and their descendants.**

If you die intestate in Scotland with no relatives, the Government scoops the lot.

You can leave your estate to be dealt with under the law of intestacy while making provision for your loved ones through a life insurance policy (see Chapter 3 for more details). Under this scenario, intestacy takes care of the basics. However, there is a drawback: The proceeds of any life insurance policy are included in your estate for inheritance tax purposes.

Planning to die intestate

What, draw up a document to say I don't want to draw up a will? Surely some misprint. This may seem like a strange idea, but bear with me. Drawing up a very simple document stating that you wish the law governing intestacy to deal with your estate is a wise move. Otherwise, family members may spend time hunting for a non-existent will. By making it plain you never made a will, you'll save them time and the heartache of rooting through your possessions.

Chapter 3

Totting Up the Value of Your Estate

*B*rits tend to keep shtum about their earnings, never mind what they're worth. It's long been frowned upon to mention the m-word in polite and not-so polite society. Mix that with a healthy fear of the grim reaper and, hey presto, no one wants to mention how much they might leave when they have passed on to the other side.

But when it comes to making plans for your loved ones when you're no longer around, you have to become a bit of a bean counter. Get your sums wrong or, just as bad, don't bother to do them in the first place and you can end up leaving too little for the upkeep of your family or leave your estate open to a smash-and-grab raid by the tax-collector.

In this chapter, I look at how to go about working out how much you're worth – from the roof over your head to the shirt on your back.

Your executors or administrators value your estate when you die and are legally bound to tell Her Majesty's Revenue & Customs (HMRC) your worth!

An Estate: Isn't That a Place in the Country?

Yes, that's one type of estate, but I'm not talking about the sort you shoot pheasants on – unless, of course, you're very well-to-do. Estate's a grand phrase but boil it down and it refers to everything you own minus whatever you owe.

You don't have to own the house or car outright for it to be considered part of your estate. Whatever fraction you own of something is given a value and included in your estate.

A great example of this is shares in a company. Say you possess 500 shares in British Petroleum (this is about 99.99999 per cent short of actually owning the company). Your tiny fraction of BP contributes to the value of your estate, as you own those shares.

You have, no doubt, at some time in the past gone through your possessions in order to give them a value for the purpose of getting a quote for home contents insurance. The final figure you came up with was probably a lot higher than you anticipated. And that's just the contents of your home! Widen that to include your bank accounts, bonds, shares, car, life insurance policies, pension pot, and your home and your original estimation when you pondered how much you're actually worth is likely to be way out.

Understanding Why You Need to Do the Sums

You need to do the sums on what your estate is worth for two very good reasons: You want your loved ones to inherit exactly what you expect to leave, and you don't want the tax authorities digging too deeply into your estate.

Leaving loved ones what they deserve

Friends, family, or perhaps even the cats' home are relying on you not to leave them in the lurch. You might think that because you left your spouse the family home they're sorted – after all, a roof overhead is a pretty fundamental human need. But you get no thanks if it turns out that the home you have left them is mortgaged up to the hilt. You may want to leave a favourite niece some shares in an Internet company you bought back in 1999 at the height of the dot.com boom – but she won't be too happy when she finds that they are worthless.

Do your financial homework by totting up your estate accurately and you should know precisely how much everyone inherits through your will. This chapter shows you how.

Avoiding the prowling tax-collector

Watch out, the tax-collector's about! Not content with collecting income tax from you when you're alive, HMRC also has its eyes on your estate once you're dead.

If your estate is worth more than £312,000 (2008/09 tax year), HMRC will take 40 per cent of anything over that magic number. If you have an estate worth £412,000, they will claim £40,000 – 40 per cent of the extra £100,000.

The number of people paying inheritance tax has skyrocketed in recent years as the rising value of people's homes has pushed more and more estates above the threshold. Your home is possibly rising in value and can act as a ticking tax time bomb for your beneficiaries. Work out what you're worth and see Chapters 13, 14, and 15 for strategies you can employ to reduce the tax liability on your estate.

The one saving grace is the fact that property left to a spouse is free of inheritance tax.

Dishing Out the Dosh with Aplomb

Armed with a reliable estimate of your true worth you can start to make plans for what to do with your dosh. You may want to sound your relatives out about what they want or need from you. Do they hope to inherit a particular item of great sentimental value? Be sensitive about broaching the subject of your demise; some relatives might feel very uncomfortable talking about this taboo subject.

Making a little stretch an awfully long way

After the totting up process you may discover that you're not worth that much. Don't panic! You don't need to get that second job to boost your estate. You can turbocharge your estate by adding life insurance and pension benefits to make sure you do what's right by your nearest and dearest. See Chapter 15 for more.

If your estate doesn't cover all your gifts, then *abatement* kicks in. Under abatement rules, if your gifts tot up to £500,000 but only £250,000 remains in the estate, then your beneficiaries can only pick up half of what you left them.

Calculating the Value of Your Assets

You can accumulate an amazing amount of stuff in one lifetime – cash, cars, property. Everything you own is counted as part of your estate. Once you've totted up the grand total of what you've got in the black, you need to look at the red, and subtract your debts.

Valuing your home

If you're a homeowner then it's a racing cert that your biggest single asset is your home. Putting the correct value on your home is absolutely key to working out the true value of your estate.

Lots of information is out there to help you work out the true value of your property – and all of it's free.

✔ Check out local newspapers for asking prices of similar properties.

✔ Search property Web sites such as `www.rightmove.co.uk`, `www.propertyfinder.co.uk`, and `www.assertahomes.com` for prices of similar homes in your area.

✔ Ask a couple of local estate agents to give you a valuation. You don't have to tell them that you have no intention of selling.

Don't waste money by asking a surveyor for a valuation. Surveyors can charge several hundred pounds for the service and you can find just as reliable information elsewhere for free.

How to leave your home in your will is covered in detail in Chapter 5.

Buy-to-let and holiday home investment properties can be valued in the same way as your main home. If possible, try to factor in the likely income earned from these investments when calculating what your estate may be worth to your beneficiaries in future. The income earned from a buy-to-let property is called a *rental yield*. Buy-to-let tycoons reckon that a rental yield of between 5 per cent and 10 per cent is usual, so if the property is worth £100,000, it should boost the estate by between £5,000 and £10,000 a year.

If you want to find out the price that homes in your area are actually selling for, check with the Land Registry – it records all sales by postcode area and property type. The Land Registry updates its records every quarter. You can check out the value of homes sold in your road by going to `www.landregisteronline.gov.uk`.

The value put on a property by an estate agent is just the asking price. But in the real world, the full asking price is rarely achieved and the seller settles for around 90–95 per cent of the amount. Knock about 5 per cent off the value of your home when figuring out what it will be worth to your beneficiaries. Remember to review this valuation every so often, as your home will probably increase in value.

The state of the housing market, the proximity of local schools, and the individual charm of a property all have a major impact on the price of a home.

Pricing pensions

As far as the tax-collector is concerned your pension is off limits. Great news! Your state and occupational pension and any *death-in-service* benefits (a lump sum paid to the beneficiary if you should die 'in the saddle') that come tacked on are not included in your estate for inheritance tax calculations. Phew.

However, it's still important to put a figure on your pension otherwise you won't get a full picture of what your loved ones will inherit.

Three main types of pension exist: State, private, and company pension.

State pensions

The pension based on your contributions made to the State Second Pension or its predecessor, the State Earnings Related Pension Scheme (SERPS), can be inherited by your spouse. This is particularly useful if your spouse hasn't worked for many years and as a result has not been paying National Insurance Contributions (NICs). (However, you can top up your NICs to receive a full pension – see www.hmrc.gov.uk/nic for more details.)

However, different rules apply according to your age, the age of your spouse, and whether you're a man or woman. The Government's Pension Service can tell you what proportion of your State Second Pension or SERPS your spouse can inherit. Call 0845 6060265 or go to www.thepensionservice.gov.uk.

When you die, the Government's Pension Service should contact your spouse to ask them to apply for a share of your state pension or State Second Pension or SERPS. Your spouse can't claim your pension until they reach retirement age. Remember, though, if you die unmarried, your state pension dies with you.

When you die, your spouse may be able to use your National Insurance Contribution (NIC) record to qualify for a full basic state pension. This can come in useful if your spouse doesn't have a full NICS contribution record of their own, perhaps because they spent a long time out of the workforce bringing up children or looking after a relative.

The State Second Pension replaced SERPS in April 2002. The differences between the two types of state pension are too boring for words, but the upshot is that they are both top-up state pensions, delivering a better state pension in old age than the standard state pension, which is currently £90.70 (2008/09 tax year).

You can find out how much your state pension is worth by writing to: The Retirement Pension Forecasting Team, Room TB001, Tyneview Park, Whitley Road, Newcastle upon Tyne, NE98 1BA. You can also get a forecast online at www.thepensionservice.gov.uk/statepensionforecast. The pension forecasting service is free.

If you live in Scotland and are deemed, under Scottish law, to be married by 'habit and repute' to the person you're living with, they can inherit your State Second Pension or SERPS.

Your spouse will not be allowed to inherit your state pension if they are not a UK taxpayer.

Private and company pensions

A *private pension* is one you start up and contribute to yourself. A *company pension*, sometimes called an *occupational pension*, is one that you and your employer pay money into.

If you sign up to a private or company pension, you'll probably be asked to state who you want to benefit from your pension when you die. Some private and occupational schemes promise to pay your spouse a pension if you die. Contact your private pension company (or, in the case of an occupational scheme, the trustees) to find out how much this pension would be.

Company schemes often come with *death-in-service* benefits. Usually these benefits involve the pension scheme promising to pay your nominated beneficiary – often, but not always, your spouse – a multiple of your annual salary if you die while employed by the firm sponsoring the scheme. Let your spouse know about these benefits.

These death-in-service benefits can be quite lucrative and are usually paid in the form of a lump sum. Best of all these benefits are considered outside your estate and HMRC won't touch 'em!

If you have a company pension, it's up to your executors, administrators, or spouse to let the pension scheme trustees know of your demise.

If you leave your job or are made redundant, you lose your death-in-service benefits.

The longer you have been paying into these schemes, the bigger the pension pot, and the more money your spouse will get.

Valuing your shares

Millions of Britons own shares. The vast majority of people only own a handful of shares in former publicly-owned companies such as BT, BP, or British Gas. If this applies to you, then it should be pretty easy for you to work out how much your total shareholding is worth. Most national newspapers list the share prices of the UK's biggest companies. Simply multiply the price printed in the paper by the number of shares you hold to calculate the total value of your shareholding. If you're not sure how many shares you own, contact the company in question and ask them.

A stockbroker charges about £15 for each share sale. So to get their hands on the dough, your beneficiary can end up paying quite a tidy sum.

If you caught the share ownership bug and bought into lots of companies, you still have plenty of painless ways of working out what your total holding is worth. Try one of the free share-tracking services offered by

- ✔ Internet service providers
- ✔ Financial Web sites such as www.MotleyFool.co.uk
- ✔ Computer programs such as Microsoft Money

You simply enter the name of the company (such as BP), and the number of shares you hold (say, 300) and these whizz-bang programs track their value. Access a tracking program every six months or so to check out what your shares are worth.

If you don't remember the name of every company that you own shares in – don't despair! You may still have the share certificates stored away in your advanced filing system – that shoebox on top of the wardrobe.

If you buy shares through a stockbroker, then it's likely that the shares are held in a *nominee account* (in the name of the stockbroking firm rather than your own name). Companies don't usually issue certificates to holders of nominee accounts. Your broker should have a record of your holding.

If you're at a complete loss, for an £18 fee the unclaimed assets register on www.uar.co.uk can help you track down lost shareholdings.

Studying your savings

Calculating how much of the 'readies' you have stashed away should be easy, as the banks and building societies send you statements.

If a bank or building society doesn't hear from you in three years (if you move house a lot and forget to notify them of your new address, or if they have had post returned to them marked 'not known at this address') the account is often made *dormant*. The money is still yours, but you must make contact with the bank or building society holding your cash and send them proof of who you are in order to get your hands on it.

Banking boffins estimate that *billions* are held in dormant accounts in the UK. The Government says that in 2009 it wants to use money in accounts that have seen no activity for 15 years removed and placed in a central pot to be used for good causes. This is a serious incentive for you to get your skates on and track down that long lost cash. However, don't panic, the Government also said that the rightful owners of the money being transferred into the central pot can come forward at anytime to be reunited with their cash.

If you can't remember where your account is held – what about that £500 your grandmother paid into that savings account in 1970 to put towards your first home? – then the Building Societies Association (www.bsa.org.uk), the British Bankers' Association (www.bba.org.uk), and National Savings and Investments (www.nationalsavings.co.uk) all offer a free dormant account tracing service.

Including your life insurance

Life insurance (sometimes referred to as *life assurance*) does exactly what it says on the tin. If you die while you have a life insurance policy in effect, the insurance company pays money to your beneficiary.

When you die, your executors, administrators, a close relative or spouse must send the life insurance company the death certificate to trigger any payout. (Chapter 11 has more on the death certificate.)

Life insurance pay-outs are part of your estate, unless written in trust (see below). Therefore, if you have life insurance set up to pay out a large sum or a regular income, expect your beneficiary to have to foot a tax bill. However, no inheritance tax is usually due if you leave your estate to your spouse.

Many different types of life insurance are available, but they all fill one or more of the following purposes:

- ✔ **Providing a lump sum.** This is the most common type of life insurance benefit. Put simply, if you die while insured your named beneficiary receives a tidy pot of cash meant to secure their future. The amount of money they receive is called the *sum assured*. The greater the sum assured, the higher the monthly insurance premium.

- ✔ **Replacing income.** This type of life insurance, often referred to as *family income benefit*, pays your beneficiary an income for life after you have gone. Again, the greater the sum assured, the higher the monthly insurance premium.

- ✔ **Paying off debts.** You may want to ensure that your family start with a clean slate financially once you're gone. Life insurance can be tied to particular debts (such as your mortgage) so that they are paid off in the event of your death.

- ✔ **Heading off the tax-collector.** Many people whose estates are large enough to attract inheritance tax often choose to take out life insurance. The idea is that the policy pays out enough to cover any tax bill that the beneficiaries face. The details of this strategy are explored in Chapter 14.

If you have life insurance, it's a good idea to have it *written in trust* so that the pay-out goes into trust rather than going straight to your beneficiaries. What's the good of that? Well, if your life insurance is written in trust the pay-out is not counted as part of your estate when it is assessed for inheritance tax. This is provided that the value of the pay-out is below the current threshold for inheritance tax (IHT), which is £312,000 in the 2008/09 tax year. If the policy pay-out is greater than the IHT threshold then a 6 per cent one-off tax charge is levied. Life insurance policies that were started before 22 March 2006 are exempt from this charge. The trustees holding the life insurance pay-out give the money to your named beneficiaries. Okay, your beneficiaries may have to wait a while for the insurance money, but it comes to them free of inheritance tax! Chapter 17 explains trusts in more detail.

Life insurers probably won't pay out if at any time you lie to them about your medical status, fail to pay premiums promptly, or commit suicide.

What on Earth Are Chattels? Looking at Moveable Possessions

Put simply, chattels are all your personal possessions. *Chattel* is a very old-fashioned word dating back to medieval times. Back in those days a typical peasant would list a couple of animals, a hair shirt, and half a turnip as their total chattels. Nowadays, the modern-day peasant (that's me and you) has oodles of chattels – CD and DVD players, Jimmy Choo shoes, sports equipment, and so on; the list goes on and on. Most of your chattels are probably only of value to you. After all, who wants to inherit your toothbrush? However, add up the value of your more expensive items, and you may be surprised at their total worth. What about that 1966 football World Cup final ticket or that signed first-edition Harry Potter book?

First you need to sort out your chattels from your chaff. Go from room to room with a pen and paper and note anything of any value. Pricing up electrical goods and furniture is easy: You may still have the receipts, or you can easily check for similar items in catalogues or shops. Remember to knock off a few quid for wear and tear.

Putting a value on unique items such as the World Cup final ticket and the first-edition Harry Potter is tougher. If you have a particularly rare collection or collectible item, you can, of course, have it valued by a professional. But there are less expensive ways of doing it yourself.

eBay is great source for finding out the value of an item. Simply type in a description of your item and Bob's your uncle: someone, somewhere in the eBay virtual universe will be selling something similar. If you use eBay to value a personal item only take the price achieved at the end of the auction. Often high bids for items don't come in until just before the auction closes.

List your chattels in a letter and keep it with your will. Refer to this letter in your will and let your executors have a copy of it.

Sometimes cash, jewellery, and cars are lumped together and called *moveable assets*. As the name suggests, these items are easier to dispose of (sell) than property.

Costing your cars

After buying your home, a car is usually the second biggest purchase you make. A new, or nearly new, car can be a very valuable gift to leave to someone in your will. However, cars lose their value very quickly, and as a result, that shiny motor that runs well and looks the part may not be worth all that much in real money terms.

Fortunately, it's very easy to find out the true worth of your car. Check out www.glass.co.uk or www.parkers.co.uk for an online valuation. Parkers and Glass also publish monthly guides outlining the precise value of every modern UK car.

If your car is a classic, then check out the owners' club Web site for an approximate value. There are owners' clubs for nearly every make and model of car, even the Austin Allegro!

If you plan to leave your new car to a relative, be aware that the value of that car is likely to fall sharply in just a few years. A car worth £15,000 this year can be worth only £5,000 two years hence. Review your car's value every couple of years to see if you need to re-jig the rest of your gifts to top up the car's cash worth to your beneficiary.

Putting a price on bling

The best way of valuing jewellery is to take it to a professional valuer. You may have had your jewellery valued for contents insurance and if it's a recent valuation you can use that.

More than any other possession, jewellery is more than just a price tag. Many people feel that their jewellery is part of them and their family history. You can't put a price on sentiment. That ring that has been passed down through your family for generations may not be worth much on the open market but to that special loved one it can simply be priceless.

The rule of thumb with bling is: If it's expensive, insure it and add its value to your final reckoning of your worth; if it's of sentimental value, then be specific about who you leave it to in your will.

Looking at art

Works of art lift the soul and help us to contemplate our place in the scheme of things. They can also be worth a big fat wad of cash! If you have any original paintings or limited edition prints literally hanging around, then try and find out their value. Works of art are included in your estate for inheritance tax purposes.

You may not have a Van Gogh above your mantelpiece, but if you have a few pieces by local artists your art can make a substantial contribution to your estate and make a tasty financial gift for a beneficiary.

The price you paid for a piece should be your guide if you bought it recently (unless you know you picked up a real bargain that's worth a lot more than what you paid for it!). If you want to value a piece you bought some time ago, then get a valuation from your local auction room. You can find them through the Yellow Pages or www.auctionguide.com. The Society of Fine Art Valuers and Auctioneers (SOFAA) Web site is at www.sofaa.org.

Art is notoriously difficult to value. Many pieces are sold at auction and it really can be pot luck if they achieve the value put on them by the auctioneers. As a general rule, art tends to increase in value at a slower rate than shares or property. What's more, tastes change: One year watercolours of idyllic pastoral scenes can be all the rage, the next some punter may be willing to part with £5,000 for a row of bricks!

Being generous can cut your tax bill. By making gifts from your estate to close relatives to mark special life events, such as a wedding, you can trim back your estate and reduce any eventual inheritance tax bill. Go on, you know your rare print of *The Scream* is the perfect gift for your in-laws' wedding anniversary. In Chapter 16, I look at some of the ways you can gift money to your loved ones tax-efficiently.

Honey, I Shrunk the Estate! Factoring in Time and Debt

Over time the property you plan to leave to your friends and family should grow in value. Shares, savings accounts, antiques, and your home should be worth more in ten or twenty years' time than today.

Most investment experts work on the assumption that an estate with a mix of all the above will grow in value by about 5 per cent a year. Such growth should help your estate keep pace with inflation, but it may move it worryingly close to the threshold above which inheritance tax is due.

The Government has raised the threshold in recent years but not by enough to keep pace with the amount people's estates are growing at – largely due to house price increases. As a result, more and more people are finding that they have to pay the tax. Head to Chapters 15 and 16 for more on reducing inheritance tax.

Keep an eye on your will to ensure it's up-to-date.

Some of your property, such as your car, electrical and household goods, is likely to reduce in value over time.

If you give away an asset, for inheritance tax purposes it is priced on the date the gift was made, not the date of death. See Chapter 16 for more on the tax due on gifts.

Not all your investments will perform well – in fact, some may turn out to be real stinkers! Check how each of your investments is doing at least once a year. Otherwise, you might find that one loved one inherits a runaway success while another gets the shares in that dot.com company that sank without trace. You may well want to change your will in order to distribute your property more fairly, if one of your investments bombs out. How to change your will is explained in Chapter 9.

Shrinking assets: Looking at what eats into your estate

In the perfect world you write your will, sit back, and watch the value of your estate grow over time. But life might bowl you a googly and you may suffer estate shrinkage.

Lots of things can happen to make you poorer. The most common include:

- ✔ **Losing your job.** If you can't work due to ill health or redundancy you are likely to have to dip into your savings to pay the household bills.

- ✔ **Being taken into a nursing home.** In England and Wales local authorities can ask you to sell some of your possessions to pay for the cost of any nursing home care they provide.

- ✔ **Being sued.** During recent times the incidents of one member of the public suing another has increased sharply, as people have used no-win no-fee law firms.

You can buy insurance to cover nursing home fees, periods of unemployment, and even costs associated with being sued. If you want to know more about these types of insurance, talk to an independent financial adviser.

The possibility of estate shrinkage is another good reason to review the contents of your will at least once a year. If you get poorer, you will have to reduce what you leave behind.

Subtracting your debts from your estate

Unfortunately, your debts don't die with you. Your creditors – the people or companies you owe money to – have the right to claim what is due them.

You must subtract your debts from your estate in order to come up with a final figure as to how much you're worth – a dead reckoning if you like!

Typical creditors include:

- Mortgage company – including the first mortgage and any subsequent re-mortgage, such as home equity release, you may have taken out.
- Credit cards.
- Personal loans.
- Overdrafts.
- Store cards.
- Student loans.

Creditors are never shy in sending you statements explaining in gory detail how much cash you owe them. Look through the statements to come up with a final figure of your debt. You never know, this can prove a wake-up call and prompt you to start paying off that store card you took out last Christmas.

If you want to pay off a loan or mortgage early you may have to pay *early redemption penalties*, or early repayment fees. Factor any such fees into your running debt total.

Don't forget to include friends and relatives who owe you money when you tot up your worth. This totting up doesn't mean Janice in the canteen to whom you lent a fiver last year but someone of whom you have documentary proof that you loaned them money, which they agreed to repay to your estate in the event of your death. If you don't have documentary proof of a loan, you're relying on the person who has borrowed the money coming forward after your death.

Many mortgage lenders insist that when you sign up to a mortgage you take out a linked life insurance policy that will pay off your debt with them if you die before the mortgage term is over.

The Grand Total: Your Net Worth

Once you have worked out the value of your home, shares, savings, pension, life insurance, jewellery, furniture, electrical goods, art, car, and other personal effects and everything else that is relevant it will probably be time for a good lie down, what with all those figures swimming around your head! After you have rested, list the value of each asset on a page of a notebook and on the opposite page list any money that is owed against that asset. If your house is valued at £180,000 but you owe the mortgage company £100,000, your house is worth £80,000 to your estate.

Tot everything up and you will come to a dead reckoning of what your estate is worth today. You now have a sound basis for deciding what to leave to your relatives and friends.

If you'd rather someone else did all the number crunching, you can pay an independent financial adviser or accountant to value your estate. However, you'll still have to do some of the legwork, such as digging out relevant paperwork.

Don't forget to factor in the costs of your funeral into the final calculation of your net worth. Funeral costs are taken out of your estate. Even a standard burial can cost several thousand pounds these days and is a major expense. See Chapter 10 for more details.

Chapter 4

Deciding Who Gets What

In This Chapter

▶ Assessing who gets what
▶ Looking at gifting to your family
▶ Avoiding gift failure

*I*n other chapters I cover totting up how much you're worth, the ins and outs of leaving your home through a will, and how to co-opt the right people into your grand designs.

But it's pointless knowing your executor from your testator or your credit from debit if you don't match up what you own to the right people.

I'm not just talking about a beneficiary getting slightly miffed that you didn't leave them that nice bone china dinner service they always admired. Make an error dishing out the dosh, and your loved ones can end up slugging it out over your property. Your will may even be declared invalid. And watch out for the tax-collector taking a whopping bite out of your estate.

Relax! In this chapter I show you how to make sure that your bequest fits your beneficiaries like a glove.

Who You Have to Include in Your Will

You can leave your estate to whomever you choose, but if you exclude your closest family they can apply to the courts to have your will changed or over-turned. The Inheritance (Provision for Family and Dependants) Act 1975 sets out that, wherever possible, your dependants should get enough to live on. So if you plan to leave everything to charity, unless you have the backing of your nearest and dearest, forget it!

Disputing your will in England and Wales

There are six groups of people who can apply to the courts for provision from your estate if you leave any of them out of your will:

- Your spouse.

- Your children (including adopted children; refer to Chapter 2 for what legally constitutes a child).

- Any person being maintained by you prior to your death, such as an infirm close relation.

- A former spouse who has not remarried.

- A partner who cohabited with you for a minimum of two years prior to your death.

- A person who, though not your child, was treated as a child by you or your family, a stepchild for example.

The court doesn't give equal weight to all of the people in these categories. If you don't leave enough for your spouse and children it's a racing certainty that the court will order that your estate be re-jigged with the aim of providing for them. But your spouse and children are very likely to be considered by the court to be more important than, say, a former spouse. Therefore, you don't have to share out your loot equally to head off any possible legal challenge.

Disputing your will in Scotland

Under the 1964 Succession (Scotland) Act (revised in 2006), in Scotland your surviving spouse or child can claim *legal rights* to your estate if you have not provided for them sufficiently in your will. The surviving spouse is entitled to claim one-half of all moveable assets (cash, jewellery, cars, and so on) if there are no children and one-third if there are children. However, by exercising any legal rights the surviving spouse or child forgo whatever has been granted to them in the will. For example, if a man leaves his wife £10,000, the widow has the choice of accepting the £10,000 or taking one-half of the estate if there are no children or one-third if there are.

If the spouse claims their legal rights, the remainder of the estate is distributed by the executors as closely as possible to the terms of the will.

Assessing What Everyone Should Have

If your goal is to look after your immediate family first and foremost, you need to consider what significant life challenges they may face when you have gone. Taking a 'what if' approach to your loved ones' finances will help you assess what you need to leave them in your will.

If you make a gift to someone in your will and subsequently sell it or dispose of it some other way, your unlucky beneficiary has no claim on it. This principle is known as *ademption* and your disappointed beneficiary won't be happy about it!

Taking care of your spouse

You probably have a pretty good idea of the financial situation of your spouse. However, it's still a good idea to discuss what they might need from your will. At the very least they are likely to want your share of the family home. You may want to leave them the whole kit and caboodle, which may be very appropriate if you have young children.

There are two ways to leave money to your spouse (or any other beneficiary) – through a lump sum or the setting up of a regular income.

✔ Leaving a **lump sum** (*capital*) gives your spouse immediate access to ready cash at a time when they need it most. You can leave a lump sum by naming your spouse as the beneficiary of a life insurance policy (refer to Chapter 3 for the tax implications of this) or you can leave them the contents of your savings accounts. Alternatively, you can simply state in your will that a percentage of your estate should pass to your spouse.

Sticking to the letter

You have the option of outlining some of your bequests in a letter attached to your will. Using a letter in this way keeps the will itself from being bogged down in a monotonous litany of who gets what. After all, does everyone present at the reading of your will have to hear who gets the cutlery?

The letter has the same legal weight as the will document itself.

Still, keep what happens to the really big stuff – your home, savings accounts, and highly personal items – in your will as they are probably of most concern to your loved ones. Just don't forget to refer to the letter in your will and make sure your executors have a copy of it.

✔ Leaving a **regular income** (*life interest*) for your spouse provides them with major reassurance. No matter what life now throws at your partner, the income you set up will provide a helping hand. You can set up a regular payment by simply leaving them an income-yielding investment such as a bond, or a fund that invests in a basket of company shares, or arrange for them to benefit from your pension. Alternatively, you can set some assets aside in trust (see Chapter 15).

Many people, provided they have assets large enough, choose to leave a lump sum *and* arrange for an income to be paid.

If you divorce your spouse, any gifts you leave them in your will are automatically cancelled. Under such a scenario the gifts given to a spouse go into the estate residue, which in turn may end up being distributed under intestacy. All in all, divorce can throw will plans into chaos, and if you take a trip to Splitsville you should seriously consider making a new will (see Chapter 9 for how to change your will).

Providing for your children

Children cost buckets of cash. They need feeding, clothing, and boy do they need entertaining! But apart from the day-to-day expense of bringing up your little treasures, you may also consider what extra cash they will need while growing up. Here are some likely areas of expenditure on them that you may want to consider including in your will:

✔ **Schooling.** Although the State provides free primary and secondary education to all, there are extra costs associated with schooling such as uniform, textbooks, home tuition, and after-school activities and trips. If you choose to have your child educated in a public school the costs can run into thousands, or even tens of thousands, of pounds per year.

✔ **Going to university.** This is a big area of concern as the cost of further education has rocketed and the old student grant – when the State paid people to drink, sorry, study – is no more. The average student now leaves university with an average debt of more than £15,000.

✔ **Buying a first home.** With house prices so high, clambering onto the property ladder is harder than ever. You may decide you would like to leave something in your will to help your child achieve their property ownership dream.

✔ **Getting married.** Seeing your child walk up the aisle is a red-letter day in any parent's life. It's no surprise, therefore, that people leave money in their will just in case they are no longer around to help with the often huge expense of the wedding day.

On one condition . . .

Sometimes gifts made to children through a will come with conditions. For example, a gift of cash can be made under the condition that it will be used for a wedding or university fees. However, conditions that are too restrictive and smack of the deceased trying to play God can be set aside by the court. What's more, the condition has to be enforceable. Who, for example, would be able to monitor if the three adult children of one Edith S of Walsall really didn't spend the £50,000 she left them on 'slow horses and fast women' as she specifically asked them not to. If you do add conditions to a gift, you should say what should happen if those conditions are not met. See Chapter 8 for more on how to make a gift conditional.

It may not be possible for you to set aside enough in your will to cover all eventualities. What's more, you may feel that there are certain things it would be good for them to provide off their own bat such as a deposit on a first home or further education.

If you want a child to use a gift for a specific purpose, such as paying university fees or funding a deposit on their first home, you may want to make the gift *conditional*. See the nearby sidebar and Chapter 8 for more on tacking conditions onto a gift.

If you make a gift in your will to a child, then the executor has to hold onto it in trust until the child turns 18. A child cannot inherit until he or she turns 18. This can be a bit of an administrative pain for the executor or trustee you appoint through your will, and there is always the possibility that the executor dies without their financial affairs being in order. The gift can conceivably be lost. The simplest way of dealing with this problem is to state in your will that if you die before the child has reached adulthood the gift should go to the child's parents with the proviso that they should hand it over to the child when the child becomes an adult.

Gifting to your grandchildren

For many, leaving something for the grandchildren to give them a head start in life is a big motivation for making a will. You must include your grandchildren in your will if you wish them to inherit, as they have no legal right to your money. If you leave your grandchildren out of your will they can't appeal to the courts for redress unless you were *maintaining* them (looking after them financially). Even through intestacy – the law that governs what happens when you die without a will – your grandchildren come way down the pecking order of beneficiaries, only inheriting if their parents are dead. There are a couple of other things you need to bear in mind when deciding how much or how little to give the grandchildren, as follows:

- ✓ **The amount you're leaving to their parents.** If you plan to leave a hefty inheritance to your children, you can, hopefully, rely on them to use it in the best interests of your grandchildren. In such circumstances you may wish to just leave a small sum to be paid when they reach a particular age or to help them buy a home or study. Make these terms clear when writing your will.

- ✓ **The age of your grandchildren.** If your grandchildren are grown up, then you probably have a good idea of what would benefit them in your will. However, if your grandchildren are minors, then they can't inherit property or cash directly, and you will have to leave the money in trust for them to access at a particular point in the future. See Chapters 15 and 16 for more details on trusts.

You can keep things simple by allowing your grandchildren to have access to the bequest on their 18th or 21st birthdays and they can then decide for themselves what to do with it.

When you put money in trust for your grandchild it is the trustees' job to invest the money until it's time for the beneficiary to inherit in their own right. Trustees are duty bound to invest the money prudently. Don't forget that your executors can double up as trustees.

Seeing your parents right

You may believe that your parents gave you everything. Hopefully they were responsible for giving you a good start in life, teaching you a moral framework to take out into the world and, when you were in trouble, who did you turn to? Although the natural scheme of things says that you outlive your parents, you may still want to include them in your will.

Born under the pound sign

A will allows you to leave something to someone not yet born. This tactic is often used by aspiring grandparents. The big advantage is that when the beneficiary is born you don't need to change the will. However, it is advisable to name someone else who should inherit just in case at the time of your death the unborn child still hasn't come along.

It may not be as easy to gauge the financial position of your parents as easily as you can your spouse's. Your parents may not feel comfortable talking about money with you. However, you can probably come up with a good guess as to what they are worth. Some factors to consider include:

- ✔ **Do they own their own home?** If your parents have lived in their house for a long time, the value has probably vastly increased, and the mortgage may be paid-off. In this case, you don't need to worry about leaving your parents without a roof over their heads.

- ✔ **Are they employed?** If your parents are still working, they are still earning. Hopefully, they have paid off the mortgage and the children have flown the nest. This time in a person's life, when they are still working but have reduced their responsibilities, is often a golden age for building up a pot of money. In short, they may not need your bequest.

- ✔ **Are they still married?** If your parents are no longer together, one parent may be poorer than the other. Bear in mind that women make up a disproportionately high percentage of the elderly poor. Your mother may have taken time off to bring you and your siblings up. As a result, she may not have paid enough National Insurance Contributions to be entitled to a full state pension. You might consider leaving more to your mother than your father, but explain to them in person or in a letter why you have done this.

If you leave money or property to an elderly relative and they end up needing local authority nursing home care, your bequest may be lost. In England and Wales the local authority (such as the town or city council) can force residents of their care homes to sell some of their assets to pay for the cost of care.

If your beneficiary's estate is over the threshold for inheritance tax (£312,000 in the 2008/09 tax year), he or she may not welcome an addition to their tax liability!

Including everyone: The catch-all approach

What about showing your feelings for that gaggle of not-so-near family?

You may only know them a little and may not be sure of their financial needs, but you might want to show that blood does indeed run thicker than water and leave them a little token. A good way to do this is to specify in your will a gift to more than one person, or group of people. For example, you may decide to leave £5,000 to be divided equally between all your surviving nieces and nephews.

Thanking those who carry out your wishes

There are a host of people who you can name in your will whose job is to ensure your wishes are carried out and your loved ones taken care of. The roles of these people are explored in Chapter 6, but you might wish to consider what to leave each one as a token of thanks.

✔ **Executors:** The executers of your will make sure your estate is distributed according to your wishes. Executors also deal with Her Majesty's Revenue & Customs (HMRC) and any creditors. It would be a nice gesture to leave them some small token for all their hard work.

✔ **Trustees:** These people administer and distribute any assets you choose to put in trust. In some cases trustees may have to look after money or property for many years. Being a trustee is a highly responsible and sometimes technical job and you may choose to leave them something in your will as a thank you. However, if the trustee is a professional (such as a solicitor or accountant), then their financial reward comes from the fees they charge. Often the same people act as both executors and trustees.

✔ **Guardians:** A guardian is the person you appoint to look after your children when you're gone. It is essential that you decide with them how much they will need from your estate to bring up your children. Leave money in trust for the child, instructing the trustees to use the money to help the guardians meet the cost of bringing up the child.

Even after you gift your home, cash, shares, items of furniture, and jewellery there may still be quite a bit left over. Instead of going into the minutiae of every golf club, handbag, and watch, you can simply use your will to gift someone the rest of your estate. What is left after all taxes and debts are paid and all specific items of property are doled out is referred to as your *residuary estate* or *estate residue*.

Solicitors refer to a gift of land as a *devise* and everything else as a *legacy*.

Gift Failure and How to Prevent It

A gift failing doesn't mean it hasn't pleased the recipient (not like those glow-in-the-dark socks you gave your father last Christmas). Instead, *gift failure* means that something has gone wrong to prevent the gift ending up in the hands of the intended beneficiary.

Gifts can fail for a number of reasons, for example:

✔ The beneficiary has died before you.

✔ The beneficiary or their spouse has acted as witness to the will and thereby lost any right to inherit.

> ✔ The gift fails as a result of divorce (see 'Taking care of your spouse' earlier in this chapter).
>
> ✔ The details of the beneficiary or gift were incomplete or incorrect.
>
> ✔ The charity you wanted to leave a gift to has ceased to exist.

If the gift was left to your child, and your child dies, the gift passes to their child (your grandchild). In other cases, a failed gift becomes part of the *residuary estate*. The residuary estate is what is left after all the beneficiaries have been paid. You may want to leave the residue of your estate to someone through your will otherwise what's left is distributed under *intestacy* (see Chapter 2 for a rundown of how this works).

The estate residue is often worth a lot of money. Think carefully about whom you want to leave your estate residue to. Most people leave the residue of their estate to the main beneficiary of their will, usually a spouse.

You can take some simple steps to stop your gifts from failing. For starters, be thorough about describing the gifts and whom you're leaving the gifts to. And whatever you do, don't get a beneficiary or the spouse of a beneficiary to witness your will signature because they then cannot inherit.

If a beneficiary dies before you, change your will and name a replacement beneficiary (see Chapter 9). Better still, name an alternative beneficiary in the original will. Naming an alternative beneficiary is a good way of ensuring that a particular asset of yours finds its way to a specific branch of your family. This measure also means you don't have to worry about changing your will every time one of your named beneficiaries dies.

Abatement: Spreading it thin

If there isn't enough money left in your estate to cover all your bequests, then it is up to your executor to apply the rules of *abatement* and reduce how much is paid to your beneficiaries. For example, if your bequests tot up to £300,000 but there is only £200,000 in the estate, then your beneficiaries will only pick up two-thirds of what you bequeathed them. This abatement process can play havoc with your best-laid plans. The only way to avoid this unforeseen event happening is to be thorough about estimating your total worth and realistic about how much you actually have to leave. In some cases, the beneficiaries are left with nothing because the deceased died with debts large enough to swallow up the whole estate. Refer to Chapter 3 for how to calculate your worth.

Don't just limit naming alternatives to your beneficiaries. Take the time to consider naming alternative executors, guardians, and trustees. All three groups have a huge role to play in securing your loved ones' future after you've gone (see Chapter 6 for more).

You can incorporate a *survivorship clause* into your will, naming an alternative beneficiary for your bequest if the first beneficiary doesn't survive for a set period of time after your death (usually 28 days). Check out Chapter 7 for how to go about wording a survivorship clause properly.

Playing the Philanthropist

After you have taken care of your nearest and dearest, you may want to leave something to charity. Hundreds of millions of pounds are left to charity each year and without this money many charities would struggle to exist.

Generally, all gifts made to charity through your will are free of inheritance tax.

Like companies, charities can fold or amalgamate with one another. If the charity you leave money to in your will ceases to exist your gift will fail. To avoid this failure, you can grant your executor the power to choose an alternative charity if needs be. That way the executor can make sure that the money finds its way to a similar charity to the one you chose originally. Add a clause to your will specifying this detail.

Specify the full name and address of the charity in your will, otherwise the gift may fail. For example, it is not enough to write 'I leave £5,000 for the prevention of heart disease'. Specify precisely which charity the cash is destined for: The British Heart Foundation, for example (with the full address of their main office).

It is a good idea to note the charity's registration number, which you can find on their Web site or stationery.

Looking after Rover, Tiger, and Smokey the rabbit

Think about what will happen to your beloved furry or feathered friend after you've gone. No, not batty Aunt Mabel with the moustache – I'm talking about your pet.

You can leave some money to a local animal sanctuary with a request that your pet is looked after for life.

Alternatively, you can instruct your executors in the will to find a suitable home for any pets, and you can set aside money to pay for their upkeep. However, with vets charging several hundred pounds for operations, you may need a tidy sum set aside to look after your four-legged friends. Just don't leave the money directly to Rover!

Gifting to Cut the Tax Bill

When deciding who gets what from your estate, bear in mind that you can give presents of cash or possessions while you're still alive. Giving gifts throughout your life – not through your will – not only makes you the generous one of the family, but also reduces your estate and any eventual inheritance tax liability. However, the tax authorities won't allow you to get away with simply giving away everything to your loved ones in your twilight years. In fact, any major gift of property or cash is still considered part of your estate for the purposes of calculating inheritance tax for seven years after it is made. (The rules on gifting and inheritance tax are explored in Chapter 14.)

Gifts you can make that are exempt of inheritance tax include:

- ✔ Gifts between spouses (as long as they both reside in the UK).
- ✔ Wedding gifts of £5,000 for each child, £2,500 for each grandchild, and £1,000 for anyone else.
- ✔ Gifts made to charities, some museums, and political parties.
- ✔ Small gifts of up to £250 in a single tax year to any number of individuals, just as long as an individual receiving a small gift doesn't also receive the £3,000 large gift too.
- ✔ Large gifts of up to a total of £3,000 in a single tax year. Any unused large gift exemption can be carried forward to the following tax year. If you haven't used your large gift exemption this tax year, you can give double (£6,000) next year. See Chapter 16 for more on gifting.

Disinheriting your not-so-loved ones

Disinheriting someone means to reject someone as your heir – it all sounds very dramatic! In effect, you disinherit someone by removing him or her from a will in which they were originally named as a beneficiary. However, there's no two ways about it, if you want to disinherit your nearest – although perhaps not dearest – relations, you probably won't be allowed to do so. The law takes a simple view: Your family are entitled to their piece of the pie.

If you really want to disinherit someone it is best to indicate in a letter addressed to the executors and the court explaining why you have taken such a drastic step. It will then be up to the court whether to overturn your decision.

See Chapter 9 for what can happen when you disinherit someone.

If you have taken full advantage of your gift exemptions, this may give you pause for thought when you consider who gets what in your will. After all, you may already have taken care of a child through a series of large gifts made over many years or a favourite niece through a £1,000 gift on her wedding day.

You can specify in your will that gifts are made *free-of-tax*. This means that any inheritance tax due on your estate is to be paid out of the residual estate. Leaving gifts free-of-tax means that the executors don't have to decide what to sell from the estate in order to meet any tax bill, they simply take it out of the residual estate. Non-residuary estate gifts are deemed to be free-of-tax unless the will indicates to the contrary.

You can make any amount of gifts from *income* (that is, not from your capital) for the upkeep of loved ones. As soon as you make gifts from income they disappear from your estate as far as HMRC is concerned.

Chapter 5

Leaving Your Home in Your Will

*H*ome is where the heart is. It's also where the bulk of your cash is tied up. According to the Halifax, the average home in Britain is around £200,000 – and that's a very tidy sum. Whoever you leave your home to is likely to be the biggest beneficiary in your will. Your home can be worth enough to secure your family's future for life. At the very least, you can leave your loved ones with a roof over their heads.

But leaving your home through a will is more than simply signing on the dotted line. You need to consider how differing types of ownership can impact your bequest. In this chapter, I look at everything you must consider when leaving your home through a will. I also show you tactics you can use to keep the family home from being sold to provide a tasty morsel for the tax authorities.

Giving the Mortgage Lender a Piece of the Pie

Your home is probably a source of pride. Being a homeowner is something special, whether you live in the grandest country mansion or the tiniest studio flat. However (and I'll whisper this very quietly), you probably aren't a bona fide homeowner. You almost certainly bought your home with a *mortgage* – a loan from a bank or building society. If you fail to keep up the repayments, the lender can repossess your home. The word 'repossess' gives the game away. You can't repossess something unless you have possessed it in the first place. Just to underline the point, many mortgage lenders insist on holding onto the title deeds of your home until you have repaid the loan – every last penny of it!

If you die still owing money on your house, the mortgage lender has first call on your home. Your mortgage lender won't demand the cash as soon as you die: They understand that it is a harrowing time for your family and are happy to let them sort out their affairs before they pay the outstanding debt. The executors or administrators of your estate will contact the mortgage lender to let them know what's happened and discuss when payment will be made.

If the property is owned on a *joint tenancy* basis, then the other tenant is liable for any outstanding mortgage. With *tenants in common* (see later in this chapter), the beneficiary is liable for any mortgage on the percentage of the property owned by the deceased. The beneficiary usually has two options: Either pay off the deceased's percentage of the mortgage, or apply to take out a new mortgage to cover the debt.

See the next section, 'Understanding How Ownership Affects Your Bequest', for more details.

Many people buy life insurance, which pays a set sum on death, so that the mortgage is paid off. The different types of life insurance are examined in Chapter 3.

The mortgage repayments *must* be met or else the lender can ask the courts for the right to repossess the property and sell it at auction to repay the outstanding balance on the mortgage. In some instances, a mortgage lender will allow a beneficiary to take on your mortgage. However, the mortgage lender checks the credit record of the beneficiary before allowing the mortgage to be transferred.

If you've taken out a second mortgage on your home, the amount borrowed has to be repaid on your death. But a second mortgage is deemed a *second charge* on your property, which means the second mortgage lender only gets their money after the main mortgage lender.

Understanding How Ownership Affects Your Bequest

You own your home so you can do what you want with it in your will, right? Wrong!

In this section I look at how different types of ownership affect who can and can't inherit your home when you're gone.

Sole tenancy

Ah, this is the easy one! You are the sole tenant, which means you personally own the house 100 per cent (not forgetting the mortgage lender, of course). But this situation doesn't mean you can leave your home to whomever you choose, not a bit of it!

If you choose not to leave your home to your spouse or children, they can ask the courts to overturn your bequest. Under the Inheritance (Provision for Family and Dependants) Act 1975, the court is likely to overturn your decision and allow them to inherit.

No direct equivalent to the Inheritance (Provision for Family and Dependents) Act 1975 exists in Scotland. Nevertheless, in Scotland, the spouse and children of the deceased are allowed to claim *temporary ailment* and *continuing ailment* from the estate (*ailment* is legal mumbo-jumbo for maintenance).

The Act may have been passed a long time ago but the idea behind it is still sound – it's designed to stop people that rely on you being left destitute or homeless as a result of the terms of your will.

As for live-in lovers, the executors or the court can still deem that they should be able to stay in your home after your death, if only for a short time while they find somewhere else to live. The court will make any such decision based on how much the person making the request to remain depended for financial support on the deceased.

If you live alone, are unmarried, and don't have children, as sole tenant you can leave your house to whomever you want.

With complex wills or a complicated estate it can take well over a year for the executor to sort everything out.

Beneficial joint tenancy

Beneficial joint tenancy means that you own the home jointly with someone else, usually a spouse or partner. When you die your share of the property automatically passes to the person who owns it with you. The surviving joint tenant becomes a sole tenant and they can dispose of the home as they wish.

Intestacy and beneficial joint tenancy

If you die without a valid will you die *intestate*. If you die intestate, strict laws governing the distribution of your estate kick in. The laws of intestacy are explained in full in Chapter 2. What happens when your home is held in beneficial joint tenancy and you die intestate? When two laws collide you only get one winner. In this case, the laws governing tenancy overrule those of intestacy.

If you die intestate, your share of the home passes to the other joint tenant and is not included in the rest of your estate that is subsequently dished out according to the laws of intestacy. This situation shouldn't matter a jot if your joint tenant is a close relative or spouse, the same person who would benefit under intestacy rules.

Joint tenancy is a painless way of leaving your home. Because joint tenancy rules take precedence, it means that you don't even have to include your home in your will. Having said that, it never hurts to make your wishes crystal clear and state that the beneficial joint tenant is to inherit. A good form of words to use is:

> *For the avoidance of doubt I give all my share and interest in the property known as (name of property) to (name of beneficial joint tenant).*

The surviving joint tenant has the legal authority to decide who can remain living in the house. If your spouse is the joint tenant and remarries, the new apple of his or her eye may become the new joint tenant. If your spouse dies, the person they have remarried takes possession of the home and can force your children to leave (if they're feeling really nasty). Such situations are more common than you may think!

The right of the surviving joint tenant is considered by law to be more important than any rights you grant a beneficiary in a will.

Joint tenancy arrangements don't offer protection for your children if your surviving spouse remarries. You may want to change the ownership basis to tenants in common and then leave your share of the property to your children. Read more about tenants in common later in this chapter.

Tenants in common

Being *tenants in common* means that you own property with one or more people upon terms that give each of you a share in it. Under this type of ownership each tenant is free to dispose of their share of the property as they see fit through their own will. If a tenant in common dies without a valid will the law of intestacy kicks in but is only applied to their share of the property. The share of one tenant in common never passes automatically on death to the other tenant or tenants in common.

Take the case of Gita and Massoud. They buy a house together worth £300,000. Gita stumps up £200,000 to fund the purchase, while Massoud scrimps together £100,000. Unless Gita is in a particularly generous mood, she will insist that as tenants in common she has a two-thirds share, leaving Massoud with the other third. If Gita then dies, her two-thirds share will pass to the named beneficiary in the will or, if there is no will, will be distributed under the laws of intestacy (refer to Chapter 2). This leaves Massoud in the position of owning the house with Gita's beneficiaries.

If you own property on a tenants in common basis, make crystal clear in a will who inherits your share. The normal options are:

- ✔ **Give your share to your surviving spouse.** If your spouse is the other tenant in common, on your death they become sole tenant (they own the family home outright), and can do with it what they want.

- ✔ **Give your share to your adult children.** If your spouse is the other tenant, your home will be owned jointly by your surviving spouse and grown-up children as tenants in common. Your spouse has the legal right to live in the property until their death.

- ✔ **Give your share to someone outside your family.** Some people choose to leave their share to charity, which is all very nice but if you plan to go down this route discuss it with your spouse and immediate family. Nasty surprises in wills can lead to legal challenges!

Dividing your property between your spouse and grown-up children can be a very smart tax play. Such a move can reduce the size of the taxable estate on the death of your surviving spouse, as half the house has already been passed to the adult children.

Looking at common property in Scotland

In Scotland a home can be owned as *common property*. Like tenants in common, each owner possesses a portion of the property and on death this is dealt with according to the terms of the will or intestacy. However, the title of the property may contain a *survivorship destination*. This means that the share of the first co-owner to die passes automatically to the surviving co-owner(s). It is not possible to change a survivorship destination except by rearranging the title, which requires the consent of all the co-owner(s). The deeds must be prepared by a solicitor. A survivorship destination normally prevents an individual from leaving his or her share of the property by will to anybody other than the co-owner(s).

Freehold or leasehold?

Property is owned on a freehold or leasehold basis. *Freehold* means you own your home lock, stock, and barrel (not forgetting the spectre of the mortgage lender), while *leasehold* means that someone else owns the land your property is built on (and often the property itself) and has agreed that you can live there for a set period of time – anything up to 999 years. Whether your house is leasehold or freehold can have a major impact on its value, but it doesn't affect your rights to leave the property in your will. If you own property on a leasehold basis your beneficiary can automatically assume the remainder of the lease.

Be realistic about the relationships your loved ones enjoy – or not – with one another. If your spouse and adult children do not get on, it's not a bright idea to write your will so that they own the family home as tenants in common.

To make life simple, you can change the terms of ownership of the property from *tenants in common* to *beneficial joint tenancy* so that your property automatically passes to your spouse. All parties must agree to this change and you need to alter the title deeds to the property. Remember, you might have to get the permission of any mortgage lender involved. After divorce, couples often go the opposite route and change from joint tenants to tenants in common. However, owning a property on a tenants in common basis is far more flexible from an inheritance tax avoidance point of view (see later in this chapter). If you're considering changing the terms of ownership, consult a solicitor.

Leaving Your Buy-to-Let Property in Your Will

More people than ever before have grown sweet on the idea of investing in bricks and mortar. For many, the combination of receiving rent for a property rising in value has been a no-brainer. If you're one of the army of private landlords, you need to consider how to dispose of your buy-to-let property through your will. Many of the factors are the same as with your main home. However, don't underestimate the differences:

  ✔ **Inheritance tax.** If you're a buy-to-let investor it's a racing certainty that your estate is large enough to put you over the threshold for inheritance tax. Don't forget that the tax liability is calculated on the market price of your property and not what you paid for it.

✔ **Mortgage.** If you own several properties it's likely you have several mortgages, too. Perhaps you took out more than one mortgage against the increased value of a buy-to-let property you bought many moons ago. Whatever the scenario, it's more complex than owning one property and means that instead of just one lender asking for cash when you die your executors and beneficiaries may have to cope with many.

✔ **Tenants.** Your contract with your tenant isn't void because you die. If your tenant signs a year-long rental agreement the day prior to your death, your tenant gets to stay put for the next 364 days under the conditions specified in the agreement. Your executors can't budge the tenant before the tenancy agreement expires, unless all parties agree to move or default on the terms of the agreement.

Buy-to-let property is not deemed a *principal private residence* (as your main home is). When your buy-to-let property is sold, the tax-collector asks for a share of the profits. This tax is called *Capital Gains Tax* (CGT). From April 2008 the rate of CGT on profit above £9,200 (2007/08 tax year) is 18 per cent, down from a whopping 40 per cent. The even better news is that CGT is not payable on assets transferred at death. See Chapter 15 for more on death and taxes.

The Other Side of the Fence: The Tenants' Story

If you're one of the millions of people who live in rental accommodation, the legal situation when you die differs depending upon whether you're a tenant of a private landlord, local authority, or housing association.

Regardless of whether you rent from a private landlord or local authority, if the property is now vacant, your executor should ask for any deposit to be returned so that it can be added to your estate.

Renting from a private landlord

If you rent from a private landlord, the circumstances when you die depend on whether you're a sole or joint tenant.

✔ **Sole tenancy.** When you die your tenancy agreement ceases. Your beneficiaries, even your spouse, do not have the right to live in the property after your death, unless they are a signature to the tenancy agreement and therefore a joint tenant. The landlord can ask that he or she is paid any outstanding rent from your estate when it goes through probate in exactly the same way as any other creditor. See Chapter 12 for more on probate.

✔ **Joint tenancy.** If you die while you're a joint tenant, the rental agreement still stands and the other tenant assumes sole responsibility for paying the rent until the end of the contract.

Renting from local authorities and housing associations

When renting from local authorities and housing associations, tenancy agreements differ depending upon whether you're a sole or joint tenant:

✔ **Sole tenants.** The agreement comes to an end unless there is a spouse, partner, or child living at the address. Often the local authority or housing association will agree to allow nearest and dearest to assume the tenancy. However, this right isn't something you can leave in your will as it is an option granted by the local authority or housing association at their discretion.

✔ **Joint tenant.** The agreement continues and the other tenant assumes sole responsibility for paying the rent.

Good deeds

A *deed of title* is the legal evidence of property ownership. If you have a mortgage, your lender may be holding onto your deeds but it's a good idea to retain a copy of them.

Keeping a copy of your deed of title with your will and a list of any debts, such as a mortgage secured on the property, makes life easier for the executors of your will.

If you sign over your deed of title to someone else the title becomes *defective* for several years at least. Most banks or building societies won't make a loan secured on the property while its title is defective. The lenders are protecting themselves just in case the courts rule that the signing over of the deed of title should be set aside.

Since 2003, the Land Registry has *dematerialised*. No, this doesn't mean it's vanished into the space-time continuum, Doctor Who style, it simply means the Registry no longer issues Land Certificates (the name for a deed of title) or Charge Certificates (which show the boundaries of a property and give details of covenants affecting it). Instead, the Land Registry relies on its computer records to keep track of who owns what.

Writing Your Home into Your Will

No set formula exists for how to write your home into your will. Just try to keep things simple for your executors – the people you appoint in your will to sort out your affairs after you've gone. See Chapter 6 for more on will-writing. If you need more detailed advice, consult a solicitor. Points to bear in mind include:

- ✔ **Make clear who gets what.** Avoid ambiguity at all costs. Don't leave your home to 'my sister' when you have two sisters. Be diligent about describing your beneficiary (put their full name and address, for example), otherwise a court fight can ensue.

- ✔ **Disclose any debts.** Alert your executors to any debts secured on your home. State clearly in your will that the home has debts secured on it, such as mortgage. Any debt secured on your home will have to be settled after your death. I look at the how's and what for's of writing up your will in Chapter 7.

When leaving your home in your will, best flag up that a mortgage or other loan is outstanding on it.

When writing your will, refer to your home as the family home or main residence rather than giving the address and an in-depth description. After all, if you move house you may have to change your will. Second homes, or buy-to-let properties, should be described in full, with the address specified.

Putting Your Faith in Trusts

A trust is a legal arrangement whereby one group of people – the *trustees* – are made legally responsible for property for the benefit of another group of people called the *beneficiaries*. You can write a trust into your own will or ask a solicitor to do it for you.

By putting your home into trust you pluck it from the rest of your estate and place it in the hands of the trustees. You rely on the trustees to follow what they see as best for the beneficiaries, or you can outline what you deem to be best under the terms of the trust. A trust can come into effect after your death or even when you're alive. This section deals solely with leaving your property in a trust. See Chapter 17 for more on trusts.

Your executors can double up as trustees; after all, both jobs require similar administrative skills as well as a hearty dose of common sense. See Chapter 6 for more on choosing the right trustee.

Less taxing times for couples

In the 2007 pre-Budget report the Chancellor announced that in future married couples and civil partners will be able to pool their inheritance tax nil-rate bands – the amount of money each can bequeath to someone other than a spouse or civil partner before it is liable to inheritance tax. What this means in practice is that married couples and civil partners can leave between them up to £600,000 (2007/08 tax year) at the time of the second death without it incurring an IHT bill. This new joint threshold is set to rise to £700,000 by the 2010/11 tax year.

You might put your home in trust for a variety of reasons, including:

- ✔ To prevent the property from being sold soon after your death.

- ✔ To ensure that the surviving spouse gets to live in the property and, on their death, an adult child or other beneficiary inherits.

- ✔ To provide a regular income for a specified beneficiary from renting out the property.

- ✔ To prevent a child from inheriting before they have reached a particular age, say 21.

- ✔ To reduce the likely inheritance tax bill on the death of the surviving spouse (see Chapter 15). A property can be *held* in trust for a set period of time or until a particular event takes place, such as the death of a surviving spouse

Putting your home into trust can make the trustees all-powerful. Under some types of trust, the trustees say what goes – not the beneficiary. Trustees have to act in the best interest of the beneficiaries but it doesn't follow that they always do what the beneficiary wants. The ins and outs of trustees are discussed in Chapter 6.

A question of trust

Theorising about leaving property in a trust is all very well, but here's an example to make things even clearer.

The no trust scenario

Nina is married to Amal and they live in a house worth £250,000 with their daughter, Jo. Nina sadly dies and Amal inherits the family home. Amal doesn't have to pay inheritance tax because he is Nina's spouse and exempt. After 15 years the value of the house shoots up to £1 million – lucky Amal. But then

Amal dies – not so lucky Amal – and leaves everything to his daughter, Jo. So Jo gets a home worth a cool million. But then the tax-collector comes knocking and demands 40 per cent of the estate over the joint married couple and civil partner inheritance tax threshold of £600,000 in the 2007/08 tax year.

Jo doesn't have that sort of money and the executor of the estate is forced to sell the family home in which Jo was brought up in order to pay the tax authorities. Jo then collects the now shrunken pot of gold.

The trust scenario

Nina leaves her half of the family home, worth £125,000, in trust. By doing this, Nina utilises her *nil-rate band* (the amount under which you don't have to pay tax), which means that she can leave property to someone other than her spouse up to the value of £312,000 (2008/09 tax year).

The trustees decide that Amal still gets to live in the home while he is alive and on his death Jo moves in. The home is valued at £1 million but half of it doesn't attract inheritance tax because it has never been in Amal's estate. This leaves a potential liability of £500,000. However, because of the recent law change allowing married couples and civil partners to pool their individual nil-rate bands, worth up to £600,000 in the 2007/08 tax year, Jo is free from having to pay IHT on the property. The type of trust that rode to Jo's rescue is a *discretionary trust*, which is explained more fully later in this chapter and also in Chapters 17 and 18.

If you set up a discretionary trust, you can appoint a beneficiary as a trustee. Discretionary trusts give ultimate power to the trustee, so by appointing a beneficiary you can make sure that they have a huge say in what happens to the asset in trust.

Helping the aged

Trusts are sometimes used to sidestep laws forcing people to sell their homes to pay for care in a local authority nursing home. In England people can only receive free local authority nursing home care if their assets are £21,500 or less. In Wales, the threshold is slightly higher at £22,000. This rule forces many people to sell the family home in their twilight years, reducing the size of their assets. By putting a home in trust it is possible to ring-fence it from any calculations the local authority makes about the value of the assets, because the property is considered to belong to someone else.

Putting your home in trust and then hobbling down to the local nursing home the next day is bound to arouse suspicion. This action is known in legal circles as *deliberate deprivation*. Local authorities and creditors can ask the court to overturn a trust in these circumstances. It's up to the court to judge whether deliberate deprivation has taken place. The Scottish executive recently introduced free personal and nursing care in homes for all adults over age 65, regardless of the size of their personal assets.

Looking closer at property trusts

Tax professionals seem in daily competition as to who can conjure up a particularly brilliant trust wheeze, ranging from the fiendishly complex to the very straightforward. But as far as putting your home in trust is concerned, you need only be concerned with three main types:

- ✔ **Discretionary trust.** Trustees of a discretionary trust have carte blanche to do what they like with the property; although they should follow your wishes they are not legally obliged to do so. This type of trust is very popular as it is flexible and gives the trustees freedom to arrange everything so that the tax collector benefits the least. This is the type of trust that Nina drew up to keep a roof over Amal's head and ensure Jo didn't receive a whopping tax bill.

Write a *letter of wishes* addressed to your trustees, outlining what you would like them to do with your money if you plan on setting up a discretionary trust. This letter is not legally binding, but at least the trustees will have your wishes in writing.

- ✔ **Accumulation and maintenance trust.** This kind of trust is primarily designed to ensure future financial provision for children or grandchildren. The property is managed to produce an income for the beneficiary, or to simply ensure it maintains or increases its value until the time when the beneficiary is allowed under the terms of the will to inherit (usually on reaching a certain age, no later than 25).

- ✔ **Interest in possession trust.** Under this type of trust a named beneficiary (usually a spouse, partner, parent, or sibling) is given the right to live in the family home for the rest of their life, but on their death the property is inherited by someone else. This type of trust does not save on IHT. See Chapters 17 and 18 for more on when to use this trust.

When generosity backfires

Simply giving away your home to children or relatives can increase your tax bill. If you remain living in the home you have given away you must prove to the tax authorities that you pay the correct market rent to the new 'owners'. What's more, the person you signed the property over to may have to pay IHT if you die within seven years of making the gift. Since April 2005, under what's called the *pre-owned assets* rules, people who continue to live in property that they have given away will be hit with an income tax bill. In short, HMRC is cracking down hard on these types of arrangements!

Check out Chapters 15 and 16 for how to protect your estate from inheritance tax pitfalls.

Part II
Writing Your Will

'Ah – my naughty grandson, Damien – If you
don't behave yourself today, Granny will
rewrite her will & not leave you anything'

In this part . . .

Make your will wishes reality! I outline a step-by-step guide to writing your own will, from appointing executors to getting the gifts down in black and white. Finally, I show you how to make your will legal and how to copperbottom it against potential legal challenges. What's more, I don't just cover simple will arrangements – A leaves everything to B – I also show you how to change your will to take account of life's changes and challenges.

Chapter 6

Choosing the Right People to Follow Your Wishes

---

*N*o one is an island and everyone needs a little help sometimes. This is never truer than when it comes to sorting out your estate after you've gone. The best-laid plans in your will can fall apart unless someone reliable is willing to follow your wishes. Picking the right people to carry out the terms of your will is as important as what goes into it in the first place. Choosing people who are on the ball will make life a lot easier for your nearest and dearest.

As you prepare your will you may need to consult a solicitor or an accountant unless your affairs are very simple – and your family may have to call in a professional for help with dealing out the dosh. Knowing when to call on the help of the professionals and ensuring you're getting the right deal is vital. Remember, forewarned is forearmed.

In this chapter, I explain the roles of everyone who makes sure your wishes make it off the page and into reality.

Considering the People Who Make Your Will Work

If you want a friend or family member to act as an executor, trustee, or guardian, make sure you're 100 per cent certain that they are up to the task. You must carefully consider if you're asking too much of them.

Talk the situation over with your nearest and dearest; be honest and upfront about what you're looking for, and stress to them that it's okay to say no. You can set out what you want from these people in writing (a job description, if you like). Even buy potential executors, trustees, and guardians a copy of *Wills, Probate & Inheritance Tax For Dummies* to read so that they know what they're letting themselves in for.

You must also make sure that you're not asking too much from any professionals – accountants and solicitors – you might employ. Yes, you pay them, but make sure that they are not advising you beyond their capabilities.

And, finally, if you decide to draw up your own will, are you asking too much of yourself? If you have complex tax and financial affairs, you might be biting off more than you can chew.

Any problems with your will are unlikely to come to light until after your death, and by then it's too late! Choose your helpers carefully.

The Big Cheese: The Executor

As the name suggests, an executor is the person whom you appoint to *execute*, or carry out, the terms of your will. The female version of executor is *executrix*, which sounds rather kinky, so for the sake of my blood pressure I stick to 'executor' in this book.

An *executor* is your representative after you die. Executors make sure all the loose ends are tied up – it's a position of considerable responsibility. In your will, your executor – a role often referred to in legal circles as *personal representative* – gets near to top billing! Executors, once they've been approved by the courts, track down all your assets and arrange for all outstanding debts and taxes to be paid. Then the executor distributes what's left of your loot according to the wishes expressed in your will.

If you did not make a valid will the court appoints a personal representative called an *administrator* for you. An administrator fulfils the same duties as an executor and, confusingly, is also sometimes referred to as the personal representative. See Chapter 12 for who can act as administrator of your estate.

Choosing an executor

When choosing an executor think organised, literate, numerate, trustworthy, good at handling money, and not afraid of a bit of hard work. As you read this, hopefully a name or two has popped into your head.

Anyone can be an executor but they have to be at least 18 years old, which is no bad thing. Would you really want Kevin the teenager sorting out your estate? In addition, they must be of *sound mind* (refer to Chapter 2 for the definition of being of sound mind).

Executors normally come from one of the following groups:

- ✔ **A beneficiary.** The executor can be a close family friend or member of the immediate family. This has the big plus that your friend or relative will want to do right by you when you've gone. But be wary of appointing the family black sheep as executor: Antagonism between the executor and the other beneficiaries can lead to delays and even legal challenges. Close family friends usually make good executors.

  Always ask the person you intend to name as your executor if they feel that they are capable of undertaking the job. A very complex estate – or one where the deceased has left an organisational mess – can take ages to execute from start to finish (although the estate should be distributed within a year). Overseeing that process is quite a lot to ask, even of a close friend or family member.

- ✔ **A professional adviser.** A solicitor or an accountant should have both the experience and knowledge to deal with your estate. Relatives and friends that you appoint may never have acted as an executor before but a professional has probably played the part hundreds of times before. However, professionals cost money – and sometimes lots of it. Some charge a fee while others will want a percentage of the estate.

- ✔ **A bank.** All high street banks offer an executor service. But as you can guess, they charge a pretty penny! Some high street banks levy a charge equivalent to 4 per cent of the value of the estate to act as executor.

- ✔ **The Public Trustee.** If you don't know anyone who can act as executor, you can appoint the Public Trustee to do the job. The Public Trustee is a Government body, set up under Act of Parliament, to deal with people's estates. They charge fees (the more work they do, the higher the fees), and cannot execute wills that involve them running a charitable trust or managing a business. Turn to the Cheat Sheet for the address and check out the Web site at www.officialsolicitor.gov.uk.

If you own your own business, try to appoint as executor someone who has experience of running a business of their own.

Appointing an older executor has the attraction that they are wise and experienced but if, fingers crossed, you live to a ripe old age, they might die before you. If the executors you appoint in your will are dead, then someone else – often a close relative of yours – steps into the breach to administer your estate.

Too many executors spoil the estate

Being an executor can be a lot of work. No surprise, then, that it is common practice to appoint more than one. You should trust your executors completely, but being trustworthy doesn't mean that they won't make mistakes. By appointing more than one executor you ensure that a second pair of eyes sees everything that is done in the name of your estate.

Often people choose to share the burden of executing their estate between a beneficiary and a professional, such as a solicitor. In theory, this choice offers the best of both worlds – the knowledge of the professional combined with the human touch of a friend or family member. If you plan on drawing up a simple will you may be best appointing just one executor, perhaps a close relative.

But remember, having too many executors can lead to delays in administrating your estate and can push up costs. You should appoint no more than four executors.

An executor cannot be sacked, even if the beneficiaries and other executors want them out. Only a court can order an executor to step aside, and that only ever happens if they are deemed guilty of misconduct.

If one of the executors *renounces* (states that he or she does not want or is unable to fulfil the duties of an executor, before they start acting as executor), the alternative or substitute named in the will automatically takes their place. If none of the executors named in the will wants the job, then the catchily named 'Non Contentious Probate Rule 20' kicks in. Under this rule, any trustee appointed in the will takes over executor duties. If the trustee refuses, then it's left up to the beneficiaries to distribute the estate. If your executor (or trustee or guardian) refuses to act, they automatically forgo any payment you set aside for them as a thank you in your will.

Your executor can claim their expenses from your estate, such as photocopying costs, buying stamps, and stationery. In addition, many people choose to leave their executor a small gift in their will, a thank you for all their hard work. Of course, if your executor is a substantial beneficiary or a professional receiving a fee, you may well think that they have already had enough of your loot.

A Matter of Faith: Trustees

Trustees run any trusts set up by your will. A *trust* is a legal device whereby a trustee is legally responsible for looking after property for a beneficiary. Property isn't just bricks and mortar – it means any type of asset, such as cash or shares. A trustee can also be a beneficiary. If you don't plan to set up a trust in your will, you won't need to name trustees. You have my full permission to skip this section!

Trusts are most commonly used to leave property to a minor (someone under 18). Trusts are explained in much greater detail in Chapter 17.

Being a trustee can be a long drawn-out process. If, for example, the minor you left property to is only a few months' old when you die, then the trustees have to look after the property for them for the best part of 18 years. In cases where a trust is set up to provide an income for the whole of the life of a beneficiary (for example, a trust set up to provide for a spouse who keeps going strong for years and years), it can end up running for decades. Often with long-running trusts the trustees retire and are replaced by someone happy to step into the void. The replacement or retirement of a trustee may require the permission of the trustees, the courts, or the trust beneficiaries.

Trustees are usually family friends, solicitors, or siblings. Choose a trustee who has all the qualities of an executor but who is also prepared to be in it for the long haul. You can use the same people as executors *and* trustees.

Trustees can be relieved of their duties by the beneficiaries, provided they are all in agreement. Furthermore, if one of your trustees refuses to act, or dies, existing trustees have the power to appoint a replacement.

Key duties of trustees

Any trustee you appoint has a duty to treat all of your beneficiaries fairly. Trustees are obliged to

- ✔ Act unanimously if there is more than one trustee.
- ✔ Ensure 'reasonable care' is taken of the assets in the trust; for example, a house in trust should be properly insured.
- ✔ Not make a profit from the trust. Nor are trustees allowed to charge for their services, unless the charges are specified in the will. Trustees, like executors, can claim their expenses, though.
- ✔ Be prepared to provide accounts if beneficiaries of the trust ask.

Protecting Your Children: Guardians

Guardians are people you appoint to look after your children in the event of your death. Your surviving spouse automatically assumes sole guardianship of your children. But you need to think of someone else to appoint as guardian if your spouse dies before you or in the nightmare scenario that you and your spouse die together.

You may have close relatives – grandparents or a brother or sister – willing to look after your children when you're gone. The courts may grant your close relatives guardianship without a hitch, but you can make their case more watertight if you name them as guardians in a will.

You can name more than one guardian or set of guardians. This provision is very useful if you want one set of relatives to look after your children during their early years and someone else to take over as they become teenagers, perhaps someone younger. You can also appoint a separate guardian for each of your children. If, for example, one child is close to one set of grandparents, while another child favours the other grandparents, you can split them up.

Eighteen is the cut-off point for a child needing a guardian, as they are considered an adult instead.

Key questions to consider when choosing a guardian include:

- ✔ Do they have experience of bringing up children?
- ✔ Do they share your world-view, values, and religious beliefs?
- ✔ Are they able to take on the responsibility of caring for your child, emotionally, financially, and physically?
- ✔ Does your child like the person, and feel comfortable with them?
- ✔ Do they live close by? If the potential guardian lives far away it may prove a real wrench for your child to up sticks, leave friends and move, particularly at such an upsetting time.
- ✔ Does the person you're considering have lots of children? Would your child get lost in the crowd or relish new siblings to play with?

If you have someone in mind to act as guardian, have a talk with them about everything you'd want them to do for your child. Tell them what you want but give them a way of refusing without any hard feelings. Being a guardian is a huge task!

Keep a letter with your will setting out how you want your child to be raised. The letter should give your guardians an idea of your hopes and aspirations for your child, rather than a prescriptive list of do's and don'ts.

Not every parent is able to appoint a guardian. In order to appoint a guardian upon death, a parent must have had *parental responsibility* for the child. Ironically, not all parents have this responsibility. If, for example, the biological father has been absent from the child for years they may not have parental responsibility.

Parental responsibility means that you have a legal duty to care for the child. You can apply to the courts for parental responsibility. Sometimes a survivor in a same-sex partnership applies for this so that the child of their deceased partner can live with them. In all cases, the court decides who has parental responsibility based on the best interests of the child.

Divorce and guardians

A mother and father are joint guardians for as long as they live together. On the death of one parent, the surviving parent becomes the sole guardian. On the death of the surviving parent, the guardian is the person(s) appointed by the surviving parent. The same is true for adopted children. That's a nice easy scenario.

The complexities kick in when the parents divorce. If the parent granted custody – through a residence order – dies, then the guardian appointed by that parent takes joint responsibility for the child with the surviving parent. If the surviving parent and the appointed guardian can't agree who should look after the child, then one party has to apply for a fresh residence order. The court decides who gets custody.

You may be vehemently opposed to your child ever living with the other parent (your ex-partner), even after your death. If you feel this way, you can explain your case in a letter kept with your will. However, it's rare for a willing biological parent to be denied the right to joint guardianship, except in cases where chronic alcoholism, drug abuse, or a history of violence is proven. Where it all gets horribly complex is when children from current and previous relationships all live under one roof as a family unit. Following the death of one parent in this type of household, several different guardians – each one most relevant to the individual child – can be appointed by the courts. At this stage it may be up to social services to step in and sort out the mess. Talk to the parties concerned and see where everyone goes from there.

No-guardian situations

If no guardian is appointed for a child, or the person appointed under a will is unable or refuses to act as guardian, the child is in effect split in two. Rest assured this isn't some wisdom-of-Solomon style ploy to get a willing guardian to step forward. The *estate of the child* – the child's property – is looked after by the Public Guardian and Trustee, while the person of the child is taken in by social services and is placed with close relatives where possible or, failing that, a foster parent. Any surviving relatives have to apply to the courts for guardianship of the child.

Appointing a guardian without using a will

It's best to make a will to make your wishes concerning your estate and your children absolutely clear. However, parents can appoint a guardian without making a will. You must draw up an *Appointment of Guardian* form, which you can write yourself. Give the full names of your children, the chosen guardian(s), and sign and date the form. But be warned that like the guardianship wishes expressed in a will, the court can overrule the parental choice of guardian. What's more, the forms cannot be used to leave property to the guardian to pay for the upkeep of the child: You can only do that through a will.

You can avoid this situation happening by naming an alternative guardian in your will just in case your first choice is unable to look after your child. Naming alternative guardians is explained in Chapter 4.

Money, money, money isn't child's play

If you're a parent you probably won't need reminding that children cost money, and lots of it – they have to be schooled, fed, clothed, and entertained. Letting the guardian(s) you appoint pay for all this from their own pocket isn't fair. You need to leave the guardian enough money in your will to cover the cost of bringing up your children.

You can use a trust to set money aside for your guardian through property or from the proceeds of a life insurance policy. The trustee can monitor what is being spent on the child. Even if you trust the appointed guardian completely – and you should do if they are to look after your little treasures – it is not a good move to name him or her as sole trustee or executor. See Chapters 15 and 16 for more on this.

As a rule of thumb, the older your children are, the less money you will have to leave behind for their upkeep, as your guardians will be looking after them for a shorter amount of time. Be open! Discuss with the guardians what they need to look after your children. If your child has a disability, your guardian probably needs more money to provide proper care. A smart move is for you all to take independent financial advice.

The Eyes Have It: Witnesses

A will in England and Wales has to be witnessed by two people, who sign their names next to the name of the *testator* (the person writing the will) at the end of the document. Witnesses do not have to read the contents of your will and dot every 'i' or cross every 't'; but they must be present when you sign your will and put their mark to that effect in your presence and the presence of each other. These two people are witnessing the signing of the will and not the drawing up of the will document. Members of the armed forces on active service can write a will without having to have it witnessed.

A witness, or their spouse, is not allowed to inherit a bean from the will, so make sure you don't ask a beneficiary or their spouse to be a witness.

As well as making sure the witnesses are not beneficiaries, bear the following in mind when choosing a witness:

- ✒ Blind people can't witness a will. (Those blind in just one eye can, though.)
- ✒ A witness must be mentally capable of understanding what is going on.
- ✒ Under 18s can act as witnesses, but the will can be challenged on the grounds that the minor did not understand what they were witnessing. Best not bother!

The witnesses you choose don't have to be pillars of the community – you aren't appointing them to look after your children, after all. What's more, the witnesses don't have to have the skills of an executor.

A close family friend, neighbour, or even a trusted work colleague makes a good witness. If any possibility exists that your mental health could be called into question, your doctor makes a good witness.

It's a good idea (although not legally required) for the witnesses to write their full names in capitals and addresses next to their signatures just in case the will is challenged and they need to be traced. Pick witnesses who are home-owners, as they are most likely to stay put.

Witnesses in Scotland

The rules on witnessing a will in Scotland are a lot less strict than in England and Wales. Only one witness is needed and he or she doesn't have to see the testator sign. All the testator has to do is indicate to the witness that they have signed their own will. What's more, the witness can benefit from the will.

However, just to confuse these simple matters, wills in Scotland made prior to 1 August 1995 must be witnessed by two people.

Considering Getting Expert Help

You've lined up your executors, trustees, and witnesses. Now what? Writing your will needs an entire chapter to itself – that's covered in Chapter 7. But for now you need to decide whether to write your will yourself, perhaps using a DIY will kit, or if you need to bring out the big guns and call in a professional to help.

If your estate is simple you can write your will yourself (see Chapter 7). If you feel you're in danger of reaching the limits of your knowledge it's time to contact a professional for help, even if it's just to check over your plans to date.

Calling in the Professionals

Many believe that the solicitor or accountant you choose to help you with your will should be an old family friend. However, in the real world few people have family solicitors or accountants and, instead, rely on personal recommendation and the Yellow Pages! But that shouldn't matter a jot as long as you approach the professional in the same way you would a plumber, electrician, or car mechanic – with healthy scepticism and unafraid to ask questions.

Many solicitors and accountants offer a free initial consultation to discuss your requirements. Go to at least two different professionals to compare the services they can offer you before choosing who to work with. Any solicitor or accountant you engage should give you a clear idea of how much they charge at the outset.

Solicitors

When it comes to writing your will or dealing with someone else's estate, the right solicitor can be very useful, even if soliciting a solicitor might be last on your list of favourite activities.

Think of a solicitor as someone you can call on when you reach the edges of your knowledge or confidence about wills and inheritance. It is up to you when you feel you have reached the limits; it can be simply how to word your will right up to including complex trusts and codicils.

Consider using a solicitor for the following situations:

- ✔ A solicitor can act as a trustee or an executor of your estate.

- ✔ The advice of a solicitor can be invaluable when you're trying to administer someone else's will, a tricky process called *probate*. (The probate process is explained in Chapters 12, 13, and 14.)

- ✔ A solicitor's office is as good a place as any to keep your will – they are used to storing many types of legal documents, such as deeds to property.

  Some solicitors charge a nominal fee, about £10–25 a year, to look after your will. The fee is often waived if you name the solicitor as an executor, as this can be quite lucrative for them.

- ✔ Above all else, a solicitor can stop you from making a horrible mistake in your will that can invalidate it or inadvertently disinherit someone precious.

Each professional you consult has their own area of expertise. A solicitor can advise on wills but may not be well-versed on the ins and outs of inheritance tax – you may be better off talking to an accountant. However, solicitors with expertise in estate planning are well honed in the art of writing a trust into your will. You can call the Society of Trust and Estate Practitioners (STEP) on 0207 838 4885 or visit their Web site at www.step.org. STEP's membership comprises both solicitors and accountants.

Lists of solicitors can be obtained from The Law Society of England and Wales on 0870 606 6565, Scotland on 0845 1130018, and in Northern Ireland on 028 90 231614. Alternatively, check out these Web sites for details of solicitors in your area: www.lawsociety.org.uk/choosingandusing/find asolicitor.law, www.lawscot.org.uk, and www.lawsoc-ni.org.

A solicitor usually charges a flat-rate fee of between £50 and £300 to draw up a will, depending on how knotty your affairs are. If you require specific legal advice on complicated issues such as trusts or administering someone else's estate, then expect to pay more.

Bargain wills ahoy! Every few years The Law Society of England and Wales runs *Make a Will Week*, when solicitors write wills for a one-off donation to charity, often less than the usual cost of making a will. Another scheme is *Will Aid*, when thousands of solicitors donate the fees they make for will work to charity during a particular month. By taking advantage of *Make a Will Week* and *Will Aid* you and a good cause can benefit at the same time.

Accountants

Accountants immerse themselves in the tax system, looking for ways to enable people to keep more of their own cash – it's not sexy but it is clever! Seeking the advice of an accountant, when you're preparing to draw up your will, can save your beneficiaries a pretty packet because they are experts in tax loopholes.

An accountant can also help with your short- and long-term estate planning.

- ✔ **Short term.** An accountant can advise you on trusts to incorporate into your will to help set in stone who gets what and when after your death.

- ✔ **Long term.** An accountant can advise you on how to distribute your estate to your nearest and dearest and reduce any eventual inheritance tax liability.

This book can help you understand the legal and financial basics so you're well informed to write your own will, but getting an accountant to check it over can put your mind at rest. After all, if you make a mistake it may only come to light when your beneficiary has an unexpected tax demand land on their doormat with an ominous thump.

Accountants charge a flat fee for completing a specific task, such as setting up a trust, or charge by the hour. Top rated accountants can charge £100 or even £150 per hour. With hourly fees like these, it is very important to agree at the outset how much work needs to be done and at what price.

You can find an accountant through the Institute of Chartered Accountants, www.icaewfirms.co.uk, or the Association of Certified Chartered Accountants (Acca) www.acca.co.uk. If you're a business owner, check out the Government's business link Web site for tips on choosing a good accountant at www.businesslink.gov.uk.

Preparing to meet the experts

Take advantage of the free initial consultation that many solicitors and accountants offer.

Take the following information with you when consulting an accountant or solicitor:

- ✔ Your personal details and those of your partner.
- ✔ Your children's details.
- ✔ Details of any stepchildren or ex-spouse.
- ✔ Details of your executors, trustees, and guardians.
- ✔ The approximate value of your home and the most recent mortgage statement.
- ✔ Life insurance policies.
- ✔ Information about your pension arrangements.
- ✔ A list of all your assets and debts.
- ✔ A list of all major gifts you have made in the past seven years (these may be subject to inheritance tax. Refer to Chapter 4 for more on gifts and their tax implications).

Before agreeing to engage the services of a particular accountant or solicitor, ask yourself the following questions:

- ✔ Do I feel confident about using this professional?
- ✔ Do I understand everything the professional told me?
- ✔ Did the professional fully understand what I am looking for?
- ✔ Am I certain how much the advice costs me?

If the answer to any of these questions is no, ask for clarification or simply don't go there! Remember, the one thing the UK definitely isn't short of is solicitors and accountants.

Making a complaint about a professional

Both the accountancy and legal professions are self-regulating. If you want to make a complaint, you have to complain to the firm in question first — then, and only then, can you take your case to the professional body that the accountant or solicitor belongs to. Accountants can belong to several different professional organisations such as the Association of Certified Chartered Accountants and the Institute of Chartered Accountants.

Solicitors belong to The Law Society. Each organisation — representing accountants or solicitors — has its own set of procedures for dealing with complaints about members. Usual complaints revolve around poor service and/or overcharging. The relevant organisation investigates your complaint and decides whether or not you can be compensated.

If you're unhappy with the response to your complaint from the organisation representing the professional, then you're free to take court action.

Going Solo: Using a Will Kit

A will kit is a legally-valid off-the-shelf pack that includes all the documents you need to complete your will yourself without using a solicitor. A will kit includes a pre-printed will form, and advice on how to fill it out.

The will form enables you to appoint executors, guardians, and trustees.

Some sections of a pre-printed will form won't be relevant to you. If you don't have young children, you don't need to appoint a guardian. Instead of leaving these sections blank, draw a line through any parts of the will form you don't fill in to make your wishes absolutely clear.

You can download pre-printed will forms and will kits from many solicitors' Web sites. Lawpack publishes DIY will kits, which are sold in Tesco, W H Smith, and Office World all for around £15. See www.lawpack.co.uk.

A will kit can't stop you from making mistakes – such as getting a beneficiary or their spouse to witness the will and thereby disinherit themselves. What's more, the advice offered in a will kit is very general and doesn't come anywhere near that of a solicitor or accountant.

A will kit saves on the hassle of drawing up will forms yourself, but can't replace professional help.

Keeping Your Will Safe

It's pointless going to the time, trouble, and expense of writing a will if you leave it lying around willy-nilly just asking to be lost.

Several options are available for safekeeping your will:

- ✔ **Your own home.** Lock away your will in a small fireproof safe, which costs about £50 from DIY shops. This action protects your will from all sorts of dangers – including your children's sticky mitts.

- ✔ **Your solicitor.** Solicitors can keep your will under lock and key. This is a particularly good idea if you want your solicitor to act as executor of your will.

- ✔ **The bank.** This is the ultra-safe option. Your bank can keep your will in their safe for a fee of around £10–25 per year. Just remember to tell your executors where the will is!

Before locking away your signed will, take two photocopies of it. Keep a copy for yourself to refer to whenever you want, without having to hassle your solicitor or bank. Give the second copy to your appointed executor so they know what to expect before the time comes to start administering your estate.

Your executors must have your original will, and not a photocopy, to have the legal muscle to administer your estate. Give your executors the photocopy purely as a sneak preview – but let them know where the original signed will is kept.

Chapter 7

Getting It in Writing: Drawing Up Your Will

In This Chapter
▶ Picking pen and paper or PC
▶ Filling in the personal details
▶ Listing who gets what
▶ Signing and witnessing your will

*Y*ou know what you own and what you want to leave everyone. You've decided who to appoint to look after your children and your estate in the event of your death.

Now it's putting pen to paper time! A will is a formal legal document and you need to follow certain rules to ensure it is valid. The legal necessities of a will aren't simply there to make hard work for you – they're in place to ensure that you set out your gifts to your loved ones in an orderly way that's easy to understand.

You can use this book to help you write your own will, and this chapter in particular gives examples of the clauses you must include. However, this book should not be used as a substitute for professional legal advice. If in doubt, give a pro a shout!

In this chapter, I take you through the process of writing your will from the first word to the final full stop. Power up your will now!

Choosing Your Materials

Proper presentation is vital when it comes to writing your will. You don't have to use perfumed paper and a quill but you do have to present your will in as legible a fashion as you can.

Thinking of leaving your mark with a video will? Exhibitionists beware: A will must be in writing to be valid (except for those on active military service).

Deciding whether to handwrite or type your will

Many people choose to write their will by hand – after all, not everyone can type. If you have good clear handwriting, then get going. Write as clearly as possible; consider using BLOCK CAPITALS. You can use pen or even a pencil, but pencil comes with the drawback – geddit? – that it can easily be erased.

If you're using a pen to write your will, don't switch colour half way through. The danger of switching colour, or from pen to pencil, is that your executors may deem that the part of the will written in a different colour was added at a later date – perhaps by someone else. As a result of this discrepancy, the executors can choose to ignore what's written in the second colour.

You may find it easier to type out your will on your computer. Using a program like Word allows you to check spelling and grammar, correcting mistakes as you go along. You can lay out your will with eye-catching bold headings.

Using a computer also allows you to save a copy of your will to hard disk, CD, or memory stick. This can be very handy if you want to print off additional copies for friends and families.

Once you've written your will, get someone who is trustworthy and intelligent to read over it to check the English. Remember: Even a misplaced comma can radically change the meaning of a sentence.

Picking out the paper

Whether you print out your will from your computer or handwrite it, use good quality, blank paper for your will. Hopefully, this document will have to survive for many years as you keep going on and on and on . . .

Ensure you have plenty of paper. When drawing up your will, allow space for the following:

- ✔ Your full name and address.
- ✔ A clause revoking all previous wills (see the following section).
- ✔ The appointment of executors, trustees, solicitors, and guardians, along with their full names and addresses.

✔ Legal clauses granting your executors the power to deal with your estate.

✔ A description of property to be inherited (such as a home, car, or savings) and the names and addresses of the beneficiaries who are to inherit this property. If you plan to do anything complex with your property, such as writing it into a trust, this is where to do it!

✔ Your signature and that of your witnesses.

Instead of writing a will from scratch, you can purchase a pre-printed will form. These forms have all the right headings with blank spaces underneath for you to fill in. Will forms and how you can get hold of one are examined in Chapter 6.

Taking Care of Preliminaries

You must obey certain rules when writing your will. Failure to follow the legal formalities of will-writing leads to confusion at best, and an invalid will at worst.

Your details

The first paragraph of your will states your personal details in order to clear any possible ambiguity. The opening line of your will is a clear statement that it is your *last will and testament*. This line tells your executors and the court that the document is the latest will you have written.

Then write that you *revoke* all previous wills. This is called a *revocation* clause and does exactly what it says on the tin: Makes any previous will and any gifts made in it automatically invalid. In addition, state clearly that you are of *sound mind* (refer to Chapter 2 for full details on what constitutes being of sound mind).

Even if the will you're writing is your first, you should still insert a revocation clause. Your executors and the courts are not to know that this is your first stab at making a will. By inserting a revocation clause you end all possibility of debate.

You must insert your full name and address and state the date on which the will is being made. These details are for clarity: If you don't put your personal details in your will no one can say legally that it is yours, even if you have it on your person when you die. Here's a sample of the first paragraph of a simple will, including the revocation clause:

> *This last will and testament made by me, NAME, of ADDRESS, being of sound mind, on DATE. I revoke any earlier will and codicils I have made.*

Keeping will-writing simple

The key to stress-free will-writing is to keep it simple. You don't need to include in-depth personal details such as your place of birth, or where you went to school. If you want to make any personal statements about your life, then write a letter and tell your executors and loved ones about it.

Similarly, don't use your will to give a detailed account of the type of funeral you want. By all means outline what type of funeral you would like (such as a burial or cremation) and allocate

money from your estate for meeting the expense. But outline precise instructions, such as music to be played and flowers displayed, in a separate letter. Go to Chapter 10 for more about making your funeral wishes clear. Keep your language simple, too. If you're unsure of the exact meaning of a particular word, look it up in the *Oxford English Dictionary* (or online at www.askoxford.com). Remember that terms are assumed to have the same meaning wherever they appear in the will.

You need to revoke *codicils* (later additions to a will) as well as any previous wills. (You can read more on codicils and how they work in Chapter 9.)

Your appointees' details

Once you've got your details down it's time to appoint those people who make your will wishes reality. Roll out your dream team – your executors, guardians, and trustees.

- ✔ **Appoint executors.** These are the people who make sure your will makes it off the page into reality. Clearly state each executors' full name and address. The address is not a legal requirement but an extra precaution. Chapter 6 explores what makes an ideal executor.)

- ✔ **Appoint solicitors.** If you want a solicitor to act as executor or trustee, give the solicitor's full name and the full address of the firm. Chapter 6 also examines the ins and outs of appointing a solicitor.

- ✔ **Appoint trustees and guardians.** Include the full names and addresses of any trustees or guardians you appoint. Your trustees may be the same people as your executors. The roles of these groups are explored in Chapter 6.

When appointing anyone to help with your will, keep it simple. You don't need to go into why you're choosing a particular person for the job.

Staying on the safe side

For safety's sake, sign and number each page of your will. This action stops anyone inserting a fraudulent page into your will. If any of the pages of your will have substantial blank spaces on them, cross a line through them to prevent someone inserting a sneaky clause and grabbing your dosh! Initial any lines you draw through your will and get your witnesses to do the same.

Avoid making any puncture marks in your will – these can be taken by your executor as indicating that there is a page or important document missing. This situation can prove a real pain to your executors as they go hunting for the missing pages. If you want to add a document put it in a separate envelope, make reference to it in your will, and give your executors a copy.

Here's an example of how to set out the details of the people who carry out your wishes:

> *I appoint EXECUTOR'S NAME of EXECUTOR'S ADDRESS and SECOND EXECUTOR'S NAME of SECOND EXECUTOR'S ADDRESS to be the executors of my will. I appoint NAME(S) of ADDRESS(ES) to be the guardians of my children.*

An appointee has the right to refuse to act, or may not be able to act due to illness or if they die before you. To cover such an eventuality you can appoint a substitute.

A form of words you can use when appointing a substitute is as follows:

> *If the appointed EXECUTOR/GUARDIAN/TRUSTEE has died at the time of my death or is unable or unwilling to fulfil the role of EXECUTOR/GUARDIAN/TRUSTEE I appoint SUBSTITUTE'S NAME of SUBSTITUTE'S ADDRESS to be the EXECUTOR/GUARDIAN/TRUSTEE.*

Giving Your Executors Elbow-Room

You've appointed your executors – now grant them the power to follow the terms of your will. Include a series of legal clauses in your will to grant your executors the right to deal with some or all of the following:

- ✔ Your personal possessions.
- ✔ Your property (such as your home, savings accounts, and shares).
- ✔ Your expenses, debts, taxes, and gifts.

If your estate doesn't cover all your bequests or debts, your executors will raise the money by selling what they need to, to meet those expenses.

You don't need to appoint an executor if you leave all your property to one person who is over the age of 18. Simply write:

I give all my property of every kind to BENEFICIARY'S NAME of BENEFICIARY'S ADDRESS.

The sole beneficiary of your estate then effectively acts as your adminstrator, gathering in your assets and paying any tax due.

Detailing Who Gets What

Now we get to the part where you divide up your goodies.

Make your bequests clear in your will. Simply list the details of the property you're giving and the person you're leaving it to, for example: *I give my sister, Andrea Hubbard of 11 Acacia Avenue, Anytown, Anyshire, my collection of rings and brooches.* You don't need to outline every piece of property in your will. For small items of property, simply detail them in a letter, which is referred to in your will, and keep the letter with the will.

Writing gifts into your will

The three types of gift you can leave are:

- ✔ **Specific gifts.** This refers to defined or identifiable possessions such as shares or a car that you leave to a beneficiary or group of beneficiaries. An example would be: *I give my car (DESCRIPTION OF CAR) to NAME OF BENEFICIARY of ADDRESS.*

- ✔ **Non-specific, or general gifts.** These are general bequests, such as *all my personal possessions*.

- ✔ **Residuary gift.** This covers whatever is left (the residue of your estate) after you dispose of all your specific and non-specific gifts. The residuary could well be the largest part of your estate. Making a residuary gift should really be a tidying-up process and the wording is easy: *I leave the residue of my estate to NAME of ADDRESS.* Job done!

Unless you say otherwise, your residuary estate is used to pay debts, funeral expenses, and usually any inheritance tax (IHT).

If you don't specify your wishes for the residue of your estate, it is dealt with under the law of intestacy. Refer to Chapter 2 for a rundown of what happens under intestacy.

In the spirit of keeping things simple – and your executors will give thanks if you do – number each specific gift. Put your major possessions, such as your house, at the top of the list and your gifts of lesser value at the bottom.

You can make your gift *free-of-tax*. This scenario sounds great but, sadly, it doesn't mean that your estate is free of tax – unless it's worth less than the starting point for IHT – it just means that your executors should make the gift from your estate after any tax has been paid. In your bequest, write:

> *I leave to my son Benjamin £10,000 free of inheritance tax.*

A beneficiary of your will may die before you. Name an alternative beneficiary to prevent the gift from failing. To name an alternative beneficiary, simply insert a line stating that in the event of the death of the named beneficiary, the property they were to inherit should pass to another named person.

You can write:

> *If my son Benjamin has died by the time of my death, the gift of £10,000 free of inheritance tax should be given to my granddaughter Helen.*

Chapter 4 has full details on what happens when a gift fails.

A big thank you

Your will is an opportunity to make clear what you think about the people who influence your life. (No, I'm not talking about disinheriting your nasty Uncle Vladimir.) Most people leave their estate to their very nearest and dearest – spouse, children, and siblings – but this can mean nothing's left to say thank you to other family members and close friends. Using your will to say thanks can ease the pain of your going. Make sure you remember everyone you need to in your will.

You may want to leave your executors a gift of some money or a personal possession. After all, your executors are going to put in a lot of work during the few months after your death. Executors aren't allowed to take money from your estate for their hard graft – although they can claim expenses – so if you don't make a gift to them in your will they get nowt! Professional executors such as solicitors and accountants charge your estate a fee so, unless you're feeling particularly generous, you don't need to leave them anything.

Leaving a gift for life

Instead of leaving your beneficiary a gift outright, you can leave him or her the *life interest* in a gift. By giving outright, you hand over the property to your beneficiary hook, line, and sinker. By creating a *life-interest gift*, you allow your beneficiary to have an income from the property but they are barred from selling it outright. The reasoning behind this action is that the property is preserved for another beneficiary. This tactic is often used by people wanting to provide an income for their spouse but desiring that their children get to inherit and dispose of the property as they wish when that spouse dies. If you want to include a life-interest gift in your will, seek legal advice.

Be careful that good intentions don't lead to the creation of an accidental life interest. Writing in your will that a beneficiary should receive an asset but on their death it should pass to someone else automatically creates a life interest. You may have been trying to make it clear what you would like the first beneficiary to do with the asset – but you can't do this without creating a life interest. Unless you want to create a life interest, be 100 per cent clear and gift to the beneficiary outright.

Being specific

When doling out your gifts to your beneficiaries when writing your will, you must make sure that you dot your i's and cross your t's:

- ✔ **Don't tack on unnecessary phrases.** A will that states: 'I leave to my brother, Paul Smith, £10,000 safe in the knowledge that he will do what is right by our sister, Maude Smith', is a recipe for disaster. The courts can interpret 'do what is right' as creating a binding legal trust, under which Paul has to use the £10,000 for Maude's upkeep.

- ✔ **Make the distribution of a joint gift crystal clear.** If you leave a gift to more than one person, tread carefully. A clause stating 'I leave £5,000 to Mr Raj and Mrs Sumi Harani' is not clear as to whether they should have the money jointly or individually. Simply inserting the words 'each' or 'divided equally' clears up any confusion.

- ✔ **Be precise about the gift itself.** If your description of the gift is incorrect or incomplete, the gift may fail. A failed gift becomes part of the residuary estate and is given to the beneficiary you have given your residue to or distributed under intestacy. If you have more than one expensive watch, make sure you give an accurate description of the Rolex intended for your nephew!

Passing the Finishing Line: Signing Your Will

Your signature breathes life into your will. Before you sign, your will is as dead as a dodo! Everyone may know that the will is yours, you may have discussed its contents with your nearest and dearest, you may even have written it in your own hand – it doesn't matter a jot. Without a properly witnessed signature, the document is not valid.

Sign your will in ink – I know you had your heart set on crayon, but resist the temptation – and use your usual signature. Ensure you are witnessed as you sign the will by two other people (see 'Getting Your Will Witnessed' later in the chapter).

You're allowed put your signature anywhere in the will document – start, middle, or end. However, signing at the end makes things much easier for all concerned. See the next section for how to word the clause before your signature.

Making your mark

You have to sign your will with your current name to make it a legally binding document. But exceptions to the rule include:

✔ If you're an actor or actress you can sign your will with your stage name. (So John Wayne didn't have to sign 'Marion Morrison', or Cary Grant 'Archie Leech'.)

✔ If you have a maiden name, you can use that if you wish.

✔ If you're illiterate, you can make a cross or a thumbprint.

✔ If you have a rubber stamp of your signature – signing things can be so tiresome, particularly cheques! – you can use that.

✔ If you're too ill or disabled to sign, someone else can sign it for you.

If you're unable to sign your own will due to illness or disability, someone has to read it to you and you must indicate that you understand and agree with its contents. This action must be done in front of your witnesses. The words you should use are as follows:

Signed by (the name of the person signing on the testator's behalf) on the direction of the testator and in the testator's presence and in our joint presence and then by us together in the presence of the testator (SIGNATURES OF WITNESSES).

✔ You're not allowed to use a seal.

Consult a solicitor for the appropriate wording if you're unsure. Doing so could save a lot of trouble and expense later.

Getting Your Will Witnessed

If your will is not witnessed properly it is invalid. If no previous witnessed will exists to replace an unwitnessed will, then you're deemed to have died intestate.

The two people you choose as witnesses must be present when you sign your will. They don't have to be present while you write your will, and they don't have to read your will – that's very boring for them – just when you sign it. Who can and can't be a witness is covered in Chapter 6. Don't forget:

- You must sign first and your witnesses after.
- You must be present when your witnesses sign.
- Each witness should be present when the other witness signs.

Don't forget the golden rule: Don't use a beneficiary or the spouse of a beneficiary to witness your will because it automatically disinherits the beneficiary.

Your will should contain an *attestation clause* to state that you and your witnesses signed it at the same time.

A simple attestation clause is:

> *Signed by the (TESTATOR/TESTATRIX) in our presence (YOUR SIGNATURE)*
>
> *and then by us in his/hers (SIGNATURES OF WITNESSES) on this day (FULL DATE).*

Get your witnesses to put their full names and address details below their signatures. Doing so isn't a legal requirement but can help your executors if the witnesses have to be traced for some reason.

Dating your attestation clause in your will is not essential under the law but makes it easier for your executors to assess whether the will in front of them really is your *last* will and testament. If the will was made a long time ago they may double check your papers to make sure that you haven't made a more recent will.

In Scotland, you only need one witness, and that witness doesn't have to be present when you sign your will. You merely have to show the witness that you have signed your will.

Chapter 8

Fine-Tuning Your Will

. . . .

In This Chapter

▶ Empowering your executors

▶ Understanding and using survivorship

▶ Adding conditions to your gifts

▶ Protecting your will from challenges

▶ Using power of attorney

. . . .

A will is far more than just a list of gifts and beneficiaries: It is a route map for your loved ones when you have gone. This chapter is about dotting the i's and crossing the t's of your will and adding those little extra clauses to take account of your unique circumstances.

If you're looking for information on trusts, turn to Chapter 17.

Powering Up Your Executors

If you tot up your estate correctly – not forgetting to subtract taxes and debts – and are realistic about leaving gifts to your nearest and dearest, your will should be carried out smoothly. However, consider for a second what would happen if you leave lots of financial bequests but have little ready cash in your estate. How are your beneficiaries going to get their hands on the readies? You need to give your executors the power to act on your behalf when you're no longer around in case something unexpected arises.

Simply by appointing executors, you give them the automatic right to deal with your estate. However, to prevent a shadow of a doubt you can include a series of legal clauses in your will to grant your executors the right to sell your personal possessions and other property to pay taxes, debts, and gifts that your estate can't otherwise cover.

To make sure your wishes are carried out, choose wise executors, power them up through your will, and put faith in their judgement.

The personal possessions clause

This clause may sound like some sort of obscure grammar rule but it isn't – or should that be ain't? A *personal possessions clause* gives your executors the right to sell some, or all, of the possessions you accumulated during your life such as furniture and jewellery. In legal circles such items are referred to as *chattels*. Your executors can sell these items to settle debts, meet a tax bill, or to gather in enough funds to pay a cash sum you left a beneficiary.

You can work a clause into your will that prevents your executor from selling property gifted in your will to a beneficiary.

You word the clause as follows:

> *I give to my executors absolutely, free of inheritance tax, all my personal chattels as defined by section 55(1) of the Administration of Estates Act 1925 which are not disposed of in my will.*

If you don't include this clause, your chattels become part of your residuary estate. The residuary estate is the prime source of funds for the payment of debts and cash legacies.

The other property clause

The *other property clause* allows your executors to sell the rest of your property, such as your home, if it is necessary to pay debts, taxes, or a beneficiary.

A form of words you can use for the clause goes as follows:

> *I give all my real and personal property of any kind, which is not disposed of in my will, to my executors. My executors must hold this property upon trust to sell the whole or any part of it or to keep the whole or any part of it in the same form as it was at the date of my death for as long as my executors decide.*

This clause is deliberately open-ended to grant the executor wriggle room. The executor can choose to sell the property if needs be; he or she can also do nothing with it for as long as they see fit.

Real property is land and *personal property* is everything else. *Upon trust* means that the property is held by one person for the benefit of another person. The testator entrusts the property to the executor, who is free to do with it as they see fit in order to ensure the beneficiaries get their gifts and that debts and taxes are paid. For example, if the executor takes possession of £10,000 worth of shares upon trust, backed up by the power of the other property clause, the executor can sell the shares and meet cash legacies for two beneficiaries of £5,000 each.

The paying of expenses, debts, taxes, and beneficiaries clause

After the sale of personal possessions or other property, the executors should have enough money to pay the outstanding debts and gifts. Add a clause to your will to make it clear that this is all the executor should spend the money on (and not a shopping trip to New York):

> *My executors must pay out of the money arising from such sale my funeral expenses, any testamentary expenses, any debts, and any legacies and taxation payable by reason of my death.*

Testamentary expenses mean the cost to your executor of gathering in and distributing your estate. *Legacies* is just another word for gifts. *Taxation payable by reason of my death* refers mainly to inheritance tax, but can also mean other tax liabilities arising from the sale of property (such as Capital Gains Tax on a second property). See Part IV for all you need to know about inheritance tax.

If you choose to go down the safety-first route of incorporating clauses in your will giving power to your executors, keep your will clear and easy for your executors to understand by inserting the legal clauses in the following order. First, grant your executors the power to sell your personal possessions, next, other property, and only then should you outline their responsibilities to pay debts, taxes, and beneficiaries.

Some solicitors prefer to use a short cut by referring to legal documents called *statutory will forms* to sum up your intentions. In effect, referring to statutory will forms acts as shorthand for your intentions. So when leaving all your personal possessions to someone, instead of listing them ad nauseum they're referred to as a gift under Form 2 of the Statutory Will Forms 1925.

Granting extra powers to your executors

You might think that having control over your personal possessions and property is quite enough power for any executor! However, the process of sorting out an estate can take over a year from start to finish and your executors need to act quickly to see that your loved ones don't suffer financially in the aftermath of your death. Write the following clauses in your will to give your executors enough power to their elbow to see your loved ones right.

> *I grant to my executors the right to invest and change any investments freely as if they were beneficially entitled to them.*
>
> *I allow my executors the right to hold investments in the name of a third party they think fit.*

The drama of reading a will

The reading of the will is a device beloved of TV drama writers. The will reading gives the writer a chance to pen a big set piece scene with the deceased springing an unpleasant surprise or two on the relatives from beyond the grave. The truth about reading a will can't be more different!

Your executor doesn't have to invite your nearest and dearest to the will reading – they can write to your beneficiaries to tell them what their entitlement is under your will. Your beneficiary can read your will after your death if they want to because it is a public document.

In this context, a third party would normally mean a stockbroker in whose name shares are traded.

Ensure your loved ones don't suffer financially by providing for them in your will in the first place.

Covering your executors' backs

By granting your executors such wide-ranging powers you can conceivably leave them liable for any loss resulting from a decision that they make. Good thing, you say, power should come with accountability. But your executor may be a friend or close family member trying to help your loved ones for no financial reward. As for professionals, they won't touch your will with a bargepole if they might be held responsible for the ups and downs of your estate.

Insert the following clause to protect your executors:

> *The decision of my executors whether to sell or to retain my property is a matter for them alone and they are not liable for any loss.*

Choose your executors with care: Incidents of executors being sued by beneficiaries for failing to administer an estate properly are fairly common.

Clinging on to a Survivorship Clause

Life doesn't always run along straight lines, and neither does death. Unexpected things can happen, such as a beneficiary named in your will dying shortly after you. The property you left this person in your will is then gifted to their beneficiaries. If the deceased beneficiary has no will, then the property you left them is distributed under the law of intestacy. (What happens under intestacy is explained in Chapter 2.)

Alarm bells are ringing! The property that belonged to you is now whisked away to the farthest reaches of your now deceased beneficiary's family and friends. If your beneficiary dies without a valid will, they die intestate and if they have no surviving relations the Government scoops the lot.

You may be comfortable with this scenario playing itself out: After all, you can't take it with you. But if you've gone to the trouble of writing a will in the first place, just a little tweaking ensures that you keep a tight rein on your property. By including a survivorship clause in your will, you can specify how long a beneficiary must survive after your death in order to inherit. If your beneficiary doesn't survive you for long enough, they don't inherit and the gift is added to the residual estate.

You can name an alternative beneficiary who inherits your gift if the original beneficiary doesn't cross the survivorship finish line. See Chapter 9 on how to name an alternative beneficiary.

Whether to roll survivorship out or not is your call. If you have a single beneficiary and are happy with the arrangements that they have in place in the event that they die very soon after you, you don't need a survivorship clause.

Wording a survivorship clause

Working a survivorship clause into your will is easy. Just write:

> *Any person who does not survive me by 28 days will be treated as having died before me.*

Although you can insert the survivorship clause anywhere in your will, the best place for it is the part where you grant your executors the powers to deal with your estate. Certainly place the survivorship clause before the part outlining your gifts.

A survivorship period usually lasts 28 or 30 days. You can choose a longer period, but bear in mind that a long survivorship period may hold up the process of distributing the estate.

If a beneficiary dies before the survivorship period has elapsed and without an alternative beneficiary in place, then they don't inherit and the property is automatically transferred into the estate residue (what's left after all beneficiaries have been paid and liabilities have been met).

A survivorship period of 28 days also applies under the law of intestacy. If the would-be beneficiary dies before the survivorship period elapses, then whoever is next in order of priority scoops the inheritance.

Thinking the unthinkable: Dying with your spouse or civil partner

If you have children the doomsday scenario of dying in an accident with your spouse or civil partner may keep you awake at night. Gear up your will to take such a horrible event into account and you can probably sleep a little easier.

Examining what would happen if you and your spouse die at the same time is the litmus test of whether your will is up to the job. Check the following list and if you realise that your will is insufficient, go back and try a rewrite.

- **Appoint guardians.** Think carefully about who will look after your children in the event of your and your spouse's death. Make sure you set enough money aside for them to bring up your children. Chapters 4 and 6 look at making proper financial provision for your children via your trustees and guardians.

- **Consider survivorship.** By incorporating a survivorship clause in your will, you can say what should happen to the property you left your spouse if he or she does not survive you for a set period of time.

- **Name alternative beneficiaries.** Your spouse is probably your main, perhaps only, beneficiary. If your spouse or civil partner dies at the same time or soon after you, even with a survivorship clause in place, the result may not be exactly what you want. By naming an alternative beneficiary, you can channel the money meant originally for your spouse to someone else of your choosing.

- **Look at tax implications.** Transfers of property between you and your spouse (and same-sex civil partnerships) are exempt from inheritance tax (IHT). However, if your spouse or civil partner dies at the same time as you, IHT can be due. The one silver lining is that a recent law changed the inheritance tax nil-rate bands – the amount of money that you can leave before IHT is applicable – when IHT calculations are made, both people in a marriage or civil partnership can be taken into account. In practice this means that up to £600,000 (2007/08 tax year) can be left to beneficiaries between both married or civil partners without IHT being due.

- **Take care of adult children.** Just because your child has grown up doesn't mean that he or she can't do with a helping hand. By leaving your child their own gift in your will or perhaps making them the beneficiary of a life insurance policy, you can help them be financially prepared for the nightmare scenario of you and your spouse dying at the same time. Bear your parents in mind, too, when allocating gifts.

Beneficiaries in Scotland

In Scotland, if you die at the same time as a beneficiary, then whoever is older is deemed to have died first. So if your beneficiary is younger than you, they are deemed to have inherited. This rule doesn't apply when spouses die together. Unless it can be proved that one spouse survived the other – only a second will suffice – they are both presumed to have died at the same time. As a result of this simultaneous death, the spouse doesn't inherit.

On One Condition: Putting Stipulations in Your Will

Some people want their will to be more than a list of gifts and beneficiaries. If you want to have more of a say about what goes on after you've gone, you can make gifts *conditional*. Making a gift conditional means that it can only be inherited when some action is performed or a specified age reached.

A will with conditions is sometimes known, for pretty obvious reasons, as a *conditional will*.

There are several reasons why you may consider working a condition into your will:

- ✔ **Protecting loved ones.** You can set in stone the responsibilities of one loved one to another to ensure a vulnerable family member is looked after.

- ✔ **Making sure the beneficiary is ready.** If a would-be beneficiary is young, you can make a judgement call as to what age they are ready to inherit responsibly.

- ✔ **Taking control from beyond the grave.** You may want to have an influence on how your beneficiary approaches life by offering the chance of scooping a gift from your will if they do or don't do something.

You can work conditions into your will in three ways:

- ✔ **Set up a life interest.** A *life interest* allows the beneficiary to benefit from the interest earned on an investment or the rental value of a property, on the condition that they do not sell up and that the gift passes to another specified individual on their death.

✔ **Write a gift into trust.** Under a trust, you sign over a property or some other asset to your appointed trustee. The trustee then distributes this property according to the conditions you set down. For example, you may not want your children to come into their inheritance until they are 25. A trustee can ensure your wishes are obeyed. See Chapter 17 for more on trusts.

✔ **Tack conditions onto a gift.** This is the 'you can't have that until you do this' tactic. Conditions range from the mundane to the simply bizarre. Back in 1862, Henry Budd left his two sons £200,000 each on condition that neither of them grew a moustache!

You can tack a condition onto a gift by writing:

> *To (name of beneficiary) I give (description of gift) on the condition that (describe condition).*

The golden rule with conditions is to be precise about what you expect your beneficiaries to do, or not do, to earn their prize.

Tacking conditions onto a gift can be fraught with danger and can even lead to your will being challenged in the courts. I go into this in the next section.

Playing God is a bad idea

The best of intentions probably lie behind a decision to work conditions into your will. However, a fine line lies between writing your will so that your nearest and dearest are protected, and playing God with people's lives. Many solicitors advise their clients to avoid making their gifts conditional because that route is so fraught with pitfalls. Consider, too, who will make sure that your conditions are met? Do you really want to lumber someone with such a task? After all, it can lead to arguments and disharmony. Ultimately, it is the court that decides whether or not a beneficiary has met any conditions set out in your will. You may also want to ask your executors to check that the beneficiary is not breaking the conditions attached to the gift.

The courts don't look kindly on wills that try to exert undue influence from beyond the grave. The days when wealthy men and women can prescribe the life choices of their beneficiaries are long gone.

Your beneficiaries have the right to ask the court for permission to collect their inheritance without having to meet your conditions. The court can deem that your condition is *reasonable* – in which case it stands – or *unreasonable* – in which case it is overturned or *voided*.

If the court decides that the condition is *open to interpretation* – not clearly defined – the condition can be overturned!

A court can void a condition if it deems that the condition is unreasonable or *contrary to public policy*. This ruling means that the condition is considered socially or morally unacceptable.

Don't be tempted to tack a condition onto a gift stating that anyone challenging the terms of your will loses his or her inheritance. The courts would probably find this *contrary to public policy*.

Typical conditions that end up being voided include:

- ✔ **Marriage break-up.** Making a gift conditional on your beneficiary divorcing their spouse is a no-no and will be given short shrift by the courts. You can't stop a beneficiary from remarrying. However, you can make a gift to a spouse on the condition that they don't remarry.

- ✔ **Chastity.** Making a gift conditional on a beneficiary remaining celibate or single isn't on either.

- ✔ **Family break-up.** You're not allowed to make a gift conditional on children being separated from their parents.

- ✔ **Criminal behaviour.** You can't make a gift conditional on your beneficiary keeping on the right side of the law (or breaking it!).

The courts can void some conditions because they are open to interpretation:

- ✔ **Religion.** Making a gift conditional that someone remains a member of a particular religion is likely to be considered reasonable by the courts. However, leaving a condition that the beneficiary should 'practise a religion' can be considered too open to interpretation and voided.

- ✔ **Good behaviour.** Making a gift conditional on your beneficiary avoiding a particular vice, such as drinking alcohol before the age of 18, is allowed. But making a catch-all statement that the beneficiary has to behave themselves will be deemed by the courts as too open to interpretation and voided.

The above is not a definitive list. It is up to the court as to what conditions are deemed contrary to public policy.

An alternative to making a gift conditional is to address a letter to your beneficiaries setting out your feelings about how you would like them to spend your gift. Keep this letter with your will to be read at the time of your death. This way your beneficiary can be in no doubt about your feelings on a particular matter.

Losing the right to a gift

As well as failing to meet a condition in your will, a beneficiary can lose the right to a gift for a number of other reasons, including:

✔ **Murder.** That's got your attention! If a beneficiary is convicted of the murder of the testator or was an accomplice to the act, they automatically lose the right to inherit. Good thing, too! However, if a beneficiary is convicted of manslaughter (non-premeditated unlawful killing such as causing death by dangerous driving), they can, under certain circumstances, still inherit.

✔ **Underhand tactics.** If the beneficiary is deemed by the courts to have exerted unreasonable influence on the person making the will, then they can lose their gift. What's more, if the beneficiary has defrauded the estate of the deceased they can have their gifts taken from them.

What happens to a gift if a condition is voided?

The court can decide to *void* (overturn) an unacceptable or vague condition. What happens to the gift depends on whether the beneficiary has by that time got their hands on it.

✔ **The beneficiary has already received the gift.** The beneficiary keeps the gift – nice and simple!

✔ **The beneficiary has not yet received the gift.** The gift is deemed to have failed and it becomes part of the estate residue and is distributed under intestacy. As a result, the beneficiary may lose any rights to the gift. If the person making the will has named an alternative beneficiary, just in case the condition isn't met, the alternative beneficiary inherits the gift – with no strings attached!

Protecting Your Will Against Challenges

Money is at the root of all evil, so it's said – it's also at the heart of most will challenges. Family niceties sometimes fly out of the window when cash is involved. Before you put your will to bed you need to double-check that your will isn't wide open to being *challenged* or *contested* through the courts, in an attempt to overturn specific terms of the will or the will in its entirety. If the terms of your will are contested successfully, then your best-laid plans can be torn to shreds.

Get your will as challenge-proof as possible by considering the following points:

- **Make sure you are of sound mind.** Okay, it sounds silly, but if you have any doubts consult your GP. Being of sound mind and who can and can't make a will are explained in Chapter 2.

- **Get the legal stuff right.** Forgetting to sign your will, or failing to have your signature properly witnessed, makes your will invalid. Check the wording of your gifts to ensure that they are crystal clear. If the description of the gift or of the beneficiaries is ambiguous, then the gift may fail, or a legal battle may flare up between your beneficiaries.

- **Don't disinherit your closest relatives.** The law almost always prevents you from cutting your spouse or dependants out of your will. Under the Inheritance (Provision for Family and Dependants) Act 1975, these people are allowed to claim money from your estate through the courts. Refer to Chapter 4 for more on this.

If you're adamant that your spouse or dependant should not inherit, write a letter addressed to your executors and the court making clear why you have taken such drastic action. If your action is deemed reasonable, the court may decide to let the terms of your will stand. If in doubt, take legal advice.

- **Don't tack unreasonable conditions onto gifts.** The types of conditions that the court may define as unreasonable are covered earlier in this chapter in the section 'Playing God is a bad idea'. Having a condition deemed unreasonable by the courts won't invalidate your entire will, but it can lead to the gift failing.

If you give away property with the aim of stopping it from passing to people who may have a claim on your estate, such as creditors, the court can order that the gifts are handed back to your estate and redistributed to meet such claims.

Letting your loved ones in on the act

Keep your loved ones informed about the contents of your will to help avoid your will being contested. Resist the temptation to spring a surprise in your will: Be honest and upfront about what you intend to do in it. You can't please all of the people all of the time, but you can take some simple steps to keep your loved ones in the loop:

- **Discuss what your loved ones need.** Find out from your nearest and dearest what they think they will need from your estate in the event of your death. These people may tell you of some expense you haven't considered or someone who should benefit from your will. Refer to Chapter 4 for the low-down on deciding who gets what from your estate.

Mentioning the unmentionables

Avoid some naughty words and actions in your will. The following can be deemed confusing by the courts and your executors, or even get your estate into legal hot water!

✔ **'About' or 'around':** Avoid words that are non-specific. 'I gift to my brother Paul Smith *around* 1,000 shares in British Telecom' is a big no-no, as it leaves the gift open to interpretation. Does 'around' mean you want to gift Paul 999 or 1001 shares? Be precise. Better wording is 'I gift to my brother Paul Smith all my shares in British Telecom.'

✔ **'Family':** Avoid the f-word like the plague. Don't write 'I leave £10,000 to be divided between my family.' One person's family member is another's distant relative. Your family is a moveable feast with potentially hundreds of people able to claim familial ties.

✔ **Libel:** A will is a public document and you cannot use it to fling out accusations or to insult someone. If you commit *libel* in your will (making a false and malicious statement to damage someone's reputation) your estate can be subject to damages. A will isn't the place for grandstanding or righting wrongs.

✔ **Let your loved ones know your worth.** You may feel embarrassed about discussing money but drop the silent act when you write your will. Tell your beneficiaries what you have in the kitty and, just as importantly, what debts and taxes your estate is liable to. Refer to Chapter 3 for how to calculate your financial worth.

✔ **Disappoint someone the right way**. If you believe your will is going to leave a friend or family member feeling out in the cold, be brave and discuss it with them. You simply may not have enough assets to please everyone. If you don't want a face-to-face discussion with your beneficiary (or non-beneficiary), write them a letter explaining your circumstances to be kept with your will for them to read after your death.

Getting to Grips with Power of Attorney

The will-writing process has probably got you thinking about life's 'what ifs?' What would happen to your estate if for some reason you became incapable of acting for yourself? Conceivably, your fortune and those of your family may go down the tubes. One way of making provision to avoid such a possibility is to create a *power of attorney*.

A power of attorney is a legal document whereby one person grants another the right to deal with their property and financial affairs.

Don't be confused by the word 'attorney': It doesn't mean that only an attorney (in North America the term means solicitor) or a legally qualified person can act for you. In fact, you can grant power of attorney to anyone, provided they're over 18 and are not bankrupt. But with such a major legal weapon it's best to choose someone very close and 100 per cent trustworthy.

Two types of power of attorney exist in England and Wales:

- ✔ **Ordinary power of attorney.** This is when someone acts on your behalf for a set period of time. Perhaps you want to go abroad for a couple of years and would like someone to take care of your affairs whilst you're away. An ordinary power of attorney becomes invalid if you become mentally incapable of managing your affairs. Ordinary power of attorney is sometimes referred to as a *general power of attorney*.

- ✔ **Lasting power of attorney.** This is when someone acts on your behalf usually for an indefinite period of time. Lasting power can kick in when you're incapable of managing your own affairs, perhaps due to serious or degenerative illness.

Unless it has been drawn up to take effect immediately, the lasting power of attorney must be activated. The attorney must apply to the *court of protection* when they feel that you may be becoming mentally incapable. If you don't appoint an attorney and own large amounts of property, the court of protection can appoint someone to manage it for you if you become mentally incapable. This person is called a *receiver*. Normally a receiver is chosen from close family. The receiver's powers are limited to dealing with your day-to-day financial affairs and property.

A solicitor can help you draw up a power of attorney. Alternatively, you can purchase a blank power of attorney form from a good stationery shop. The wording for appointing someone to act under an ordinary power of attorney is:

I appoint (name of person) to be my attorney in accordance with Section 10 of the Powers of Attorney Act 1971.

To appoint someone to act under enduring power of attorney, use the following wording:

I appoint (name of person) to be my attorney for the purposes of the Enduring Powers of Attorney Act 1985 with general authority to act on my behalf.

Granting someone *general authority* means that that person is free to do what they want with your property – they could even sell your home! If this thought terrifies you, instead of writing 'with general authority to act on my behalf' write: 'With authority to do the following on my behalf'. Then list the property you want the attorney to have control over. Talk the situation through with a solicitor and have them draw up the enduring power of attorney.

Get your signature and that of the attorney witnessed (but not by each other or by your spouse).

A person granting power of attorney is referred to as the *donor*. The person receiving the power is referred to as an *attorney*.

You can cancel any power of attorney by using a *deed of revocation*. This deed is a separate legal document revoking the power of attorney. You can download a blank deed of revocation from www.clickdocs.co.uk or www.lawpack.co.uk.

To cancel an enduring power, however, you must be mentally capable. You must inform the attorney that you are cancelling the power of attorney. Both powers of attorney become invalid on your death.

Creating power of attorney in Scotland

Laws governing power of attorney in Scotland contain key differences to those in England and Wales, although you appoint an attorney in the same way. In Scotland, the types of power of attorney are more numerous:

- ✔ A *welfare power of attorney* allows you to grant up to four attorneys to look after your personal welfare, such as deciding on care arrangements. A welfare power has to be registered with the Office of the Public Guardian and must incorporate a certificate signed by a solicitor or medical doctor. You can contact the Office of the Public Guardian via their Web site at www.publicguardian-scotland.gov.uk or by phoning 01324 678300.

- ✔ A *continuing power of attorney* is for all intents and purposes the same as lasting power of attorney in England and Wales. The attorney has the right to operate your bank accounts, sell property, and deal with all your financial affairs.

A person can grant a power of attorney only if capable of understanding what he or she is doing. No one, not even close family, can arrange power of attorney for someone else, so you must do it while you're able to express your own wishes.

The end of endurance?

Lasting power of attorney replaced *enduring power of attorney* in late 2007. What's the difference between the two types of power? Very little indeed except that when the attorney applies to the court of protection for the power of attorney, someone must certify (called the certifier, funnily enough) that the donor knows that this new power is about to come into force.

The certifier is left alone with the donor to explain the situation, without the attorney present. The court appoints the certifier.

Lasting power of attorney tends to be more complex and time-consuming to draw up than an enduring power. Expect to pay between £200–£300 to get a solicitor to draw up a watertight lasting power of attorney.

Chapter 9

Ringing the Changes: When and How to Change a Will

*L*ife doesn't stand still and changes in your personal circumstances may cause you to amend or even *revoke* (cancel) your will. Changing a will isn't straightforward: Get it wrong and your beneficiaries may miss out on your pot of gold. Likewise, if you revoke a will incorrectly your estate may end up in the wrong hands – such as the tax-collector's.

Added to all that, your will can be changed after your death if you have not left enough money for your dependants or have tacked unreasonable conditions onto your gifts.

In this chapter, I look at what may prompt you to change your will, how to go about doing it properly, and what circumstances can lead to the terms of your will being altered after death.

Changing a will at a drop of a hat can be even worse than never reviewing it at all. All changes to your existing will must be signed and witnessed in the same way as your original will. This is a time-consuming and, if you use a solicitor, expensive process. Always ask yourself: Is the change really necessary?

Love Changes Everything . . . Even Your Will

Marriage and divorce are the two most common reasons for changing a will.

Marriage

If you get married after making your will, by law your will is *revoked* (cancelled). The law presumes that your wishes have changed, as you now have a spouse. If you die without making a fresh will – preferably before you go on that dangerous sports honeymoon – you are deemed to have died *intestate*, with all the potentially troublesome consequences that can entail (refer to Chapter 2). If you have a complex estate with lots of different assets and beneficiaries and you get married, you're probably best off drawing up a new will. However, if you have a simple estate you can use a *codicil*, simply inserting the new love of your life as the main beneficiary of your estate.

Divorce

Divorce has the effect of cutting your ex out of your will entirely. The law presumes you don't want to give your ex a cut of your estate. Instead their share of your estate goes to whoever would have inherited had your ex died at the date of divorce. Therefore, if you named an alternative beneficiary to your spouse, the gift passes to them. Alternatively, if you haven't named a beneficiary, the gift becomes part of your estate residue. The remainder of your will remains valid.

If you are still on good terms with your ex and/or children are involved, you may still want your ex to benefit from your estate. In these circumstances you must amend your will by adding a *codicil* (an addition to your will). See 'Wording a codicil' later in this chapter.

You can negate the effects of divorce on your will by stating in your will that your spouse should inherit even if you're no longer married to them.

If you named your spouse as an executor in your will, they are barred from acting as executor if you divorce.

Expecting to get hitched?

You can make a will *in expectation of marriage*, also referred to as *contemplation of marriage*. This type of will enables you to leave property and assets to your intended spouse and won't be instantly revoked on your wedding day. To make sure that your will in expectation of marriage does what you want it to do, write in the opening clauses of your will:

'This will is made by me, (your name), in expectation of my marriage to (your intended spouse's name).'

If the marriage doesn't take place – for example, heaven forbid, you are stood up at the altar – a will in expectation of marriage is not automatically revoked. You can revoke the will in the normal way (covered later in this chapter).

If you then marry someone else other than the person named as your intended spouse – perhaps the attractive would-be bridesmaid or the lantern-jawed best man you met on your aborted wedding day – your will made in expectation of marriage is automatically revoked.

If you own property on a *beneficial joint-ownership basis* with your ex-spouse, he or she automatically inherits your part when you die. If you don't want this to happen, amend the terms on which you own the property. Refer to Chapter 5 for how to leave your home through your will and how to change ownership on the deeds of the property.

Marriage, kids, divorce, and Scottish wills

In Scotland, getting married doesn't automatically revoke your existing will, as it does in England. However, under Scottish law your spouse is allowed to make a claim against your estate of up to half of its value after your death.

If you have children after making a will and have not made any mention of them, the will is considered void. In such a situation you must make a new will taking the wee ones into account.

In Scotland, divorce doesn't bar your ex-spouse from inheriting. To stop your spouse from benefiting if you subsequently divorce, add the phrase 'on condition that we are still married at the time of my death' to any gift made to your spouse.

Having Children: Sleepless Nights and Altered Wills

Anyone who has heard the patter of tiny feet knows it changes life's priorities. Suddenly you're not the most important person in the world; your son or daughter is, and naturally you want to see them right.

You may think that by leaving everything to your spouse all will be taken care of. But your spouse might have different priorities to you. If you want to be absolutely sure that your children have enough money for further education or to travel the world, make specific provision for them. Head to Chapter 4 to find out about dividing up your estate.

Also bear in mind the awful scenario that you and your spouse might die together. You may want to amend your will to appoint a guardian if you haven't already done so. Refer to Chapter 6 for more on the role of guardians.

You can alter your will to appoint a guardian by adding a codicil. 'Wording a codicil' later in this chapter tells you how.

The early transfer of property and gifting of cash, such as through a trust to a child, can help reduce the eventual inheritance tax (IHT) bill on your estate. Chapter 17 explains how trusts can help your family and reduce IHT.

Your children growing up should prompt a review of your will. Any guardianship or trusts that you set up when your children were little sprogs may no longer be needed. Your kids might have started to strike out on their own and you may want to amend your will to ensure your estate helps them get on the property ladder or undertake that career-enhancing course. (You can change a trust into a gift through a codicil, but it's best to get a solicitor to do this.)

On the flipside, however, your once angel-faced cherub may have turned into a hormone-ravaged malcontent who couldn't be trusted with a penny of your cash. In this case, you may want to raise the age on which your child can inherit the goodies. You can make this change by adding a codicil to your will.

Get a solicitor to draw up any changes to trusts written into your will. A solicitor will charge a fee but will ensure that the wording is spot on so that your trust does exactly what you want it to do.

Correcting Mistakes in Your Unsigned Will

The golden rule here is simple: You can make changes to your will at any time, *prior* to it being signed and witnessed. After signing, you must tread very carefully or else the changes you make will not be recognised by the court.

Before signing and having your will witnessed, get someone to read it to check for clarity. A friend or family member with experience of writing their own will can tell you if what you've written makes sense to them. You can ask your executors to read through the will; after all, it's up to them to deal with your estate when you've gone. You can also use a solicitor to check that your will is correct but they charge for this service.

You are unlikely to get everything right first time – nobody's perfect. If you have to make corrections, be careful how you go about it:

✔ Use the same colour pen that you used to write your will to make any alterations, otherwise your executors may deem that the changes were added by another person and so ignore them.

✔ If the alterations are considerable, you might want to start again from scratch – if you start crossing out huge swathes of your will it can become very messy and difficult to understand. What's more, your executor may decide someone else made the changes.

✔ If you make any obvious changes to your will document, then sign the changes and have your witnesses sign them, too.

✔ If your unsigned will is on a computer simply replace unwanted passages with the ones you want. Drawing up your will on a computer means it's easy to make changes.

Changing a Beneficiary

If you leave some money to your cherished octogenarian Great-Aunt Mabel, the chances are that she will shuffle off this mortal coil before you.

If you haven't named alternative beneficiaries in your will, any cash gift left to someone who has died becomes part of your residuary estate and is divided up amongst all the living beneficiaries of your residuary estate. The residue of your estate is often worth a lot of money, so it's a good idea to gift it to a beneficiary or beneficiaries.

If you bequeathed an item such as a painting or other family heirloom to a beneficiary who has since died, the gift forms part of the residuary estate. The executor may order that the item is sold and the proceeds divided amongst the living beneficiaries. If this item is something that you are keen to keep within the family, then make an amendment after the death of the beneficiary leaving it to a new beneficiary. You can do this by adding a codicil to your will (see 'Wording a codicil' later in this chapter).

If you have a child who has children of his or her own, and your child sadly predeceases you, any benefit he or she was due to receive from your will goes automatically to their own children (or grandchildren, if their children have died). The partner of your child has no rights to your estate – it is entirely up to you to name them as a beneficiary.

Make life easier on yourself: Name an alternative beneficiary when you write your will in case your first choice dies before you. Naming an alternative should cut down on the number of times you have to change your will.

When reviewing your will, check to see if any of the charities you left money to are still in existence. Charities merge and fold and if you don't get the details right in your will the gift could fail.

Snip, Snip: Cutting Someone Out of Your Will

Disinheriting someone is fraught with danger and shouldn't be done in a fit of pique! Think carefully before changing your will to remove a beneficiary. Ask yourself the following questions:

- ✔ **Will the disinheritance work?** It may feel good to disinherit a beneficiary who has angered you, but they may have legal rights to your estate. (See Chapter 4 for who can put in a claim from your estate.)

- ✔ **Is the split irrevocable?** If you might see eye-to-eye again with your beneficiary, think twice before cutting them out of your will. You may, for example, see your troubled relationship improve very late in life – even on your deathbed – by which time you may not be physically up to the job of putting the person you disinherited back in your will!

- ✔ **What happens to the gift?** If you cut someone out of your will you have to do something with the gift that you had intended them to have. If the beneficiary was only in line for a small gift, then simply sign it over to someone else using a codicil (see the section on codicils later in this chapter). However, if the person cut out of your will was one of your main beneficiaries perhaps you should conduct a root-and-branch review of the gifts made in your will, even going as far as writing a new will (see the section on writing a new will further on in this chapter).

Getting by with a little help from a pro

If you're planning to make changes to your will, seek out the advice of a solicitor or accountant, even if you didn't use one to draw up your will in the first place. You may welcome what a professional brings to the will review process. A professional can alert you to the implications of some of the changes in your life since you drew up your original will. What's more, a professional can stop you from making mistakes when changing your will.

How to get the best from solicitors and accountants is dealt with in Chapter 6.

If you're sure you want to cut someone out of your will, resist the temptation to pick up a pair of scissors and snip out the unwanted name – doing that would infuriate your executors and you'd be remembered as a fruit cake. If you want to cut someone out of your will, you must use a codicil or write a new will.

Avoid writing your reasons for disinheriting someone in your will. Put your reasons in a letter and keep it with your will. The letter may be used in court if your unlucky beneficiary contests your decision.

Changing Financial Circumstances

Any major changes in your financial circumstances, however slowly they materialise, should prompt you to take another look at your will. Such changes include:

- **Getting richer.** If you've owned your own home for more than five years its value has probably more than doubled. Happy days! However, inheritance tax is no longer simply for rich toffs and city slickers. If your property is worth over £312,000 (2008/09 tax year), it is liable for IHT.

  Perhaps you inherit a big pot of cash from that uncle who lived in Los Angeles and did something with computers. Your estate is suddenly pushed over the IHT threshold. You may want to revisit your will and increase the gifts to beneficiaries. Chapter 16 covers getting your estate into tax-saving shape.

- **Getting poorer.** You could be unlucky enough to suffer a downturn in your financial fortunes. All that money you planned to leave your nearest and dearest is spent! Add a codicil to your will to take account of your new lowly circumstances.

Perfect percentages

Bequeathing a percentage of your estate instead of a specific amount of money or shares should reduce the likelihood of you having to make later changes.

However, no matter how you word your will, there is no 100 per cent guarantee that life's ups and downs won't make a change necessary.

Keep a copy of your will close at hand and give it the once over each year to see if a change needs to be made to ensure your family and friends are properly provided for.

Bear in mind that the younger you are when you make your will, the more likely you are to have to change it.

If you become poorer and don't change your will, your beneficiaries could suffer *ademption*. Ademption means that your beneficiaries inherit gifts that are no longer in your estate and under such circumstances they get zilch. Always keep an eye on your wealth and be prepared to reduce your gifts or cut some beneficiaries out of your will if your estate shrinks.

✔ **Retiring:** If you take early retirement, living off your savings means you have less to leave to your beneficiaries. You never know; you may have to raid an account earmarked for a particular loved one. If you need to alter your will to reduce your too-generous gifts, see 'Wording a codicil' later in this chapter.

Changes of circumstance can creep up on you. Read over your will once a year just to check that its terms are still relevant. Consider how your loved ones' circumstances may also have altered, such as a marriage or imminent bankruptcy, which might require a change in your will.

Appointing New Appointees

Over time, the people you originally chose to carry out the wishes expressed in your will – executors and trustees – may no longer be up to the job. These people may have died, become incapable through age or illness, or simply not be keen on the task in hand any more.

Perhaps your children have grown up and flown the nest and, fingers crossed, made a success of things, and don't need a guardian appointed for them, or a trustee to look after their gift. (Take a look at Chapter 6 for tips on how to choose the right appointee.)

As with the other changes outlined in this chapter, you need to write a codicil to change an appointee (see the section on codicils a bit further on in this chapter).

If you make changes to your team of executors, trustees, or guardians, if possible let the person you're taking out of your will know what you're planning. This measure is polite, and also means that the ex-executor or whatever can now rest easy in the knowledge that their help won't be called upon if you die. But don't talk to the original person until you discuss your plans with the person you're planning to appoint in their stead!

Writing Changes into Your Will

You can make changes to your will arrangements in two ways: By using a *codicil* or by making a new will. A codicil is a separate document drawn up after the original will that adds to or alters that will.

In order to make a change to your will you have to be of *sound mind*. If you suffer from some form of mental illness, ask your GP if you're fit to make changes to a will.

Introducing codicils

A *codicil* is an addition to a previously written will. Codicils are often used to add a new beneficiary to a will or to change the amount of someone's legacy. A codicil carries the same legal clout as the original will but can cause complications – so some solicitors advise their clients to destroy or revoke their will and write a new one (perhaps earning them a nice fee in the process). Certainly, if you want to make more than one or two changes, then a new will could be the best option. (Read 'Destroying Your Will' later in this chapter.)

A codicil needs to be on a separate sheet of paper and must be signed and witnessed in the same way as your original will. (Chapter 7 covers witnessing your will.)

Legally, you can write as many codicils as you like, but most solicitors advise that you stick to making one or two changes to your original will through a single codicil. Write a new will if you need to make lots of changes.

Wording a codicil

A codicil should start by stating that it is made *in addition* to your will.

A codicil needs to make clear what you want to leave and to whom. If you have to change the details of your gifts, the same care should be taken as when you wrote your original will. Be precise about the gift and to whom you're leaving it. Give your beneficiary's full name and their relationship to you.

If you don't describe your gift or beneficiary properly, you run the risk that your executors will deem that the gift has failed. (Chapter 4 has more on how gift failure works.)

You can make two types of codicil; the first simply *adds a clause* to your original will, while the second *revokes a previous clause* and replaces it with another.

Adding a clause

In the example below, the testator wants to gift some shares that they forgot about at the time of drawing up their original will.

The simple codicil is written as follows:

> *This codicil is made by me (testator's name and address), as an addition to my will dated (date of will).*
>
> *1. I give 1,000 shares in British Petroleum to my cousin (name of beneficiary).*
>
> *2. In all other respects I confirm my will.*

Revoking a clause

In this example, the testator revokes a beneficiary's gift – perhaps the property is no longer in the estate or the beneficiary has died – but wants to add a new gift and beneficiary into their will.

The codicil is written as follows:

> *This codicil is made by me (testator's name and address), as an addition to my will dated (date of will).*
>
> *I revoke my gift of my mountain bike to my niece (name of beneficiary).*
>
> *I give £500 to my sister (name of beneficiary).*
>
> *In all other respects I confirm my will.*

The phrase 'In all other respects I confirm my will', tacked onto both types of codicil, tells the executors that the clauses not affected by the codicil in the original will still stand.

Witnessing the codicil

The signature to the codicil must be witnessed in exactly the same way as when signing a new will, even down to the *attestation clause* (refer to Chapter 7). A form of words when witnessing a codicil that is acceptable to the courts is:

> *Signed by the testator in our joint presence (your signature) and then by us together in the testator's presence (signatures of your witnesses).*

Get your witnesses to write their address details with their signatures. A dispute may arise after your death over the changes you made to your will, particularly if you remove a beneficiary following a falling out. In such circumstances, your executors may have to track down your witnesses. Cover all the bases and make life easier for your executors!

Don't get your codicil witnessed by any beneficiaries or their spouses, or else you automatically disinherit them.

Having Your Will Changed by the Courts

Now the situation gets tricky, because to get to grips with this topic you have to pretend you've written a will and now popped your clogs. So forgive me for talking about you as if you're no longer around.

Under certain circumstances the courts can decide that your will should be changed after your death. A court doesn't simply decide a will should be changed: Someone has to apply to have it altered. Applications to have your will changed usually come from three distinct groups of people, each with their own reasons for asking for your will to be changed:

- A dependant who feels that you haven't left them enough property in your will.
- A beneficiary who is unhappy at a condition you attached to your gift to them.
- An executor or beneficiary who wants to have a mistake in your will rectified.

Unhappy dependants

Certain groups of people, such as your spouse and children, can ask the courts for more money from your estate than you left them.

Your spouse is in pole position for putting in a claim from your estate, even if he or she remarries after you die. The court can settle any amount of money from your estate on your spouse, regardless of their financial position. Your spouse could be rolling in it yet still have a claim upheld.

The other groups which can claim from your estate – children, stepchildren, former spouse, and anyone who has been maintained by you prior to your death – can only claim on the basis of hardship. Your former dependants may be broke and have to rely on the state for help if they are denied a slice of your estate, for example. Chapter 4 explores the rights of your dependants.

The court has the power to take whatever money is needed to meet the claims of creditors from any part of your estate.

If the debts of the estate are larger than the assets, an estate is *insolvent*. Putting in a claim against an insolvent estate is pointless.

Unreasonable conditions

If a beneficiary feels that a condition tacked onto your gift to them is unreasonable, then they can ask the court to set the condition aside. The sorts of conditions that the courts are likely to deem unreasonable are explored in Chapter 8.

Rectifying a will

If the wording of your will is ambiguous or contains a clear mistake, an executor or beneficiary can ask the courts to *rectify* your will.

The court won't just take the executor's or beneficiary's word for it; evidence must be produced to show that what you wrote isn't really what was meant. Typical types of evidence that may be acceptable to the court are an *affidavit* – a sworn statement – that you made a contrary statement of intent to that made in your will, or a letter outlining a similar circumstance.

Anyone seeking to have your will rectified has to get their skates on. The courts take a dim view on attempts to rectify a will long after the death of the testator (the person who wrote the will).

Changing a living will

Living wills allow you to tell loved ones and doctors what treatment you do not want to receive if you're so ill that you cannot communicate your wishes. (Chapter 10 has lots more on living wills.)

Review your living will at regular intervals – at the same time as you give your standard will the once over.

The way in which the law regards living wills may change and this may cause you to revise your living will.

In theory, changing a living will shouldn't be as dicey as making alterations to a standard will. A living will has no weight in law anyway and so the document may not be challenged in court. Nevertheless, if you want to change the terms of your living will it is best to draw up an entirely new one – you don't want crossings out and added text to make it look like you had a change of heart.

If you read over your living will and are still happy with its terms, why not date and sign it again (not forgetting the witnesses)? Doing so lets your loved ones know that you've reviewed it since drawing it up and are still happy with it.

Clubbing Together to Change Your Will

If your executors and adult beneficiaries agree, they are allowed to change the terms of your will after your death. What? How dare they? You go to the trouble of drawing up a valid will, taking care to distribute your property to your nearest and dearest, and the ingrates go and move the goalposts.

But hang on a minute. Usually your executors and beneficiaries club together to change your will for a good cause such as beating the tax inspector or righting a mistake in your will. Now that's better, isn't it?

Your executors and beneficiaries can use a *deed of variation*, also referred to as a *deed of family arrangement*, to alter the terms of your will.

The purpose of the deed is to change the way your property is distributed under your will. Usually a deed of variation is used with two goals in mind:

- ✔ **Improving tax planning.** You may not have left your property in a tax-efficient manner – naughty you! Your beneficiaries may want to perform some jiggery-pokery with your will to repair the damage and ensure that the taxman gets as little of your loot as possible – good on them!

- ✔ **Making provision for another beneficiary.** If you drew up your will a long time ago you may have left someone important out of your will. Or perhaps a beneficiary needs more from your will. If so, terms can be altered.

Alternatively, you may have forgotten to provide for someone who has a legal claim on your estate. A deed of variation can head off a legal challenge.

You need a solicitor to draw up a deed of variation. See Chapter 14 for more on how deeds of variation can be used to save tax.

Your executors and beneficiaries can enter into a deed of variation provided that its terms don't reduce the share of any beneficiary under 18. A deed of variation must be in writing, signed by beneficiaries making the variation (and by the executors if the variation means that more tax will be payable), and executed within two years of the testator's death.

Once a beneficiary has been changed through a deed of variation, it is set in stone – no second chances exist.

By drawing up your will properly, working out the tax implications, and regularly reviewing your will, you should be able to negate the need for your beneficiaries to resort to a deed of variation.

Ka-Boom! Destroying Your Will

It sounds a bit dramatic, but deliberately destroying your will is a legitimate way of revoking it. According to the absolutely ancient Wills Act of 1837, you can revoke your will by 'burning, tearing or otherwise destroying it'. Whichever way you choose to destroy your will – flushing it down the toilet, or feeding it to a goat are two possible, if rarely used, methods – just make sure you do it properly; no legible text should survive! Destroy *all* copies of your will – not just the original.

If you deliberately destroy your will and then die without replacing it, you are deemed to have died intestate – without a will. Dying intestate can have major consequences on how your estate is dished out (check out Chapter 2 for full details).

If someone else destroys your will without your say-so, your will is still valid. Any evidence that exists of its contents – such as a letter written by you outlining the will – can be used to decide who inherits. If you are concerned that your will is at risk of being destroyed by an irate relative, keep it locked away in a fireproof safe, or stash it away at your bank (refer to Chapter 6 for more ideas on safekeeping your will).

Starting Over: Creating a New Will

If you decide to destroy or revoke your old will and opt for writing a new one, always start with the legal jargon: 'I revoke all previous wills and codicils.' If you don't make that position clear, then only the parts of the old will that conflict with the new will are cancelled.

The rules for writing a new will are the same as for making the first one. How much extra work making a new will involves depends largely on how long it is since you drew up your original will. If you decide to draw up a new will soon after your original one, many of the assumptions that you made about your estate could still hold water. But if it's been five or more years since you drew up your original will, you need to evaluate your estate from scratch. Follow these simple steps:

1. **Work out how much your estate is now worth.** Your house may be substantially higher in value, or perhaps those shares you earmarked for your son or daughter are now worthless after a stock market crash.

2. **Decide what your beneficiaries need.** The financial circumstances of your loved ones can change dramatically. Consider your loved ones' new financial situations in a new will.

3. **Take account of tax changes.** The Chancellor changes – okay, usually increases – taxes in the spring budget each year. Work out how any tax changes affect your plans.

Don't forget to sign and witness your new will (Chapter 7 has the details).

Chapter 10

Making Clear Your Funeral Wishes

*Y*ou can use your will to dictate your basic funeral wishes. You can outline whether you want to be buried or cremated, any hymns you want sung or music played. You might even take the opportunity to detail the type of gravestone and inscription you want, perhaps even incorporating a best before date if you so desire!

Incorporating your funeral wishes into your will comes with the danger that you may be buried or cremated before the will is read. Let your executors and loved ones know that your will contains your funeral wishes. Even better, go for the belt-and-braces approach and write your funeral wishes into a letter and give your loved ones a copy.

Your will is not the place to go into pages of detail about your funeral. By all means state your basic requests, but save the finer points for a letter.

Web sites can give you inspiration for readings, hymns, and music for funerals. For example, check out the Church Music Site for suitable Christian hymns at www.cul.co.uk/music/funeral.htm. It can be comforting for your loved ones for someone to give a *eulogy* – which literally means a good word – about you and your life.

It's your funeral

Your funeral can be as individual as the life you lead. A little research can turn up some unconventional ideas for ceremonies to celebrate your life.

If you're not religious and would like to keep the big bloke in the sky out of your funeral, contact the British Humanist Association for a list of people who can conduct non-religious funeral services. Get in touch with them at www.humanism.org.uk.

The Lesbian and Gay Christian Movement has lists of ordained ministers who are happy to conduct ceremonies – check out their Web site at www.lgcm.org.uk.

Some people of a nautical bent want to be buried at sea. Sadly, the authorities don't look kindly on sea burial and have imposed stringent guidelines. Currently there are only three sites around the UK where sea burials are allowed: off the Isle of Wight and East Sussex.

In addition, a special licence must be obtained for a sea burial from the Department for Environment, Food and Rural Affairs (DEFRA). Look on the DEFRA Web site for more details: www.defra.gov.uk.

Those with one eye on future generations may want to arrange an environmentally friendly funeral; a green funeral. Green funerals involve the use of biodegradable material such as willow or chipboard and even the use of horses to pull a funeral cortege instead of a gas-guzzling hearse!

Remember, though, that in most green burial sites (usually woodland rather than a cemetery) the use of headstones is usually not permitted.

You don't need an 'official' at your funeral; you can choose to rely on a loved one to say a few words if you wish. However, if you're buried in a churchyard it follows that a minister will conduct the proceedings.

Paying for Your Funeral

The cost of your funeral can be taken out of your estate. (Remember the clause about *funeral expenses and testamentary expenses* in Chapter 8?) Alternatively, you can purchase a prepaid funeral plan from a funeral director. This does exactly what it says on the tin – or should that be lid? – you pay an agreed sum in advance for an agreed service. The plan usually includes the cost of cremation or burial and the services of a minister. Plans start at around £1,500.

Let your loved ones know if you purchase a prepaid funeral plan otherwise you might end up with two funerals. (Didn't they make a film about that?)

The Office of Fair Trading Web site (www.oft.gov.uk) offers free leaflets to download on choosing a funeral director, funeral costs, and prepaid funeral plans. Also check out the Age Concern England Web site at www.ace.org.uk for advice on arranging a funeral.

Going out in a blaze of glory

If you have a yen to leave this world with a bang, a company in Essex can mix your ashes with fireworks for an unforgettable send-off. Check out www.heavensabove fireworks.com for more.

Americans are innovators in many ways, and our friends in the States have gone a step further in alternative send-offs. A company in California can scatter cremated remains from a helium balloon that bursts at 30,000 feet. If that isn't high enough, Celestis Services in Texas can pop human ashes into a small tube attached to a satellite that orbits Earth.

For a more down-to-earth approach, ashes can be mixed with molten glass into a decorative 3-inch sphere mounted on a base bearing your name, or whipped up with oil paints for a commemorative portrait.

And finally, for a watery grave, a company in Georgia can mix cremated remains with cement and sink the block to the bottom of the deep blue sea to form habitats for corals and sponges.

If you were claiming state benefits at the time of your death your loved ones may be able to obtain a grant from the Benefits Agency Social Fund to help with the costs of your funeral. Contact them through the Department for Work and Pensions, the Web site to try is www.dwp.gov.uk.

Remember to check out what happens if the funeral director goes bust. Is the money you have prepaid for your funeral ring-fenced? What's more, if you pay by instalments, will your policy be invalidated if you die before you have made the final instalment?

Your next of kin are not legally bound to follow your wishes for your funeral or the disposal of your remains, even if you put them in a will.

Donating Your Body to Medical Science

It's not very nice to think about your body being operated on after your death, but you can save a life, help research into diseases, and train the next generation of doctors by donating your body. The three types of donation you can make are:

- ✔ **Organ donation.** Parts of your body, such as kidneys, heart or lungs are removed for transplantation to someone in need. Check out www. uktransplant.org.uk to register as an organ donor.

✔ **Tissue donation.** Tissue from your body and organs is used in research experiments. Donations of human tissue can help doctors get to grips with killer diseases. You can find out more about tissue donation from the Tissue Bank Web site on `www.bodydonation.org.uk`.

✔ **Whole-body donation.** You can leave your body to medical science for teaching anatomy to medical students. Contact your local medical school (usually the medicine department in your local university) for more information. It's absolutely essential that you tell your loved ones your intentions. If not, it will come as a very nasty shock when the local medical school comes to claim your corpse.

You can use your will to make an organ donation but by the time the will is read it's possible that the organs are no longer useful for transplantation. It's best to keep a *donor card* with you (available from `www.uktransplant.org.uk`) and essential to let your next of kin know your wishes. Ultimately, your family must sign over your body, as a donor card is not a legal document, just proof of your intention to donate.

You can ask the medical school to return your ashes – or your body – to your loved ones when it is finished with your body. Make such a wish clear on the medical school's donation form. Don't forget to explain in a separate letter what you want to happen to your remains after the medical school has finished with them. This gives your loved ones the heads-up that they must prepare themselves to do something with your remains.

If any doubt about the cause of death exists, the coroner has lawful possession of the body. Any wishes made in a will for the disposal of the body are, quite literally, put on ice!

Breathing Easier with a Living Will

Advances in medical science make it possible to prolong life as never before. That reality pleases many, but what if the quality of the life being prolonged is poor? In fact, what if you're kept alive purely by medical science and have no genuine prospect of recovery?

A *living will* is designed to let loved ones and doctors know what your wishes are in the event of a serious illness rendering you incapable of communication. In a living will, you can outline under what circumstances you would like medical treatment to be withdrawn and let nature take its course. You can have a living will and a standard will.

Living wills are very individual and need precise wording – after all, when they kick in it's probably too late for you to make changes. As a result, you may want to seek legal advice when drawing up a living will.

Understanding the living will dilemma

Legally speaking, a living will is a pale imitation of a standard will. A standard will has a multitude of laws backing it up but a living will has very little apart from the recent Mental Capacity Act.

As a result, your living will can be ignored by all and sundry. Doctors take the Hippocratic oath, which binds them to serve their patients to the best of their ability. For many doctors this means doing their utmost to keep their patients alive.

However, living wills are growing in importance and real decisions are made based on their contents. They provide a firm guide to your loved ones and doctors are increasingly taking them into account when deciding treatment. Many doctors now believe that if the patient has gone to the trouble of drawing up a living will, their feelings shouldn't be ignored. The British Medical Association has said of living wills '...where incompetent or unconscious patients have made a formal and specific statement applicable to the circumstances, doctors should regard it as potentially legally binding'.

The recently introduced Mental Capacity Act means that healthcare professionals have to take the terms of a living will into consideration when deciding upon medical treatment. If you're making a will you can make a decision now about treatment you wouldn't want in future when you have lost capacity. A living will must be in writing, signed and witnessed, and if it applies to life-sustaining treatment there must be a statement that the decision stands even if life is at risk.

If you go into hospital or a nursing home and have not made clear what treatment you want to refuse, the authorities are legally bound to keep you alive by whatever means necessary.

Don't leave it too late to make a living will. If you make one when you're in good health, it will be seen as a strong indication of your true feelings.

Writing your living will

If you want to take the plunge and write a living will then follow some simple steps to help it punch its weight:

- ✔ Keep your living will concise, clear, and ensure you give your full name and address.

- ✔ Make clear the circumstances under which you want its terms to become active, such as if you become terminally ill and have no means of communicating.

- ✔ Outline the sorts of treatments you don't want, such as being fed by tube. This is called an *advance directive*. Make your advance directive as clear as possible.

   The withdrawal of food or water under the terms of your living will may hasten your death but at the same time lead to severe discomfort. If you don't want fluid and nutrition to be withdrawn, say so in your living will.

- ✔ Get the document witnessed by two people, in exactly the same way – including attestation clause – as a standard will. Make sure the persons witnessing your living will are not beneficiaries under your standard will, if you have one. (Refer to Chapter 7.)

- ✔ Keep the living will with your standard will and let your nearest and dearest know where it is.

- ✔ Let your GP know that you have made a living will. If the time comes, your GP can let the hospital know that a living will is in play. You can discuss the medical profession's attitude to living wills with your GP, or check out the British Medical Association's Web site at www.bma.org.uk or The Law Society's Web site at www.lawsociety.org.uk.

- ✔ In a pinch, check out the Web site for the Terrence Higgins Trust, which, in conjunction with Kings College, London, Centre of Medical Law and Ethics, has published a good living will form, including forms of advance directive and health care proxy, at www.tht.org.uk. You need to make a donation to access the form.

Any request you make to have basic medical treatment withdrawn can be ignored, even if it is in the form of an *advance directive*. Basic medical treatment includes pain relief and hygiene measures. However, medical staff have to take your wishes – as expressed through a living will – into account.

Keep a card in your wallet stating where you keep your living will. This can prove very wise if you have a bad accident and rendered unable to communicate your wishes.

An advance directive not to receive certain types of health care is not the same as *euthanasia* (painlessly killing someone who is severely disabled or terminally ill). Euthanasia and assisted suicide are both illegal. If you say in your living will that you want to be helped to die then your doctors will ignore it and it may bring the rest of the document into disrepute. Information is available from the Voluntary Euthanasia Society's Web site at www.ves.org.uk.

Dictating the medical treatment you want to receive

Not only can you use a living will to tell doctors what sorts of treatment you *don't* want, you can also use it to make clear any treatment you would prefer to receive. Such a clause in a living will is called an *advance statement*.

An advance statement can be worded as follows:

> *I refuse medical procedures to prolong my life or keep me alive by artificial means if I have a severe physical illness which in the opinion of two independent medical practitioners, it is unlikely that I will ever recover.*

If this is too open-ended you may wish to make your advance statement more specific, in this example prolonged coma is taken into account:

> *I refuse medical procedures to prolong my life or keep me alive by artificial means if I have been permanently unconscious for a period of 6 months and in the opinion of two independent medical practitioners there is no likelihood that I will recover.*

An advance statement does not carry the same weight as an *advance directive* (a request not to receive certain treatment). In the final analysis it's up to the doctor what treatment you receive, provided, of course, it doesn't go against any advance directive you may have made.

If you're pregnant at the time when a living will comes into force, the doctors are bound to do their utmost to keep your child alive. If that means ignoring the terms of your living will then they will.

Appointing medical proxies

You can use your living will to appoint a *medical proxy*. A medical proxy, sometimes called a *health care proxy*, is someone who communicates the wishes expressed in your living will to the doctors or who can make decisions about your medical care on your behalf. A trusted friend or close relative make good medical proxies, especially if they have some sort of medical background. Doctors don't have to follow your medical proxy, particularly if the wishes of the next of kin are different.

You can appoint a medical proxy by writing:

> *I wish to appoint (name and address of proxy) as my medical proxy. The proxy should be involved in any decisions about my health care options if I am physically or mentally incapable of making my views known. He or she is fully aware of my medical wishes.*

Make sure that your proxy is happy to do what you ask of them. Give them a copy of your living will and make sure your next of kin know who they are and what their role will be, if the time comes. Your proxy only has a say in your medical treatment, not your assets, so there is no risk of legal wrangling between your proxy and the person with power of attorney, if they're different people.

Part III
Managing Probate

'First of all, the good news – You have been
left a very large old estate...'

In this part . . .

The chapters in this part show you what to do when someone close to you dies. I take you through all the things you may have to do to make sure the deceased's estate goes to all the beneficiaries rather than the taxman. No stone is left unturned in this part to make sure you're well equipped to deal with the estate of someone who has died, from tracking down creditors and beneficiaries through selling property to – boo hiss! – paying any tax that may be due.

Chapter 11

What to Do When Someone Dies

In This Chapter

▶ Registering the death

▶ Organising the funeral

▶ Considering burial or cremation

*T*he death of a spouse, parent, close relation, or good friend is a desperately sad time. Your emotions can run riot, but many people find some solace in having practical steps to take which occupy their mind. This chapter helps you understand what steps need to be taken immediately following someone's death.

Some duties, such as registering the death or arranging the funeral, can be undertaken by an executor or administrator, although it is not strictly their job. If you are the nearest and dearest of the deceased, you may want to take care of these arrangements yourself. But if you're acting as an executor, the golden rule is to be prepared; be ready to step up if you're needed.

Registering the Death

When someone dies a doctor should be called. The doctor issues a certificate stating the cause of death, along with a document outlining who is eligible to *register* the death.

The local Registrar of Births, Deaths and Marriages has to be told when anyone in their catchment area dies. The local registrar, or Registry Office, is listed in the Yellow Pages.

In England and Wales, the registrar in the district in which the death occurred must be informed within five days.

If the doctor sends the medical certificate direct to the registrar, allow a few days for it to arrive before going to the Registry Office to officially register the death.

The person who informs the registrar of the death is officially called an *informant*. Who can act as an informant partly depends on where the deceased died. Most deaths occur at home or in a public building such as a nursing home or hospital. Under such circumstances, the following people may act as informant, in this order:

- A relative of the deceased who was present at the death.

- A relative who was present during the final illness and who perhaps had visited on the day of the death.

- A relative living nearby to the place of death.

- Anyone who was present at the death.

- A person in authority in the building where the death occurred; if the death took place in a nursing home the owner can act as informant.

- The people the deceased shared a building with.

- The person who is arranging the funeral.

If the death takes place in a place other than the deceased's home or a public building, the following people can register the death in the following order:

- A relative of the deceased.

- Anyone present at the death.

- The person who found the body.

- The police (if the body is unidentified).

- Whoever is arranging the funeral.

If the deceased dies abroad, perhaps on holiday, the death is first registered in that country. In some countries, the local British Consul should be able to register the death. Eventually, a copy of this certificate becomes available from the UK's General Register Office. Dying abroad may cause some delay, but nothing too drastic provided the death is not suspicious. But don't forget that the Consul usually won't pay for the body to be sent home.

Documents needed to register the death

You are interviewed by the registrar, during which he or she asks you to provide the following information and documents:

- The medical certificate outlining the cause of death (unless this was sent directly to the registrar by the doctor).

- The full name, address, and occupation of the deceased.

- The date and place of death, as well as the date and place of birth (take the birth certificate of the deceased along with you if you can).
- The deceased's state pension or benefits documents.
- The names and dates of birth of the deceased's spouse and children under 16, and the spouse's occupation.
- The NHS medical card of the deceased, if you have it.

Provided the information you supply is up to scratch and you have the right to act as informant, the registrar will ask you to check over the details provided and sign the register. The registrar then gives you a death certificate, stating the name of the deceased, date, place, and cause of death. The death certificate is a copy of the entry on the register of births, deaths, and marriages.

Carefully check what's written in the register before you sign it. Once the register is signed, an order of the Registrar General – a sort of super-registrar for the whole country – may be required to correct it.

Ask for several copies of the death certificate from the registrar. Several different institutions you need to inform of the death will probably need to see a death certificate at the same time. A nominal fee is levied for each extra copy of the death certificate.

The disposal certificate

While you're with the registrar ask for the *disposal certificate* – a rather unsympathetic term for a certificate of burial and cremation, also known as a green form. You need to give this certificate to the funeral director so that he or she can collect the deceased from the mortuary and organise the funeral arrangements. If the body is to be cremated, ask for an application for cremation, too. (See 'Returning to the air: Cremation' later in this chapter.)

The funeral director passes on the disposal certificate to the cemetery authority or the vicar or priest of the churchyard where burial is to take place.

Deaths involving the coroner

When a death that may not be due to natural causes occurs, it must be reported to the coroner. The coroner is a type of judge who is obliged to hold an inquest into any violent or unnatural death or a sudden death of unknown cause. Deaths as a result of accident, suicide, poisoning, surgery, murder, or while the deceased was in prison or police custody must be reported. The police will usually do the reporting.

Registering a death in Scotland

In Scotland the rules governing the registering of a death are more flexible than those in England and Wales. For starters, the registrar must be informed of death taking place within eight days, not five. What's more, the death can be registered in the district where the death occurred or where the deceased usually resided. However, the death of a visitor to Scotland must be registered where the death took place.

Deaths can be registered by relatives of the deceased, a person present at the death, an executor or legal representative of the deceased, an occupier of the building in which the death occurred, or anyone with the paperwork needed to register the death.

The information that the registrar needs is the same as in England, except that the time of death must be given too.

As in England, the informant is given a certificate allowing the funeral director they choose to collect the deceased's remains.

The coroner sends a letter to the registrar saying that the death can be recorded. If a coroner's inquest must take place, the coroner acts as informant for the purpose of registering the death. It is then up to the family to obtain copies of the death certificate from the Registry Office, which is listed in the Yellow Pages.

If the deceased had not been treated by a doctor during his or her illness or hadn't seen a doctor within 14 days of death, the death is reported to the coroner.

Breaking the News: Informing People of the Death

When the death occurs you may need to let the wider world know what's happened. Putting a notice in a local or national paper makes friends and distant family aware of the deceased's passing. You can call the newspaper yourself or ask the funeral director to do so.

As a general rule, let the following people and institutions know:

- Her Majesty's Revenue & Customs (HMRC).
- Bank and credit card companies.
- The deceased's doctor (if a different doctor provided the medical certificate).

✔ Employer or pension scheme.

✔ Council Tax and Housing Benefit office.

✔ The solicitor of the deceased if they had one.

✔ The Department for Work and Pensions if the deceased received a state pension or benefits; the registrar issues a free death certificate for this.

You should return the deceased's passport, driving licence, and any benefit or pension books to the relevant authorities.

Celebrating a Life: Planning the Send-off

You don't need this book to tell you the importance of getting funeral arrangements right. Many funerals are planned right down to the tiniest detail to minimise the distress of loved ones and ensure a proper celebration of the life of the departed. Chapter 10 has more on funerals.

The executor must tell the deceased's next of kin any funeral wishes that are outlined in the will. However, these wishes have no weight in law. The person organising the funeral can do what he or she wants, even if they go against the deceased's wishes.

Picking a funeral director

The person who died may have a prepaid funeral plan and left the policy documents with their will (refer to Chapter 8). If not, you must employ a funeral director, or undertaker, to take care of all the funeral arrangements for you in return for a fee.

A good funeral director should provide the following:

✔ A written estimate of how much the funeral will cost at the outset.

✔ A basic and comparatively inexpensive service, which may just involve a simple coffin.

✔ A detailed account of what each item has cost after the funeral.

Some funeral directors break their services down so that you can choose what you would like them to do, others simply offer a range of all-in packages, ranging from the elaborate and expensive to the simple and less costly.

Look for a funeral director who is a member of one of the three trade associations, who have procedures in place to resolve disputes between funeral directors and clients:

- ✔ **The National Association of Funeral Directors:** www.nafd.org.uk
- ✔ **The Society of Allied and Independent Funeral Directors (SAIF):** www.saif.org.uk
- ✔ **The Funeral Standards Council:** www.funeral-standards-council.co.uk

The amount spent on the funeral in no way reflects how much the deceased was loved. Funeral directors may market their most expensive packages with flowery language – the subtext being that the more you spend, the more special the person was – but try and ignore it. Buy a package that fulfils the needs of the family and friends but still leaves enough in the kitty to pay tax, creditors, and beneficiaries.

Returning to the air: Cremation

Like miniskirts, cappuccino, and Microsoft, *cremation* (reducing the body to ash) was unheard of back in Victorian times. When someone died they were buried and that was that. However, attitudes change and cremation is now more popular than burial. The local parish church is no longer a focal point of everyone's life. To be buried in the grounds of a building that many may never have visited strikes some people as odd, even hypocritical. What's more, cremation is far cheaper than burial and therefore less of a financial strain on those left behind.

More form filling

A body that is cremated cannot be exhumed so the law demands that those wanting to lay their loved ones to rest in this way have to jump through a few administrative hoops. As well as getting the registrar's burial and cremation (disposal) form, an *application for cremation*, which you can get from the funeral director, must be completed by the next of kin or the executor. This application has to be countersigned, usually by the funeral director.

The deceased's doctor has to fill in a form outlining certain medical information. If the deceased has a pacemaker fitted it must be removed prior to cremation or else it can cause an explosion. Quite a dramatic way to go! A second doctor has to offer a second opinion.

Costs of cremation

Most crematoria are run by local authorities, which have a scale of fees for a cremation. Crematoria charge for the cremation, use of the on-site chapel, storage of ashes, and a memorial.

Cremation comes with many of the trappings of a traditional burial. Crematoria offer plots in their gardens of remembrance where the urn containing the ashes can be buried. Loved ones can mark the plot with a plaque – although the crematorium is likely to insist on a uniform type of plaque and even inscription.

Most crematoria are open Monday to Friday, but some offer cremation services at the weekend (these usually cost more). Crematoria operate to a very tight schedule and services usually have to be very short. Often a funeral service takes place in a church and then the mourners move on to the crematorium. For more details, see the Web site of the Cremation Society of Great Britain at www.srgw.demon.co.uk/CremSoc.

Before cremation can take place, the cause of death has to be established beyond reasonable doubt by the doctors. A coroner can order that only a burial should take place – to allow for the body to be exhumed at a later date, if necessary.

Returning to the earth: Burial

Burial usually means less upfront administration but more expense. The only piece of documentation you need is the registrar's disposal form. The expenses associated with burial are legion. Buying a plot and gravestone alone can run into many thousands of pounds.

Those wanting a grave to be the final testament to someone's life may be in for a surprise or two. You must follow the churchyard rules on what can be carved on a gravestone, and how the surrounding grave must look – usually lawn so that it doesn't get in the way of mowing. A good funeral director should know the rules of the local churchyard. After all, they arrange funerals every day; you may only have to do it once.

Paying for the Funeral

A bill for even the simplest funeral can run into many thousands of pounds. The funeral director's account should be very detailed – outlining money paid out to the crematorium, the vicar, even the florist.

You should not have to settle the bill out of your own pocket. Major banks and building societies release cash from the deceased's accounts to enable funeral expenses to be paid after they've seen the funeral director's bill.

The payment of funeral expenses is the first claim on the estate of the deceased. That means that the cost of a funeral is met before HMRC, creditors, or beneficiaries get any loot.

You can ask the funeral director to wait to bill you until you have been granted probate or letters of administration. Funeral directors are pretty used to waiting for their money. However, settling their bill immediately can prove less distressing to the next of kin, not to say fairer to the funeral director who has overheads to meet. Some funeral directors offer a discount for quick payment.

Check the will to see if the deceased specified which account should be used to cover the funeral expenses.

If the deceased's next of kin are on benefits they can ask the Social Fund for a loan to cover funeral costs. You can get more information from the Department for Work and Pensions on www.dwp.gov.uk or Citizens Advice on www.citizenadvice.org.uk.

Chapter 12

Pro-what? The Basics of the Probate Process

*P*robate is all about dealing with the estate of someone who has died. Looking after someone's estate (being the *executor*) is a major responsibility. Whether the estate is worth a few thousand quid or millions of pounds, everyone involved pins their hopes on everything going well.

Being chosen as an executor is a real vote of confidence in your character. The person who named you in their will trusted you to do what is right. If you step into the breach and administer the estate of someone who has died without a will, then the onus is on you to get it right.

In this chapter, I show you what probate is and the processes you can expect to face when you administer someone else's estate.

Starting at the Beginning: What Is Probate?

Apparently, only two certainties exist in life: Death and taxes. But to that short list you can add probate.

The word *probate* comes from the Latin 'to prove' as probate is the legal recognition that the will is valid and the executors can deal with the estate. Nowadays, probate has come to mean the process of gathering up the property of someone who has died and then distributing it to creditors, the tax-collector, and finally beneficiaries. Whether a valid will exists or not, this process is called the *administration* of an estate.

The person or people who deal with the deceased's estate are called *personal representatives*. Personal representatives come from one of three distinct groups:

- **Executor.** Someone appointed in a will to oversee the probate process by distributing the estate. The executor is duty bound to follow the wishes expressed in the will. If, for example, the will states that a beneficiary should not get a gift until a specific age, it's up to the executor to make sure this happens.

- **Administrator.** If no valid will exists naming executors, someone must come forward to take the deceased's estate through probate. More often than not a close relative volunteers to administer the estate. This person is called – wait for it – an administrator. Instead of getting *grant of probate* (explained below), an administrator applies for *grant of letters of administration*. An administrator doesn't have the terms of a will to follow. Instead, the administrator is legally bound to distribute the deceased's property under the rules of intestacy (refer to Chapter 2 for how intestacy works).

If a will exists but doesn't name executors, an administrator must dole out the estate according to the terms of the will, rather than intestacy, as the will is still valid – just not perfect.

- **Courts.** If no one comes forward to take an estate through probate, then the courts step into the breach. Everything is done by the letter of the law, but without the human touch. This is the last you'll hear about this situation here, as this book presumes someone – maybe you – is willing to act as a personal representative.

If the executors appointed in a will have died or are unwilling to act, then a beneficiary steps into the breach and acts as an administrator of the estate. Under such circumstances, the would-be administrator has to apply for *grant of letters of administration with will annexed*. Many wills make provision for an executor being unable to act by naming an alternative. Alternatives have exactly the same powers as the first choice executor.

An important difference between administrators and executors is that some of the powers of an executor kick in on the testator's death. An administrator has to wait for grant of letters of administration before they can act.

Ideally a beneficiary should be paid their inheritance within a year of the testator's death. This time period is often referred to as the *executor's year* but also applies to people administering the estate under letters of administration. So get moving!

Understanding Grant of Probate and Letters of Administration

As an executor or administrator you can't fulfil your duties without first getting confirmation or permission from the courts to do so. *Grant of probate* is the official seal of approval for an executor to deal with the estate. Without grant of probate, you can't get down to sorting out much of the deceased's estate, such as selling shares and getting your hands on money held in some bank accounts.

In situations where no will exists, the person looking to administer the estate must apply for *letters of administration*. Letters of administration, like a grant of probate, is the official go-ahead to allow a person to act on behalf of the deceased.

In England and Wales both grants of probate and letters of administration are doled out by the High Court through a network of *probate registries*. You can find the address of your nearest probate registry in the Yellow Pages or by checking out www.hmcourts-service.gov.uk/cms/wills.htm.

A Highland thing

In Scotland, the terms used to describe the people involved in the administration process are different to those used in England and Wales:

✔ An executor appointed in a will is an *executor-nominate*.

✔ Someone appointed by the court to act as administrator (for example, if no will exists) is an *executor-dative*.

✔ Grant of probate is called *confirmation*.

✔ Letters of administration are called by the same name but are issued by the Commissary Department of the Sheriff Court.

You don't have to sit twiddling your thumbs until you receive the grant of probate. Typical jobs an executor can get on with prior to obtaining grant of probate include organising the funeral arrangements, getting a death certificate, and securing the property of the deceased.

Applying for grant of probate and letters of administration are explored in greater detail in Chapter 13.

Knowing When You Don't Need a Grant of Probate

If the estate is small and simple, then it may not need a grant of probate.

The following rules apply:

- ✔ No asset in the estate is worth more than £5,000
- ✔ All the property in the estate is held on a beneficial joint tenancy basis (see below for more)

Under such circumstances, the executor can crack on with the job of gathering in the assets, paying debts, and making sure the beneficiaries get what they are due. However, you must have a copy of the death certificate to take to the bank before they hand over the cash. With small estates, the administration process you need to follow is set out during the next few chapters (such as gathering in the estate and tracking down and paying creditors); you're just relieved of the tiresome job of obtaining grant of probate or letters of administration. Now isn't that nice?

Property owned on a *beneficial joint tenancy* basis isn't subject to probate. On the death of one joint tenant, the ownership of the entire interest in the property automatically passes to the surviving joint tenants. (Chapter 5 covers leaving a home in a will.)

Even if the estate doesn't require a grant of probate, Her Majesty's Revenue & Customs (HMRC) may need to see a set of estate accounts. So keep a record of all the money gathered in and paid out during the administration process. Check out Chapter 14 for how to draw up estate accounts.

Even if the estate doesn't have to go through probate, keep a copy of the will, or the original if you can, so that it can be produced – hey presto! – if a dispute arises.

Team Executor: Working Together

Most wills appoint more than one executor to share the workload and keep an eye on one another. Also, it's common for more than one person to apply for letters of administration.

Meet up with your fellow executors or administrators at the start of the process to divide up the work. One of you may have experience of dealing with tax, while another may be very close to the deceased's nearest and dearest. Talk it over and decide who is comfortable doing what – it's useful if one executor or administrator takes a leading role in the process to make sure the estate is administered as quickly and smoothly as possible.

Stay in touch with your fellow executors and administrators. Some key documents need to be signed by all the executors or administrators; for example, all the executors have to attend the probate registry when applying for grant of probate (see Chapter 13).

Treat the probate process as you would work. Agree to an agenda and follow it through. After all, it's a solemn process. Put your decisions about dividing up the work in writing and get all executors or administrators to sign. The document isn't legally binding, but it's good to set out clearly what everyone's responsibilities are.

Just because another executor or administrator takes on a particular area of work doesn't absolve you of any blame if something goes wrong – not a bit of it! A creditor or beneficiary doesn't care who deals with what, just as long as they get what they are due under intestacy or the terms of a will. If another executor makes a mistake, you may be liable too.

Turning down the job of executor

Just because you're named as an executor of a will doesn't mean you have to take on the job. Perhaps you have too much on your plate to take on the job or you're suffering ill health. Be honest with yourself early on – it's better not to take on the role than to do a rushed, slipshod job.

If you want to renounce your executor status, contact your local probate registry (you can find the details in the Yellow Pages or visit `www.hmcourts-service.gov.uk/cms/wills.htm`). Alternatively, if you don't want

to take the option of renouncing your right to act, ask for a *power reserved letter* from the probate registry, fill it in and return it. By using a power reserved letter you retain the right to step back into the role of executor at a later date, perhaps if another executor dies.

If you believe you may have difficulty acting as an executor but don't want to go to the extreme of getting a power reserved letter, you can appoint a solicitor to do all the legwork for you. See the section 'Using a Solicitor' later in this chapter for more on this option.

Four is the maximum number of executors. If more than four executors are appointed in the will, an executor must renounce or reserve their rights to act. The non-acting executor can step back into the breach at a later date if one of the acting executors can no longer do the job.

Following the Duties of an Executor and Administrator

The tasks of an executor and administrator are the same (for the sake of simplicity, I just use the term 'executor' rather than 'executor and administrator' in this section). I give an overview of the duties here, and go into more detail in Chapters 11 and 13.

Dealing with the deceased

An executor often takes a hand in sorting out the funeral arrangements of the deceased. For example, the will may outline the funeral wishes of the deceased or mention a pot of money to cover the expense of the funeral. How much of a role an executor plays in the funeral arrangements depends on the wishes of the next of kin. The family may want to take care of every little detail themselves. As an executor, it's best to make yourself available to the deceased's nearest and dearest, and be ready, willing, and able to take some of the administrative strain if they wish.

Registering the death and obtaining a death certificate can be dealt with by the executor or by the deceased's nearest and dearest.

 The death certificate is essential to administer the estate as no one is legally dead until it has been issued —a very strange scenario! Head to Chapter 11 for more on getting hold of the death certificate.

Obtaining the legal power to act

You must get hold of the original will – if one was written – and obtain the necessary legal powers to administer the deceased's estate. You need to obtain grant of probate (if a will exists) or letters of administration (if it doesn't) from your local probate registry to assume legal responsibility.

If you are one of two or more executors, check that the other executors are willing to act. Then sort out how you're going to divvy up the work. If any trustees or guardians are named in the will, let them know the terms of the will.

Valuing the estate of the deceased

Before you're granted the power to administer the estate by the probate registry, you need to put a figure on the estate. This is necessary for working out the tax bill (explained in Chapter 15). You must track down the deceased's bank accounts, savings, and shares. In addition, you need to work out whether the home of the deceased is subject to probate – it won't be if it's owned on a joint tenancy basis.

You then need to subtract any debts. If it is a large or complex estate you may have to advertise in the local paper to alert creditors to what has happened so that they can come forward and put in a claim (see Chapter 14 for how to go about this).

If the estate is worth more than £300,000 (2007/08 tax year) or £312,000 (2008/09 tax year) and not going straight to a spouse, charity, or political party, then inheritance tax may have to be paid. See Chapter 15 for more on IHT.

How to go about valuing the estate of the deceased is explained in Chapter 13.

Taking care of the tax-collector

As executor, you must sort out any tax bill arising from the estate. Tax bills might include income tax, Capital Gains Tax, and inheritance tax. You have the power to raise money from the sale of assets and even to borrow in your role as executor in order to meet an IHT bill. The tax-collector may not just take the executor's word on how much tax is owed; it may be up to you, as executor, to submit IHT accounts. The tax-collector may come back to the executor with a different figure – no doubt higher! – for what is owed in tax. As executor, you must fight the corner if the tax-collector tries to take too much of the loot.

Check out Chapter 13 for more on calculating the tax due on the estate.

Good will hunting

One of your first jobs as executor is to find the will. The will is essential for proceeding to grant of probate. Hopefully, the person who made the will told you where they kept the original. However, if the whereabouts of the will is a mystery, and you can't find the document in the deceased's home, try looking in the following places:

- ✔ **Solicitor's office.** If the will was drawn up with the help of a solicitor, then the original may be held in the solicitor's office.

- ✔ **The bank.** Wills are sometimes kept safely in a bank. If a bank is named as an executor in a will they often allow the will to be deposited with them for free.

- ✔ **Principal registry.** The will might be deposited at the Safe Custody Department of the Principal Registry in London, which is the granddaddy registry of them all. If the will is kept at the Principal Registry you should find a deposit certificate in the possessions of the deceased. The will can be reclaimed by sending the certificate to: Principal Registry, Family Division, Safe Custody Department, First Avenue House, 42–49 High Holborn, London WC1V 2NP.

If you can't find the original will, don't panic. In England and Wales, a photocopy of a signed and witnessed will is acceptable. The probate registry may ask for proof that the original will was not destroyed on purpose to revoke or annul it. If, for example, the will was destroyed in a house fire, the registry may want proof that the fire took place. (Refer to Chapter 9 for more on what constitutes a revocation of a will.)

Distributing the estate

You must pay the tax-collector and creditors from the deceased's estate. Don't forget, of course, to subtract your expenses from the estate. Then it's time to dish out the dosh to the beneficiaries named in the will. If no will was left, the administrator has to distribute the estate according to intestacy rules.

The final duty of an executor is to draw up a set of *estate accounts*. These give a rundown of what you've done, from paying tax to collecting and distributing the deceased's assets. Give a copy of these accounts to the beneficiaries and then keep the accounts safely for a minimum of 12 years.

With the agreement of all adult beneficiaries affected, it's possible for an executor to vary the terms of a will through a *deed of variation* to make the estate more tax efficient. Chapter 14 explains this process.

Executors are expected to make a decent fist of the job. If you are negligent, beneficiaries and creditors can take court action against you.

Using a Solicitor

Executors and administrators can instruct a solicitor to help them administer the estate – it's up to you whether you feel you need to call in the professionals. This book helps you through administering an estate and gives you pointers on where to go when things get more complex.

Certain situations may give you pause for thought, and make you consider calling on the help of a solicitor:

- ✔ **Missing essentials.** If you can't find a beneficiary or the original will, a solicitor can advise you on the best course of action.

- ✔ **The will is challenged.** If someone questions the terms of the will or if you think it has been drawn up incorrectly, a solicitor can utilise his or her previous experience to sort out the situation.

- ✔ **Complex financial affairs.** If the deceased owned a business or if the will contains a trust, you may want to call on the expertise of a pro.

Chapter 6 explores how to go about choosing a good solicitor.

If you use a solicitor, ask them at the outset how much they charge. Solicitors are likely to have set fees for carrying out particular work, plus an hourly fee. Keep control of costs: Some of the beneficiaries have to approve the accounts at the end of the administration process and they won't be pleased if you lavish lots of cash on legal eagles.

Let your fellow executors and administrators know that you want to use a solicitor. However, even if they disagree, the other executors or administrators can't forbid you from getting help from a solicitor or any other type of adviser.

Chapter 13

Dealing with the Estate: First Steps

*I*f you're an executor of someone's will or plan to put yourself forward to act as administrator of someone's estate (both also known as the personal representatives), the onus is now on you to get things right. In this chapter, I take you through what you, as an executor or administrator, need to do following a death.

Taking Stock of the Estate Assets

One of your key jobs as an executor or administrator is to work out the value of the assets of the deceased at the time of their death. You must be thorough about this job because the deceased's beneficiaries and creditors are relying on you. Even the tax-collector is relying on you – now isn't that a novel situation?

When applying for grant of probate or letters of administration (explained below), you have to give the precise value of all the deceased's main assets. How to value an estate is explained in Chapter 3, but for the purposes of applying for probate you need to know the value of the following assets:

✓ **Property.** Obtain a value of any houses or flats owned by the deceased. You can do this yourself by researching the local market or ask an estate agent for a valuation. Check out on what terms the property was owned. If the property's in the deceased's sole name, then it goes straight into the estate pot; if not, then it may not be counted as part of the estate. Refer to Chapter 5 for different types of ownership.

✔ **Foreign assets.** You must get a valuation of any property owned abroad, or money or shares tied up in another country. It can be tricky to work out how much property or other assets owned abroad are worth. Hopefully, the deceased's papers hold a clue, or perhaps the spouse knows the value of the property or asset. If you still cannot value foreign assets, take legal advice.

✔ **Current and savings account.** Ask the banks or building societies of the deceased for an account statement and a list of all the deeds and share certificates held by the deceased. In addition, ask for any information the banks might have on tax paid on the deceased's savings during the tax year of their death.

Take this opportunity to stop any direct debits and standing orders from the deceased's accounts.

✔ **Shares.** The deceased may hold shares in their own name (in which case share certificates will be in their possession) or through a nominee account with a stockbroker. A stockbroker should be able to provide you with a valuation of any shares owned by the deceased. Alternatively, Chapter 3 shows how you can research the shares' value yourself.

✔ **National savings.** NS&I offers a free tracing service of any National Savings held by the deceased, or you can fill out Form NSA 904, available from the Post Office. Check out `www.nationalsavings.co.uk` for more details.

You can cash in Premium Bonds, or keep them running for 12 months after the death of the holder. You never know, they may strike the jackpot during that time!

✔ **Wages.** It's unusual that someone dies on pay day – even when out celebrating. As a result, the deceased's employer probably owes the estate some cash, whether in wages, expenses, pension, or some other type of benefit. Contact the employer but remember, they won't make a payment until they see grant of probate or letters of administration.

✔ **State benefits.** If the deceased was in receipt of the state pension or any other benefit, you need to write to the Department for Work and Pensions to let them know what has happened. Ask them to outline any pension or benefit owing to the deceased. The address is in the back of this book.

✔ **Life insurance.** Write to the life insurer to notify them of the death, quoting any policy numbers and enclosing a copy of the death certificate. Ask how much money is payable and whether the insurance is written in trust for a named person. If it is written in trust, then the policy may pay out directly to the named beneficiary; if not, the money forms part of the estate for inheritance tax (IHT) purposes. Alternatively, the policy may pay out to a creditor such as a mortgage provider.

✔ **Tax refund.** Her Majesty's Revenue & Customs (HMRC) may owe the deceased's estate money rather than the other way around. Whatever the scenario, write to the local tax office informing them of the death and ask for a tax return which you have to fill in and return.

✔ **Business interests.** If the deceased owned all or part of a business, then ask the firm's accountant for a precise value of what it's worth. Hire an accountant to do the sums if the firm doesn't have one.

✔ **Personal possessions.** You don't have to research the value of every little item the deceased owned: That would be time-consuming and perhaps intrusive. However, the value of cars, jewellery, and works of art can all add up to a pretty penny so get a reliable valuation. Consult people in the know: Garages, jewellers, and art dealers. Try and give your best guesstimate for the total value of small possessions.

Assessing the value of the deceased's estate will be a lot easier if the deceased made a recent list of their property. If someone asks you to act as their executor, if possible ask them to compile an up-to-date list of their property.

When assessing the estate of someone who leaves a spouse, household items are presumed to be owned jointly between them – so divide each item's value in two. If the household items are worth £1,000, for example, assume the deceased's share to be worth £500.

The price you put on an asset is what it would fetch if sold on the open market at the date of death.

As executor or administrator, you need to open up a new bank account to receive the assets of the deceased and pay expenses, creditors, tax, and beneficiaries. For the sake of ease of administration, open the account with the same branch that the deceased had his or her current account with. Once the grant of probate or letters of administration are received, the bank transfers whatever it holds in the deceased's name over to the executor's account.

Using the death certificate

All the trouble you took to obtain official copies of the death certificate will now pay off, as banks, building societies, stockbrokers, and life insurers won't think about paying up without seeing a copy of the death certificate.

Sending a copy of the death certificate ensures that you are put in the picture. However, most institutions wait for grant of probate or letters of administration as well before letting you get your hands on the deceased's possessions.

Deducting the Debts

Most people, even multimillionaires, die with some form of debt, whether a whopping mortgage, credit card, or just an unpaid gas bill. You need to subtract any debts from the assets to come up with a true reckoning of what the deceased's estate was worth at death.

Possible areas of debt include:

- ✔ **Mortgage.** This is usually the big one! Send the mortgage lender a copy of the death certificate and ask them to outline how much capital and interest is left on the mortgage. If the deceased had an endowment policy, include the policy number and ask what it's worth.

- ✔ **Utility bills.** Take an electric, gas, and, if applicable, water meter reading as close to the date of death as possible and ask for a bill to that date. Ask the phone company to supply a bill up to the date of death.

- ✔ **Loan, overdraft, and credit card bills.** Write to the banks or building societies concerned and ask how much they are owed.

- ✔ **Tax debt.** The deceased may owe income tax or Capital Gains Tax. Write to the tax office informing them of the deceased's demise and ask for a tax return to fill in and send back.

Most creditors won't chase up a debt until after grant of probate or letters of administration have been obtained. After all, it doesn't make good public relations to go chasing a deceased's next of kin for money in the immediate aftermath of a death.

If the deceased's financial affairs are very complex, you may want to advertise for creditors to come forward. Chapter 14 looks at dealing with creditors coming out of the woodwork.

Applying for Probate

You need to obtain special powers to be able to gather in the assets of the deceased and then pay tax, creditors, and beneficiaries. The special powers you need aren't the ability to look through walls or scale tall buildings like Superman. You need the courts to grant you the power to administer the estate of the deceased.

If you're a named executor in a valid will, then you must ask the court for *grant of probate*. In cases where no will exists but you want to administer the estate, ask the court to grant you *letters of administration*. Chapter 12 covers the basics of both of these ways of administering an estate.

Essentially, the process of applying for probate and letters of administration is the same. Only when it comes to distributing the estate – one way according to the will (probate), the other by the law of intestacy (administration) – do key differences emerge.

If the value of the deceased's assets is less than £5,000, probate is not required. However, the executor is still duty bound to follow the terms of the deceased's will.

Understanding probate forms

When applying for grant of probate or letters of administration, you face an alphabet soup of forms with catchy titles like PA1 or IHT 205.

You need to fill in both:

- **Form PA1.** This form asks for information about the deceased and the names and addresses of executors.

- **Form IHT 205.** In short, this form asks for the low-down on the deceased's estate and is used by HMRC's Capital Taxes Office to work out how much inheritance tax is due. Their useful Web site is www.hmrc.gov.uk/cto. The size of a person's estate also dictates the size of the fees charged by the Probate Registry. You can get the forms free-of-charge from the Personal Applications Department of the Principal Probate Registry in London, your local District Probate Registry, or HMRC's Capital Taxes Office. You can also download them at www.hmrc.gov.uk/cto/pa1.htm. The contact details are in the back of this book.

You can get more details on how to apply for probate by downloading Form PA2, 'How to Obtain Probate', from www.hmcourts-service.gov.uk.

Before you can get a grant of probate or letters of administration, you'll probably need to pay a percentage of any inheritance tax due on the estate, or show that there is no IHT to pay. See Chapter 15 for more on IHT.

Filling out Form PA1

Form PA1 is the *Probate Application Form* and you need to enter the following information:

- **Deceased's details.** Provide the full name, address, occupation, marital status, and date of birth and date of death of the deceased. In addition, the form asks whether any assets of the deceased's estate are held in another name, such as that of a business partner.

✔ **Details of the will.** Does a will exist and if so, are any of the beneficiaries under 18? Also state the names of the executors and which of them are applying for probate.

✔ **Details of any relatives of the deceased.** These details are essential, especially when there is no will and the relatives inherit under intestacy. Lead with the spouse, parents, brothers, and sisters. If people from these groups no longer survive, include the details of any of their surviving children.

✔ **Applicant's relationship to the deceased.** This information helps clarify if the person applying for probate or letters of administration is allowed to do so. Refer to Chapter 12 for more on who can apply.

✔ **Interview location.** Unfortunately, you can't conduct the entire probate application process through the post, via e-mail, or over the phone. You and any fellow executors must attend your local Probate Registry Office and take the scary-sounding executor's oath. The oath binds you to perform your duties in a reasonable time and to submit proper accounts.

You can use Form PA1 if you decide *not* to act as executor. This is called *power reserved*. Power reserved is explained further in Chapter 12.

Filling out Form IHT 205

The three dread letters I-H-T give a clue to what Form IHT 205 is all about – inheritance tax! Cue lots of booing and hissing.

Form IHT 205 is a preliminary form used by the Probate Registry to weed out those estates that are likely to be subject to inheritance tax. This form is submitted at the same time as Form PA1.

If you want to know more about filling in Form IHT 205 – and frankly, who wouldn't? – you can download free guidance notes from HMRC's Web site at www.hmrc.gov.uk.

Part 1

The first part of Form IHT 205 asks a host of yes-no questions, such as:

✔ Did the deceased make any gifts or transfers totalling more than £3,000 a year, other than normal birthday, festive, or wedding gifts?

✔ Did the deceased own or benefit from any assets held outside the UK, such as business interests or foreign property rentals?

✔ Did the deceased pay premiums on any life insurance policies that were not for the deceased's own benefit or which did not pay out to the estate?

If you answer 'yes' to any of these questions, then the tax authorities would like to know more about the estate – isn't that nice? Form IHT 200 now has to be filled out (see Chapter 14). However, inheritance tax may not necessarily be due.

Even if you answered 'yes' to any of the questions in the first part of Form IHT 205, you may not have to fill out the second part of the form (see below in Part 2). Instead, you may have to submit Form IHT 200 – a full account. A note on the form tells you when to switch from filling in IHT 205 to IHT 200. Confused yet?

Form IHT 205 is often called a *short form for personal representatives* (you'll see the irony of this when you come to gaze on it). When reading Form IHT 205 and the accompanying notes, you may find that the estate is an *excepted estate*. Being an excepted estate means that the estate is not too large and is relatively uncomplicated (no substantial foreign property, for example) and this excuses you from having to fill in full account Form IHT 200.

Part 2

The second part of Form 205 asks you to state how much each part of the deceased's estate is worth. The assets that you must give a value to include:

- ✔ Cash held in bank and building society accounts.
- ✔ National Savings and Investments accounts.
- ✔ Share accounts and money from insurance policies.
- ✔ Any property owned solely by the deceased.
- ✔ Any assets held as tenants in common.
- ✔ Property owned as part of a business partnership.
- ✔ Household goods such as furniture, jewellery, or cars.

If the deceased doesn't own particular assets mentioned in the form, simply write 'nil' on the space provided.

Part 3

The third part of Form IHT 205 asks for details of any assets passing automatically to a surviving joint owner. You also have to provide details of any debts and funeral expenses.

Debts and funeral expenses are subtracted from the estate total to result in a final total. The final total is then considered for inheritance tax purposes. If the estate is worth more than £312,000 (from April 2008), the threshold for IHT, then a full account – Form IHT 200 – has to be submitted to the tax-collector. See Chapter 14 for more on how to fill this form in.

The final part of the form is a space for the executors or administrators to sign and date. If you're acting with other executors or administrators, you'll have to meet up to check over the forms. The two forms, PA1 and IHT 205, along with the will and death certificate, are then sent to the Controlling Probate Registry Office. Most major cities have a Controlling Probate Registry Office.

Take a photocopy of the probate forms before submitting them.

You can find a helpful guide to correctly filling out form IHT 205 on the HMRC Web site. The notes form is catchily called IHT 206 – those wacky tax people, eh?

Even if you make it crystal clear that the deceased's estate is too small to attract inheritance tax, you may still have to submit accounts to HMRC at the end of the probate process. Turn to Chapter 14 for more on submitting the accounts.

Attending the probate interview

A few weeks after submitting your probate forms, you and your fellow executors or administrators will be asked to attend an interview at the Probate Registry Office you nominated in Form PA1.

All the information that you supplied in the probate forms is transferred onto a formal printed legal document. You and your fellow executors or administrators will be asked to check this document for any errors. You must then take the *executor's oath*, swearing to perform your duties in a reasonable time and submit accounts.

At the interview you must pay a fee to the Probate Registry for the administration involved in the grant of probate. The fee is currently £130. Payment can be made by cheque, banker's draft, or postal order. If you set up an executor's account you should draw money from this to cover probate fees, as it will be paid back from the deceased's estate. Probate fees in Scotland are levied according to the size of the estate: Estates worth less than £5,000 don't incur a fee; those above £5,000 incur a £90 charge.

The watchful eyes of the tax-collector

Every year the tax-collector very obligingly scrutinises a number of small estates in the same way as a large estate. This means that even if the estate is below the inheritance tax threshold, the tax-collector can ask that Form IHT 200 – the full account – be filled in. Any request to fill in a full account has to be made by HMRC within 35 days of grant of probate.

Hey presto – you now have probate and are free to deal with the estate.

Take all the papers relating to the estate with you to the meeting, just in case you need to clear up any discrepancies. Ask for plenty of copies of the grant of probate or letters of administration, as you may need to send off several copies at the same time.

Applying for Confirmation in Scotland

In Scotland, instead of obtaining a grant of probate the executors and administrators have to apply for *confirmation*. Confirmation is explained in Chapter 12.

Filling out Form C1

Under confirmation, you fill in Form C1. Essentially, this form fulfils the same role as Forms PA1 and IHT 205 in England, Northern Ireland, and Wales. Form C1 establishes the details of the deceased, the executor, and the contents of the estate and their value.

Form C1 asks if the estate is *excepted* (exempt from having to submit a full account and therefore, in effect, free from inheritance tax). In order for an estate to be *excepted*, it has to fulfil the following conditions:

- ✔ The deceased lived in the UK at the time of death.

- ✔ The estate before deduction of any debts or gifts is worth less than the threshold for inheritance tax (£312,000 from April 2008).

- ✔ The estate is worth less than £1,000,000 but passes to the deceased's spouse or civil partner – who must be living in the UK – or to charity.

- ✔ Assets held outside the UK are not worth more than £100,000.

- ✔ The deceased had not made any substantial transfers within seven years of their death.

If you answer 'no' to any of the above statements, then move on to fill in Form IHT 200 (see Chapter 14). Bad luck!

The excepted estate rules are a bit of a minefield. If you're at all unsure as to whether the estate is excepted or not, contact your local tax office for clarification.

Proceeding with caution

If no will exists and you apply for confirmation, you may have to obtain a *Bond of Caution*. A Bond of Caution is a guarantee given by an insurance company that you will distribute the estate according to intestacy and not try and pocket the lot yourself – it should really be called a bond of good behaviour! Of course, an insurer won't simply issue a Bond of Caution gratis; sometimes it can cost several hundred pounds to obtain.

If you're the spouse of the deceased administering the estate, then you won't need a Bond of Caution. Why not? Under Scotland's intestacy rules the spouse is in pole position to scoop all or most of the deceased's estate anyway – so why would you cheat?

Confirmation forms are available from the sheriff clerk's office or the sheriff's court in the area the deceased lived in at the date of death. You can find these addresses in the Yellow Pages.

If the estate is worth less than £25,000, you can obtain confirmation under the Small Estates Act. Ask the sheriff's clerk to prepare Form C1 for you. For more details on dealing with small estates in Scotland, check out the Scottish Court Service Web site on www.scotscourt.gov.uk.

In Scotland, a person who applies to administer an estate when there is no will is called an *executive dative*, while a person who is appointed under the terms of a will is called an *executive nominee*.

Dealing with the sheriff

Scottish sheriffs are far removed from their Wild West namesakes, such as Wyatt Earp and that large chap from *Bonanza*. Scottish sheriffs run the sheriff's court and it's through this court that confirmation is granted.

Send completed confirmation forms to the sheriff's clerk of your local sheriff's court along with a copy of the will, if there is one. As with probate, obtaining confirmation incurs a fee. Pay this fee from any money held in the executor's account. The fee is waived for estates worth less than £5,000. A few weeks after submitting your confirmation forms, you should receive your confirmation forms and any extra copies you have requested. You are now free to deal with the deceased's estate.

If you discover that you underestimated or overestimated the size of the deceased's estate after you have submitted Form C1, you can amend it. Ask for Form C4 and submit this to the Capital Taxes Office. You have six months after discovering the mistake to complete C4 or else you can face a fine!

You Have the Power: What Next?

Grant of probate, letters of administration, and confirmation all act as proof that you're legally allowed to gather in the deceased's assets.

Armed with any of these papers, you can ask all and sundry for any money due the estate. Pay this money into your executor's bank account. From this account you can pay any outstanding debts, and ensure the beneficiaries get their due.

A beneficiary has the right to their inheritance within a 'reasonable' time-frame. What is deemed reasonable varies, of course, from case to case, but usually the beneficiaries should get their money within a year. This is why the 12 months following the death is often referred to as an *executor's year*. Obtaining probate can take a couple of months, particularly if the deceased's tax affairs are complex, and by then some beneficiaries may be wondering when they'll see their inheritance. So get your skates on!

Turn to Chapter 14 to discover how to distribute the estate.

Chapter 14

Distributing the Estate

- -

In This Chapter

▶ Paying inheritance tax, Capital Gains Tax, and income tax

▶ Keeping creditors sweet

▶ Seeing the beneficiaries right

▶ Changing who inherits what

▶ Producing the estate accounts

- -

*B*eing an executor or administrator of an estate means that you can't hang about. Once you've dealt with the immediate aftermath of the death and with the submission of the probate or administration forms it's time to get your hands dirty with the estate. You have to pay the taxes due, keep the creditors sweet, and distribute the gifts to the beneficiaries.

In this chapter, I take you through dishing out the dosh with aplomb!

Paying Out in Sequence

The order in which the tax-collector, creditors, and beneficiaries receive money from the deceased's estate is set out in law. As an executor or administrator it's your legal responsibility to ensure that you follow this order of priority when distributing the estate:

✔ **Her Majesty's Revenue & Customs (HMRC).** If inheritance tax is due on the estate, then it has to be paid before probate or letters of administration are granted (refer to Chapter 12 for more on these).

✔ **Creditors.** Next in line, this description covers anyone who can prove that they are owed money by the deceased.

✔ **Beneficiaries.** Finally comes anyone set to inherit under the terms of a will or under intestacy (where there is no will).

First and foremost the deceased's remains must be disposed of properly. The cost of the funeral may swallow a small estate. If this happens, then the beneficiaries, creditors, and even the tax authorities miss out.

Inheritance tax (IHT) is due on the estate after funeral expenses and money owed to creditors is subtracted. So if the assets of the estate are worth £317,000 – £17,000 above the starting level for IHT (£300,000 2007/08 tax year) – but the deceased owed £20,000 and £5,000 was spent on the funeral, then the estate for IHT purposes is valued at £292,000 and no tax is due. Or, stated another way, deduct the liabilities from the assets to calculate the net estate. IHT is due if the net estate exceeds the threshold.

Form-filling for HM Revenue & Customs

In Chapter 13, I showed you how to go about letting the tax-collector know the value of the deceased's estate. Form IHT 205 in England and Wales, and Form C1 in Scotland set out the assets of the deceased. If, after any debts and transfer of property to a spouse was taken into account, the estate was worth less than £300,000 (2007/08), rising to £312,000 in April 2008 then you have finished with the tax-collector as far as IHT is concerned.

Otherwise, the tax-collector wants to know more – aren't you lucky!

You need to fill in and submit form IHT 200, a full statement of the deceased's accounts. In short, the snappily-named Form IHT 200 is a souped-up version of Form IHT 205 and the Scot's Form C1. Similar areas are covered but in greater depth. Form IHT 200, which covers England, Wales, and Scotland, comes with lots of *supplementary pages*.

The supplementary pages that you're most likely to use cover the following areas:

- ✔ **Pages D3, D4, D5, and D6** ask for details of gifted property and assets held in trust, death benefits paid under pension policies, plus any property held on a joint tenancy basis.

- ✔ **Page D7** relates to stocks and shares and asks for a rundown of all the deceased's holdings. If the deceased held any investment trusts or unit trusts, then the fund manager will supply a valuation but they need to see a copy of the death certificate before doing so.

- ✔ **Page D12** asks for details of any buildings and land owned by the deceased. You need the property's open market value and a copy of the tenancy agreement if it's let.

  Don't deduct the mortgage from the valuation. However, if the deceased only owned a share of the property, just give the value of that share and not the value of the whole property.

Doing it by the numbers

Before you send HMRC Form IHT 200 you need a reference number that's unique to the deceased's estate. You have to use this reference number on any form or written communication with the HMRC. They may ask you for the reference if you have to call the HMRC to ask them a question. You get the unique reference online through the HMRC Web site. When applying for the reference number you're asked to give your own personal details and those of the deceased. The reference number makes it easier for HMRC officials to keep track of the paperwork. Eventually the HMRC is looking to move to online filing of inheritance tax forms but it'll take a few years before the paperless dream becomes reality.

All the executors or administrators must sign Form IHT 200. This form must be submitted before probate, letters of administration, or confirmation (in Scotland) can be granted.

If you need help, then Form IHT 210 explains how to fill out Form IHT 200, while Form IHT 213 helps you work out if any tax is due. You can get the forms from your local tax office or download them from www.hmrc.gov.uk. If you'd like over-the-phone guidance, call the HMRC helpline on 0845 30 20 900.

Calculating Inheritance Tax

Chapter 13 shows you how to tot up the assets of the estate for calculating IHT. As an executor or administrator you can work out the IHT bill yourself or ask the tax office to do it for you. If you decide on DIY, then you fill out supplementary page D18 and submit it at the same time as Form IHT 200.

Gifts made to a spouse, charities, and political parties, the debts of the deceased, and 'reasonable' funeral expenses – no hiring out Westminster Abbey – are deducted from the estate.

If the total value of the estate is greater than £300,000 (2007/08 tax year) rising to £312,000 in April 2008, then IHT kicks in at a rate of 40 per cent. If the estate is worth £400,000, the IHT bill will be 40 per cent of £100,000, or £112,000 from April 2008.

You may want to ask a solicitor or an accountant to give your Form IHT 200 and your tax liability calculation the once over. If the estate is a very complex one, you may choose to leave the tax-collector to work out the IHT bill.

Paying IHT in instalments

Usually, inheritance tax has to be paid in full prior to grant of probate or letters of administration (refer to Chapter 12 for details of how probate works). However, for family businesses and farmland, HMRC accepts payment in instalments for up to ten years. Otherwise, the costs of meeting the IHT bill could drive some farms and family businesses to the wall. See Chapter 19 for the low-down on how to use instalments to the estate's advantage.

If you inherit property that has recently been subject to an IHT charge – in other words, the person leaving the gift to you recently inherited it themselves after IHT had been levied on it – then you're entitled to claim IHT relief. (Check out Chapter 16 for more on this important tax relief.)

If the deceased gave away any substantial assets during the seven years prior to death they may still attract IHT. This situation is called a *potentially exempt transfer* (PET) and is explored in full in Chapters 15 and 16. Crucially, the level of IHT paid on a PET reduces between three and seven years.

When the tax-collector comes knocking

Dealings with HMRC don't always run smoothly! You may have gone about filling out your forms in good faith and even paid the IHT due, but that won't stop the tax-collector from picking holes in your calculations. HMRC will be in touch if:

- ✔ A mistake was made when totting up the value of property, shares, or other assets.

- ✔ The value you put on an asset is disputed.

- ✔ HMRC believes that the deceased's estate is bigger than you said. This doesn't mean they think you lied, but perhaps they think the deceased broke some tax rule to reduce their estate's exposure to inheritance tax.

A dispute often occurs when the deceased gifted a large asset less than seven years before he or she died. For example, the deceased may have given the family home to a close relative with the ultimate aim of keeping it out of the tax firing line. However, if the deceased continued to live in the home after gifting it then the gift can be considered a *gift with reservation of benefit*. As a result, the gift (the house in this case) may still be liable to some sort of IHT charge. Chapters 15 and 16 have more on this sort of gift.

Going head to head with the tax-collector

Just because the tax-collector says more tax is owed than you anticipated doesn't mean you have to take their word for it. You're free to fight back!

If HMRC comes up with a radically different tax bill for the estate, seek advice from a solicitor or an accountant. If the difference between your two positions is small, discuss it with the tax office; they may see the sense of your argument.

HMRC has *district valuers* whose job it is to assess the value of assets such as buildings and land in their locality.

Don't delay in finalising your tax business. Interest will be charged on any IHT left outstanding six months after the date of death.

Preparing to cough up the inheritance tax

Once you have come up with an IHT figure that you and the tax inspector are happy with, it's time to pay what's due.

HMRC issues calculations or a *notice of determination* if IHT is due, which sounds very ominous!

If you disagree with the IHT figure, you can lodge an appeal against a notice of determination within 30 days of it being issued, otherwise the notice is final. Appeals are made to special independent HMRC commissioners and can only be based on a point of tax law. Under exceptional circumstances an appeal could be taken to the High Court, but that could be ruinously expensive.

Ask HMRC for three copies of *IHT 30*, an application to be discharged from further IHT. All the executors or administrators need to sign the three copies of IHT 30 – keep one for your records and return the other two to HMRC.

The executors or administrators armed with grant of probate or letters of administration can now start gathering in and distributing the estate. Phew!

If you fail to pay inheritance tax by the due date then HMRC starts charging interest on what's owed. Interest starts to apply automatically seven months after the deceased's death. At present, the HMRC charges 5 per cent interest a year.

Re-evaluating the estate

Even after probate or letters of administration are granted, the tax inspector reserves the right to come knocking again. HMRC may have further questions about the value of property reported in Form IHT 200. Ultimately, a fresh IHT bill could be levied on the estate, in which case it's wise to get advice from a solicitor on how to deal with this fresh claim.

If you discover that the deceased had hidden assets that you weren't aware of when probate or letters of administration were granted, you're legally bound to let HMRC know. Again, an extra IHT charge could be due.

Fortunately, this is a two-way street. If you underestimated the deceased's debt you can ask for an IHT rebate.

Whatever the scenario, if you discover that the reality of the deceased's estate doesn't match what you set out in Form IHT 200, let the tax office know sharpish!

If you sell any of the deceased's share investments at a loss within three years of the date of death, you can claim relief against IHT. Likewise, if land or buildings are sold at a loss within four years of the death, you can claim IHT relief. Ask your local tax office for more information.

Raising Money to Pay Inheritance Tax

You can't get your hands on the money or property of the deceased until you obtain grant of probate or letters of administration. However, before you can be granted probate or letters of administration you must pay the tax-collector if the estate is worth more than $300,000 (2007/08 tax year) or $312,000 from April 2008.

This leaves you in a catch-22 situation. If you can't sell bits of the estate or access the deceased's bank accounts, how on earth do you raise the cash to pay any tax due?

Don't worry – you can call on the following people and organisations to give you a helping hand with meeting the IHT bill:

- **National Savings.** If the deceased had National Savings accounts, you can ask to use the funds to pay HMRC. In effect, what you're doing is getting one branch of the Government to pay another.

- **Beneficiaries.** If a beneficiary has already financially benefited from the deceased's death – such as a lump sum payment from a pension provider, which is not included in the probate process – you could ask him or her to use this money to meet the IHT bill. The beneficiary will get their money back from the estate when it has gone through probate.

✔ **Building society and bank accounts.** Most building societies and some banks will release money to pay IHT without a grant of probate or letters of administration. However, the building society or bank may insist on sending the money directly to HMRC.

✔ **Personal possessions.** As an executor, you have the right to sell the furniture and personal possessions of the deceased from the moment of death. However, administrators (where there's no will) are not allowed to sell the personal possessions of the deceased until they have obtained letters of administration.

If you need to sell the personal possessions of the deceased, make sure you let the nearest and dearest know what you're up to. They can let you know if an item has some sentimental value and shouldn't leave the confines of the family. Also, check that the deceased didn't leave the item to someone in the will!

If you can't raise enough cash to meet the IHT bill through these measures, you will have to borrow the funds.

Some bright sparks take out a life insurance policy specifically designed to cover any IHT bill due on their death. Head to Chapter 16 for more on this tactic.

Gathering in the Assets

Once you've got your hands on grant of probate or letters of administration – Chapter 12 tells you how – it's time to collect the deceased's assets to pay beneficiaries and creditors.

Borrowing to meet the tax bill

The deceased's bank may be willing to lend the money to cover the IHT bill. As the estate is large enough to attract inheritance tax in the first place, it's a racing certainty that they'll get their money back once the estate goes through probate. The bank may charge a fee for arranging the loan, and you'll have to pay interest. However, it shouldn't take too long to pay back the loan once probate or letters of administration have been granted and the money from the deceased's estate starts rolling into the executor's account.

You may be able to claim income tax relief on any interest payments on a loan to cover IHT. Call your local tax office for full details.

You should already have a very good idea of what the deceased is worth. In order to complete probate forms PA1 and IHT 205, you provided a value for the following:

- ✔ Cash held in bank and building society accounts
- ✔ National Savings investments accounts
- ✔ Share accounts and money from insurance policies
- ✔ Any property owned solely by the deceased
- ✔ Any assets held as tenants in common (refer to Chapter 5 for more on this)
- ✔ Property owned as part of a business partnership
- ✔ Household goods such as furniture, jewellery, or cars

As part of the estate assessment process, you have already written to all organisations with which the deceased held money, investments, or property. Provided you sent these organisations a copy of the death certificate they should have supplied you with the details of any property, cash, or shares the deceased held with them. However, in most cases financial institutions won't let you have access to the deceased's cash, property, or shares until you send them a copy of grant of probate or letters of administration.

As soon as you've got your hands on it, send these organisations an official copy of your grant of probate or letters of administration and full details of the executor's account. Sending photocopies won't do: Obtain official copies from the probate registry. Enclose a covering letter clearly stating your details and the deceased's details. The organisations should then make the assets available to you, transferring any cash accounts straight into the executor's account. Job done!

The organisations should provide you with a copy of the deceased's accounts and files. Hold on to these copies for when you compile the executor's account. See 'Producing the Final Accounts' later in this chapter for more.

If you don't have plenty of copies of grant of probate or letters of administration, then you must send the original. You then have to wait for the organisation you contacted to return it to you so that you can send it off to the next organisation. This is the administrative version of death by a thousand cuts. Spend a few pounds extra and get plenty of copies of grant of probate or letters of administration from the probate registry. The current fee is £1 per copy.

Check to see if the deceased's employer owed them any money. The State may owe the deceased's estate some cash through a pension or tax rebate.

Claiming life insurance

If the deceased had a life insurance policy you won't need grant of probate or letters of administration to activate the pay-out. Simply send an official copy of the death certificate along with the original policy document. If the original policy document can't be found, then fill out a *lost policy indemnity form*, available from the insurer. If the policy doesn't clearly state the date of birth of the deceased, you may have to send a copy of the birth certificate, too.

If the life insurance policy is written in *trust*, then it may pay out directly to the named person. If the policy is not written in trust, it forms part of the estate for inheritance tax purposes and should be included in Form IHT 200. Alternatively, the policy may be written so that it pays out to a creditor such as a mortgage lender.

If the life insurance policy was a *with-profits* policy, an investment bonus payment may be due on top of the standard pay-out on the death of the policyholder.

Your job as an executor or administrator is to ensure that no stone is left unturned in the effort to squeeze as much out of the estate as you can for the beneficiaries.

Paying Off the Debts

Once you've paid any tax due and obtained grant of probate or letters of administration, it's time to meet the deceased's debts.

The biggest debt due on an estate is usually the mortgage. The mortgage lender usually insists on one of three things:

- ✔ The person who inherits the property pays off the mortgage in full immediately.

- ✔ The person who inherits the property takes on the mortgage on the same terms as the deceased.

- ✔ The property is sold to repay the lender. This action is usually a last resort.

Which one of these three options gets the green light depends on a combination of factors such as the size of the loan, the attitude of the mortgage company, the value of the property relative to the mortgage, and the financial position of the person inheriting the home. Call the mortgage lender to discuss the options.

If the will states that the property should pass to the beneficiary 'free from any mortgage debt outstanding on the property', then you must do your best to ensure that the mortgage debt is paid off from the residuary estate.

The deceased may have more than one mortgage, perhaps from separate lenders. The first lender has *first charge* on the property, which means they get their money, you guessed it, first. Once the first lender is satisfied, you have to see to the second mortgage. If the second mortgage can't be met in full, the second mortgage lender may insist that the property is sold.

Other debts such as credit cards, loans, and household bills should be paid out of the *residuary estate*. The estate residue is whatever remains after factoring in gifts made in the will. If the residue isn't large enough to cover the debts, you have no option but to use some of the assets gifted through the will to meet the debts (I cover this in 'Selling the Assets to Pay the Debts' later in this chapter).

Ask creditors for a receipt when you repay them; this is important for when you draw up your final accounts.

Locating Missing Creditors

As an executor or administrator, a big part of your job is to alert would-be creditors of the demise of the deceased.

A quick hunt of the deceased's papers should reveal most creditors' details as lenders are super-keen on sending reminders of how much money is owed. But your creditor-hunting job may not stop there, particularly if the deceased had complex financial affairs.

You have to let the wider world know of the deceased's demise by advertising. I don't mean taking a 30-second commercial slot in *Coronation Street*. No, follow the legally recognised way of informing the wider world of a death and take out a press advert.

Place one advert in the *London Gazette* (PO Box 7923, London, SW8 5WF, telephone 0207 394 4580). The *London Gazette* is ancient and has a tiny circulation, but it's traditional to list deaths in it and creditors know to keep an eye on its pages. Edinburgh and Belfast versions of the Gazette are published; check out the group's Web site at `www.gazettes-online.co.uk` for details about how to advertise. Also advertise in the deceased's local paper to give everyone a chance to know what's happened.

An administrator is only permitted to advertise for creditors after being granted letters of administration. Executors, though, can take out an advert at any stage of the process, even prior to being granted probate.

All adverts should clearly state the name and address of the deceased and an address to write to for anyone owed money by the deceased. Set a deadline for when creditors should put in their claim – two months after the advert is placed is usual.

Executors and administrators in Northern Ireland can protect themselves in the same way as those in England and Wales by advertising for creditors in the _Belfast Gazette_. In Scotland, the onus is on the creditors to discover the death and they have six months from the date of death to come forward. After six months, creditors are only paid if the executor or administrator still has the funds to do so.

Check out the notices section of your local paper for an idea of the style and wording of a death notice – hardly a thumping good read, I know, but worth the effort.

Don't be tempted to do half a job. Locating missing creditors is a key part of your duties. If a creditor comes out of the woodwork late in the day it could throw all your plans and hard work in the air. Even worse, if the creditor can prove that you didn't take proper steps to let them know of the death, he or she could sue!

If a creditor does come forward after seeing your advert, check that the claim is legitimate and backed up with documentary evidence, such as a signed credit agreement – not 'I once lent him £5 in the pub and never got it back'!

Coping with an Insolvent Estate

If the deceased's debts are larger than the assets, then the estate is _insolvent_. If the estate is insolvent, not all the creditors will get what's owed to them. Nevertheless, as an executor or administrator it's up to you to make the best of a bad job. If in doubt, consult a solicitor.

In cases of estate insolvency, you don't simply pay out to the creditor that shouts the loudest. You're bound by Act of Parliament to pay the debts in a certain order:

 ✔ **Mortgage.** The lender will insist that the property is sold to repay the mortgage. The lender is known as a secured creditor.

✔ **Tax authorities.** If the deceased owed money to the tax-collector (such as VAT), then this has to be paid next.

✔ **Other creditors.** These are also called *unsecured* creditors. These debts can include credit cards, personal loans, and utility bills. Work out what percentage of all the debt can be met from the proceeds of the estate. Then offer the creditors an equal percentage. If the debts are £40,000 and the money available is just £20,000, offer all creditors 50 per cent of their money back.

Play fair: Picking and choosing which creditors to pay from the estate could lead to you being sued.

Where an estate is clearly insolvent you may decide not to bother applying for grant of probate or letters of administration. Instead, you can leave it up to the deceased's creditors to apply for letters of administration – it will then be up to them to do the legwork.

Tracking down beneficiaries

Whether you're administering an estate according to the terms of a will or the law of intestacy, you may encounter difficulty tracking down a beneficiary. After all, people are more mobile than ever before.

From a legal standpoint you're duty bound to make certain efforts to track down a beneficiary. As with tracking down creditors, advertise in the *London Gazette* (England and Wales) or the *Edinburgh Gazette* in Scotland, or the *Belfast Gazette* in Northern Ireland, plus the deceased's local paper.

If you don't have any luck this way, try the following:

✔ If you have a rough idea of where the beneficiary lives, you can advertise in their local newspaper.

✔ The Web site www.192.com has a people finder function, which, for a fee, allows access to the electoral register database.

✔ If the beneficiary has an uncommon name, you may be able to find them by typing the surname into the search engine www.google.co.uk.

✔ If you know the school the beneficiary attended, try the search facility on www.friendsreunited.co.uk.

✔ Check out www.titleresearch.com that can trace missing heirs and next of kin.

✔ If the inheritance is substantial, hire a private detective who is used to tracking down missing people. Just don't trust anyone in a long trench coat and dark glasses calling themselves Mr Snoop.

Selling the Assets to Pay the Debts

Only sell anything of the deceased's after you've explored all other avenues of raising the necessary cash. The will should give you full rights to dispose of the deceased's property as you see fit.

You may need to sell the deceased's assets for a number of reasons, including paying for the funeral, meeting creditors' demands, or paying the IHT bill.

Discuss with the other executors which parts of the estate should be sold so that the deceased's wishes can most closely be met. Don't just pick on one beneficiary and start selling off their gifts while leaving everyone else's intact, unless of course you have their consent.

Get three written quotes for the items you sell. Accept the highest and keep all three quotes on file, just in case someone checks that you got the best possible price.

You must try and get the best possible price for the deceased's assets. If you fail to do so, then the beneficiaries may have a case to sue you!

Paying the Beneficiaries

You're on the home straight now! You've paid off the debts in full and now it's time to distribute the deceased's estate. You distribute the estate according to the terms of the will or, if there's no will, under the law of intestacy. Whatever scenario you're working under, the basics of paying the beneficiaries are the same:

- ✔ **Personal property.** You can physically hand these over to the beneficiaries or simply arrange for the beneficiaries to collect the property.
- ✔ **Cash gifts.** You should already have the money from bank and building society accounts paid into the executor's account. To fulfil a cash gift, simply give the beneficiary a cheque drawn from this account.

As you distribute each gift to the beneficiary, ask them to sign a receipt clearly describing the gift and its value. Keep one copy and give another copy to the beneficiary. The beneficiary may need this receipt when filling out their tax return, for example.

Transferring shares and property, and fulfilling gifts to children require a little more work, as I explain below.

Sharing out the shares

You need a *stock transfer* form from the company registrars or a blank form downloaded from www.lawpack.co.uk to sign shares over to the beneficiary. All the executors must sign this form. Send the stock transfer form to the registrar of the company in question, together with the original share certificate and the obligatory copy of the grant of probate or letters of administration.

If the deceased's share holding is to be split between two or more beneficiaries, a separate stock transfer form is needed in each case.

If the shares are registered in the name of a stockbroker – this is often called a nominee account – you don't have to go to all the rigmarole with the stock transfer form. Instead, simply write to the stockbroker and ask them to hold the shares in the name of the beneficiary.

Good news! No stamp duty is payable on the transfer of shares to a beneficiary.

Passing on property

If the deceased left a gift of property or land in England or Wales in the will, follow these steps to formally transfer the property to the beneficiary:

1. **Fill in Form AS1 from the Land Registry.** Tell the Land Registry if the mortgage on the property has been paid off. The form can be downloaded from the Land Registry Web site at www.landreg.gov.uk or contact your local Land Registry office (the address is available from the Web site or in your local telephone book).

2. **Make sure the completed form is signed by each executor in the presence of a witness, and by the beneficiary who inherits the property.**

3. **Return the form to the Land Registry along with a copy of the grant of probate and the fee** – dealing with a government agency always involves a fee! As long as all the documents are in order, the transfer of the legal ownership of the property from the deceased to the beneficiary takes place.

A docket for the Scots

Transferring a home or land can be a little more complex in Scotland. The Certificate of Confirmation – the Scottish equivalent of grant of probate – has a *Form of Docket* attached, which you fill in and keep with the title deeds of the property. This Form of Docket transfers ownership from the deceased to the nominated beneficiary. The docket has to be signed by the executors and the beneficiary and the signatures must be witnessed.

Register the transfer in the Books of Council and Session in case the form is destroyed or lost. You can do this by applying to the Keeper of the Registers of Scotland, Meadowbank House, 153 London Road, Edinburgh EH8 7AU.

If the property is registered at the Scottish Land Registry let them know of the transfer of ownership. The Web site `www.scotland landregistry.co.uk` explains how to go about this.

You don't need a Form of Docket if the property automatically transfers to someone else under joint tenancy. This is often referred to in Scotland as transfer of property under a *survivorship destination*.

In some unusual cases the land gifted is not registered with the Land Registry. If this is the case, you must go about the painstaking task of registering the property in the name of the beneficiary. If you find yourself having to deal with unregistered land, seek the advice of a solicitor.

Transferring an inheritance to a child

Children under the age of 18 can't inherit in their own right. As an executor, you may need to invest their money for them to inherit when they reach maturity.

The safest place for the cash is a building society deposit account, where it should keep pace with inflation. If the child is very young and has a long time before they inherit, you might consider investing in shares, which, historically, tend to show bigger growth. Remember that share prices can decrease as well as increase!

Seek independent financial advice if you have a large inheritance to invest.

Avoid risky investments. If you blow the child's inheritance on a 'get rich quick' scheme they won't thank you for it; in fact, they may well sue!

Dishing out the estate under intestacy

If there is no will the property of the deceased is distributed under the laws of intestacy. It is your duty as an administrator to ensure that this law is followed to the letter. Who gets what under intestacy is explained in great detail in Chapter 2. In brief, under intestacy the estate should be distributed in the following way in England and Wales.

- If there is a surviving spouse but no children, the spouse takes personal possessions plus the first £200,000 and half of what is left of the estate. The other half goes to the parents of the deceased. If there aren't any parents alive, then the siblings of the deceased inherit.

- If there's a surviving spouse and children, then the spouse takes the personal possessions and gets the first £125,000 plus a life interest – income – in half the remaining estate. The children take the other half of what's left.

- If there's no surviving spouse but there are children, then the estate is divided equally between them.

- If there are no spouse or children, a strict order of priority applies where relations inherit according to their proximity in blood to the deceased. Check out Chapter 2 for a full rundown.

In Scotland, who inherits what under intestacy is very similar to England and Wales except that the surviving spouse has more rights to the property. Check out Chapter 2 for the low-down on Scotland's intestacy laws.

If you invest for a child's benefit, ask the building society for a *self-certification form*. This form exempts the savings from having tax deducted.

Facing Up to a Will Challenge

Being an executor isn't all tax forms, tracking down creditors, and dividing out the estate. Sometimes you have to face up to a will challenge, where the terms of the will are contested.

As an executor it's your job to ensure that the terms of the will are followed. However, there may be times when you, and the beneficiaries, feel that the person challenging the will has a legitimate claim.

Under such circumstances the executors and beneficiaries can agree to alter the terms of the will with the aim of meeting the claim. I cover changing a will in the next section.

The usual suspects who challenge a will include:

▸ **A dependant who feels that they haven't been left enough property in the will.** Under the Inheritance (Provision for Family and Dependants) Act 1975, people deemed dependant on the deceased at the time of death may have the right to a share of the estate. Refer to Chapter 8 for how this works.

▸ **A beneficiary who is unhappy at a condition made on the gift to them.** If the beneficiary feels that a condition tacked onto their gift to them is unreasonable, then they can ask the court to set it aside. Conditional wills are explored in Chapter 8.

▸ **A beneficiary or executor who seeks to have a mistake rectified in the will.** If the wording of the will is ambiguous or a clear mistake is in the will, an executor or beneficiary can ask the courts to rectify it. See below for correcting a will.

If the situation looks like it could all turn nasty, talk to a solicitor who can advise you on what to do next.

Fighting a will challenge can be very expensive. If the claim is not substantial it may not be worthwhile going to court. Talk to a solicitor and the beneficiaries to look at simply coughing up what is requested.

A will challenge can hold up the distribution of the estate for several months and, in some exceptional circumstances, even longer.

Not only the terms of the will can be challenged – your actions as an executor or administrator can also come under scrutiny. Creditors and beneficiaries have been known to take executors and administrators to court over what they see as an unfair act or sloppy, expensive administration. If you find that your actions are called into question, consult a solicitor.

Sneaky! Changing Who Gets What in a Will

Three reasons for altering a will are, to correct a mistake, to put right an injustice, or to reduce the tax liability of the estate:

▸ **Correcting a mistake.** If the wording of the will is ambiguous or a mistake is made, as an executor you can ask the court to *rectify* the will.

However, the court won't just take your word that a mistake has occurred. You must provide the court with other evidence such as a letter you have from the deceased, or a sworn statement from someone saying that the testator made a contrary statement of intent.

✔ **Righting a wrong.** Perhaps the deceased has not provided enough for a dependant. In the interests of natural justice or to simply avoid a will challenge, the executors and the beneficiaries can alter who gets what. You can do this through a *deed of variation*, sometimes called a *deed of family arrangement*. If you want to draw up a deed, see a solicitor.

A deed of variation is a very complex device and should not be entered into without first taking legal advice.

✔ **Reducing tax.** The inheritance tax liability may have been settled at the time probate was granted, but guess what? You do have a chance of some comeback. You can draw up a *deed of variation* and re-jig who gets what in the will to reduce the IHT bill. You can also keep to a minimum any possible future inheritance liability – for example, on the death of the testator's spouse. Once a deed of variation is drawn up and agreed to by the beneficiaries it's time to let Her Majesty's Revenue & Customs (HMRC) know what the new arrangement is. Fingers crossed, a tasty tax rebate could result!

Under tax rules, no beneficiary is allowed to receive payment in cash or kind for agreeing to give up their inheritance through a deed of variation.

Your executors and beneficiaries can enter into a deed of variation provided that its terms don't reduce the share of any beneficiary under 18. If a child is involved, then you must seek the consent of the courts to the deed of variation.

The Tax-Collector's Second Coming

Inheritance tax may be the biggie as far as the probate process is concerned, but it's not the only tax to rear its ugly head. While in the throes of distributing the estate, watch out in case the following taxes become due:

✔ **Capital Gains Tax.** If the deceased's assets are sold for more than the value at the deceased's death, then Capital Gains Tax (CGT) may be payable.

✔ **Income tax.** Income from the estate is liable for tax from the date of death until it has been fully administered.

I delve deeper into both scenarios below.

Beating the Capital Gains Tax rap

In life, CGT occurs when an asset is sold for more than was paid for it. But something rather nifty happens in death: The executor or administrator is treated as having acquired the deceased's asset at its *market value* (the value of the asset at the date of death, not the date of purchase). As a result, assets that naturally increase in value over time and have a CGT liability hanging over them – sword of Damocles style – are usually free of CGT!

However, if the asset increases further in value during the probate process (remember, the whole operation can take over a year), then CGT may be chargeable. But the executor or administrator is granted a CGT allowance of £9,200 in a tax year – if the CGT gain is less than £9,200, hey presto, no CGT is due.

If the deceased's assets increase more than £9,200 since the death and before leaving the estate, capital gains are now taxed at a flat rate of 18 per cent.

The deceased's main residence is usually free of CGT, but a second home isn't.

If the asset falls in value during the probate process, then you can offset this loss against a capital gain made on the sale of another asset.

Bracing yourself for income-ing tax

You must pay income tax on any income received during the probate process, such as rents from property and interest from National Savings accounts. Unfortunately, when the deceased dies, so does their income tax personal allowance.

Income earned on the estate is never taxed at the higher band of 40 per cent – so be grateful for small mercies.

Ask your local tax office for an *income tax return* and fill it in with all the income that the deceased's estate has earned.

If the estate borrowed in order to pay an inheritance tax bill, the interest payments on this loan for the first 12 months can be offset against any income tax due.

If the estate is largely made up of savings accounts, then tax is deducted at source. That makes things easier!

Working with the Residuary Estate

The residuary estate is whatever is left after the tax authorities, creditors, and beneficiaries receive payment.

Don't forget to deduct the expenses that you incurred as an executor from the residuary estate. You're not allowed to deduct any *payment* for your services, but hopefully the person making the will was kind enough to leave a little gift as a thank you for all your hard work.

Three things may happen to the residuary estate:

- ✔ The testator may have said in their will what should happen to the residuary estate. If so, tot up how much is left after everything else has been paid from the estate, and arrange for payment to go to the named beneficiary.

- ✔ The testator may leave the residue to meet the estate's tax liability. For example, the residuary estate can be used to pay back a loan taken out to pay inheritance tax prior to grant of probate.

- ✔ The testator may have forgotten about the residuary estate. If this is the case, they are deemed to have died *partly intestate*. You must distribute this portion of the estate according to the laws of intestacy, explored in greater detail in Chapter 2.

Send the beneficiary or beneficiaries of the residuary estate a completed copy of Form R185 from HMRC. This form shows the income that the residuary estate earned during the year and any tax paid on that income. I'm sure they'll be thrilled to receive it!

Producing the Final Accounts

You're nearly over the finishing line; just one last effort! Your final job as an executor or administrator is to produce the estate accounts for the main beneficiaries. If you've been thorough during the probate process and kept all the paperwork tight, this should be a breeze.

The accounts should set out clearly the following information:

- ✔ **All taxes paid.** In the case of inheritance tax, this means keeping a copy of Form IHT 30 showing that no more IHT is due.

- ✔ **All creditor accounts settled**. You should have receipts from creditors.

✔ **All beneficiaries receiving a gift.** You should have got all the beneficiaries to sign a receipt for their gift.

✔ **All testamentary expenses.** In short, every penny you spent as an executor or administrator should be accounted for, from postage stamps to the paying of solicitor's fees.

Once you have drawn up your accounts, send all the beneficiaries a copy. The beneficiaries should indicate that they are happy with the way in which these accounts are set out.

Her Majesty's Revenue & Customs (HMRC) may request a copy of the estate accounts for their files.

A copy of the estate accounts must be kept for 12 years after probate.

That's it – your job's over. Put your feet up, have a nice rest; after all that hard work, you deserve it!

Part IV
Taxing Times: Inheritance Planning

In this part . . .

Watch out, watch out, the taxman's about! Don't fall victim to the great post-death tax grab: read this part and see how you can put plans in place to make sure that any tax due on your estate is kept to the absolute minimum. I explain how inheritance tax works and show you how to put simple plans in place to protect your family's finances, home, and business. What's more, trusts – the heavy guns of estate planning – are laid bare. The legal eagles will try to persuade you that trusts are super-complex things only to be understood by them – for a whopping fee, of course. I debunk this myth by showing you how and when to use carefully targeted trust weapons. If you're looking to secure your family's future, this is the part for you.

Chapter 15

Introducing Inheritance Tax

Death may be inevitable but huge tax bills don't have to be. Even if you're quite well off – lucky you – you can minimise the amount of tax your estate has to face.

But before you can make the right tax-saving moves you have to know your enemy – inheritance tax (IHT) – and what weapons you can utilise from your armoury.

If you're serious about avoiding IHT, you really need to make a will to use all your IHT-busting weapons.

In this chapter, I explain how IHT works.

Making Sense of Inheritance Tax

Inheritance tax has been called many things over the years, some printable, some not. During the hundred-odd years IHT's been around it's been called 'estate duty' and 'capital transfer tax'.

Whatever its name, IHT has always amounted to the same thing. When you die the executors or administrators of your estate are legally bound to assess your wealth and if your estate is worth more than a particular amount of money, then it's IHT time!

IHT may seem unfair. After all, you pay taxes throughout your life. You earn money at work, you pay income tax; buy something in a shop, you pay VAT; buy a house, you pay stamp duty – tax, tax, and more tax.

However, IHT is a crucial revenue-raiser for the Government to pay for hospitals, schools, and the subsidised bar in the House of Commons! So don't hide under the covers hoping that the IHT bogeyman will go away – he won't.

IHT is the looming iceberg on the horizon for your estate, and you need to plot a course to steer well clear of it. Forewarned is forearmed. Fortunately, you can employ all sorts of tactics to deny Her Majesty's Revenue & Customs (HMRC) a piece of your estate.

Your executors or administrators will probably have to pay some or all of the IHT due on your estate before they can obtain grant of probate or letters of administration (refer to Chapter 12 for more on these). HMRC get their money first!

The estate of any member of the armed forces who dies while on active service (or later from wounds received on active service) is totally exempt from IHT.

Doing the Inheritance Tax Sums

If your estate is worth more than £312,000 (from April 2008) when you die it may be liable to IHT. The starting point for paying IHT is called the *IHT threshold*.

IHT is charged at 40 per cent, the same as the top rate of income tax. So if your estate is worth £500,000 the tax hit could be a whopping £80,000 – ouch! This sum works as follows: £500,000 (£300,000 IHT threshold = £200,000; 40 per cent of £200,000 = £80,000.) The people inheriting your estate have to find that money somehow. (Refer to Chapter 13 on how your executors can raise money from your estate.)

The threshold for IHT is raised by the Chancellor every year. The idea of raising the threshold is to keep pace with inflation or, in another word, prices. Inflation has been stable in recent years, bobbing along between 2 to 4 per cent. All very good you might think.

However, your financial worth probably rises faster than inflation. For starters, wages normally rise slightly quicker than inflation, and if you're savvy and shop around for the best savings account then it's probably paying comfortably more than inflation. What's more, share investments over the long term tend to beat inflation hands down.

Don't forget the daddy of all your assets: Your home. According to the Halifax, the average UK house price has more than doubled in the past five years. In parts of London and the south-east just an *average* home is now worth more then the IHT threshold. The number of estates that attract IHT is predicted to grow during the next ten years. One of these estates could be yours!

The message is clear: What used to be a tax for the mega-rich and toffs with a huge ancestral pile is now stalking the ordinary man or woman on the street.

Individuals who are *domiciled* in the UK – regard the UK as their permanent home and pay tax in the UK – are liable for IHT on all their worldwide assets. Yes, that includes your gîte in France!

Everyone has a *nil-rate band*. This is the amount of money you can leave in your will before it becomes subject to IHT (the same as the IHT threshold).

The tax year doesn't run like a calendar year; it runs from the 6 April in one year to 5 April the next.

I know it's boring, but try to study the Chancellor's Budget speech, which usually takes place sometime in March. The Chancellor often uses the speech to announce any increase in the IHT threshold. Alternatively, if the idea of a man in a suit droning on about 'fiscal prudence' and 'inflation targets' isn't your cup of tea, check out the HMRC Web site for the latest information on tax thresholds, www.hmrc.gov.uk.

Working Out Your Tax Liability

Your first move in the IHT avoidance programme is working out your estate's potential liability. Chapter 3 explains how to go about valuing your estate. In brief, try and arrive at a value for the following assets:

- ✔ Property, such as your main home and any holiday property
- ✔ Business interests
- ✔ Cash held in bank and building society accounts
- ✔ Stocks and shares
- ✔ Life insurance benefits
- ✔ Personal possessions, such as your car and jewellery
- ✔ Collectibles, such as works of art or expensive wine

If after doing the maths your estate is worth more than the IHT threshold (£300,000 2007/08 tax year rising to £312,000 from April 2008), the alarm bells should start ringing – it's time to get your estate into a tax-efficient state.

As far as HMRC is concerned your estate doesn't just include all your property at your death. Your estate may include property that you gave away during the seven years prior to your death.

You only need a bit of time and application to work out what your estate is worth today. But working out what your estate may be worth in future takes a little bit of crystal-ball gazing. Fortunately, you can use some likely estate growth scenarios to work out if you have to worry about IHT:

- **Savings growth.** Most safe investments – savings accounts, bonds, and the like – are reckoned to grow in value at around 5 per cent a year.

- **Share growth.** Insurance companies believe that share prices grow by between 5 and 9 per cent a year over a long period of time. Financial advisers reckon that 7 per cent a year is a good ball-park figure.

- **Property growth.** The stellar growth of the past five years has been unusual, but over the last 40 years, house prices have increased on average by more than 10 per cent per year.

It doesn't take a rocket scientist to work out that if your main assets grow by 5, 7, or 10 per cent a year while the IHT threshold increases by 3 or 4 per cent a year, then sooner or later your estate might well catch up with the IHT threshold.

Recognising the 'Must Plan' Scenarios

Some situations should make you ponder planning to avoid IHT, even if the value of your estate is currently below the IHT threshold. See if you fit into one of the following scenarios:

- **Age can equal wealth.** Age is supposed to make you wiser. It can also super-charge your estate. As people enter their fifties they often enjoy a golden financial era – assuming they're in good health and still working. Fifty-somethings are at the height of their career, their mortgage is probably paid off, and the children have flown the nest!

- **Marriage and children.** At first glance, marriage and children seem good things for your estate. Property that passes to your spouse on your death is free of IHT. However, this increase in wealth means that your spouse's estate can be burdened for IHT purposes when your spouse dies. If your spouse dies without taking IHT avoidance measures and the value of the estate has grown then the beneficiaries – perhaps your children – could face a nasty tax bill.

Hold the front page! Tax break for couples

In October 2007, the Chancellor gave married and civil partners a major tax break. The IHT nil-rate band (the value of assets that you can pass on free of IHT) of the deceased spouse or civil partner now passes onto the surviving spouse or civil partner. In effect, this means that on the death of the second spouse or civil partner his or hers nil-rate band is doubled. In the 2007/08 tax year the nil-rate band of a surviving spouse or civil partner is £600,000, by the 2010/11 tax year the Government has said this combined nil-rate band will have risen to £700,000. However, if you're married or in a civil partnership and the combined value of your estates is worth more than £600,000, you'd be wise to take measures to reduce your IHT liability now.

If you're young, free, single, and poor IHT should be the last of your worries, unless you're set to inherit a substantial sum from a close relative!

The Cruellest Cut of All: Tax and the Family Home

Becoming a homeowner is very exciting, from the moment you move in and discover the previous occupier has taken everything to bringing up a family there. But on becoming a homeowner you have suddenly made it more likely that one day – hopefully many years off – your estate will be subject to inheritance tax.

If you don't plan properly, your estate's executors or administrators may have no option but to sell the family home – even if your nearest and dearest have their hearts set on continuing to live there. Of course, this action is a last resort, but if most of your wealth is tied up in your home then it may have to be sold. Sadly, the incidence of homes being sold to meet an IHT bill is on the increase.

Facing Up to an Inheritance Tax Bill

Chapter 16 is chock-full of ideas on how to avoid IHT. But, hey, maybe you're simply loaded and you've got to face the IHT music. So be it! But nothing's stopping you from taking steps to ensure that any IHT bill is sorted out with the minimum of fuss and financial pain. The following sections offer some ideas to make the tax-paying job easier.

Build up a handsome estate residue

The estate residue is everything that's left after funeral expenses, prior gifts, and payments to creditors. By having a healthy estate residue you're leaving your estate's executors with the wherewithal to pay HMRC. The estate residue often makes up the majority of the estate.

Check your estate and will at least once a year so you can get a handle on whether the residue will be large enough to cover the tax bill.

Squeeze the life out of life insurance

You can take out life insurance with the aim that on death it pays out enough to cover any IHT bill.

The proceeds of the life insurance policy may be subject to IHT itself. Ironic, eh? The way around this situation is to write your policy in trust to a beneficiary (perhaps one who is also your executor) and they can use the proceeds to pay the tax bill. Head to Chapter 17 for the low-down on trusts.

Below are two insurance options – it's crucial that you purchase the right insurance to meet your specific IHT needs.

- ✔ **Term insurance.** This pays out for a fixed period of time, say, until you're 65. Once the time period has expired and you turn 65, that's it, all bets are off and you're no longer insured!

- ✔ **Whole-life policy.** This pays out when you die whether it's the day after the policy is taken out, or a hundred years hence. This type of policy is particularly useful when looking to cover the total IHT bill on an estate. As a rule of thumb, whole-life insurance is more expensive than term insurance.

If you decide to buy life insurance, obtain advice from an independent financial adviser, especially if you decide to write the policy into trust. Check out www.unbiased.co.uk for a list of independent financial advisers in your local area.

Life insurers don't require grant of probate or letters of administration to pay out if the policy is not payable to the estate; all they need is a copy of the death certificate. As a result, the money can be there to meet any IHT bill in double-quick time.

Tax: A question of morality?

In this book I go on and on about being boxing clever to avoid IHT. However, tax avoidance has a moral dimension. Although you may not always recognise it, the State provides us with a lot during our lives – the school system may have taught you how to read this book; the National Health Service may have helped you or a loved one get over a serious ailment; and the armed forces have defended your liberty, often with their lives.

You may think that taxing an estate in excess of a quarter of a million pounds is fair enough, and why shouldn't you contribute to your country from beyond the grave through IHT? For one thing, the tax-collector would be proud of you!

Life insurance tax rules have changed. If the proceeds of the life policy take the value of the deceased's estate above the IHT tax threshold (£312,000 from April 2008) and the policy pays into a trust to be distributed gradually to beneficiaries rather than in one go at the time of the policyholders death, then IHT is due. However, policies written in trust, which are more straight-forward and pay out to the estate at the policyholder's death are still exempt from IHT.

A Taxing Question: Avoidance or Evasion?

Question: What's the difference between inheritance tax avoidance and evasion?

Answer: Fines and possibly a spell in prison.

Both avoidance and evasion are about making the estate seem smaller than it actually is for tax calculation purposes. In this book, and especially in Chapter 16, I give you heaps of tips about how to avoid paying tax and how to pass on as much of your loot as possible to your loved ones. But I tell you about ways to *avoid* tax, not ways to *evade* it.

Avoidance is about getting the tax laws to work for the good of the estate. IHT exemptions exist for good reason and you're free to use them.

Essentially, *evasion* amounts to the non-disclosure of assets to HMRC and the illegal spiriting away of parts of the estate. These actions are underhand and if HMRC find out they crack down hard!

Any IHT evasion you commit probably won't be discovered until after your death when HMRC looks at the accounts submitted by your executors or administrators. And although you can't be punished, your estate can be. Likewise, if your executors are found to be complicit in your tax evasion or undertake their own naughty tricks, they could face fines and, in extreme cases, even be thrown in jail.

Tax Planning: An Act of Faith

Whatever method you choose to keep your estate out of the clutches of HMRC, you need to have faith. Don't worry, this book hasn't suddenly started diving headlong into new-age philosophising – I'll save that for *Spotting Someone's Aura For Dummies.* You have to have faith in your executors, trustees, and, above all, yourself to play the best role in the tax-avoidance drama.

- ✔ **Executors.** These people are your estate watchdogs; they see the terms of your estate through and deal with HMRC. Executors can also help vary the terms of your will post-mortem so that the estate can save tax. See Chapter 16 for more on how they can do this.

- ✔ **Trustees.** If you use a trust to reduce your estate's exposure to IHT you're going to need trustees. As a rule of thumb, the greater flexibility you grant your trustees, the greater potential they have for avoiding tax on behalf of the beneficiaries. Trust them to do this!

- ✔ **Yourself.** If you're embarking on tax-saving tactics such as using your exempt gifts to the maximum, making a potentially exempt transfer, or putting your assets into trust (all explained in Chapter 16), you need to be 100 per cent sure that you won't change your mind. Once you start down the tax-saving road and ridding yourself of assets it can be very difficult to backtrack.

Chapter 6 gives the low-down on what to look for when appointing an executor or trustee. As for finding a spouse or civil partner who you can have faith in, best ask your mum!

In your enthusiasm to get your estate into tax-saving shape, be careful not to leave your spouse short of money in the event of your death.

If you're looking for a root and branch review of your tax position, seek advice from a solicitor or accountant.

Chapter 16

Simple Steps to Reduce Inheritance Tax

*F*ighting the tax-collector to protect your hard-earned dough from inheritance tax (IHT) has a downside and an upside. The downside is that you won't be around to pull on your boxing gloves if any problems with your IHT planning come to light; it's up to others to sort out how any tax bill is paid. The upside is that you can work out if IHT is coming (head to Chapter 3 for help valuing your estate) and you can start planning now on ways to reduce the tax liability on your estate for the ultimate benefit of your nearest and dearest.

If you're a beneficiary, executor, or administrator for someone's estate and they weren't very switched on to tax avoidance, you can use a deed of variation to claw back some cash from Her Majesty's Revenue & Customs (HMRC); Chapter 9 shows you how.

In this chapter, I show you lots of different tactics you can use to sidestep IHT: It's time to get with the tax-fighting programme!

Exploiting the Combined Nil-Rate Band

This book does not condone spouse exploitation, even if it's to get your hands on the TV remote control!

However, you can do a certain sort of exploitation together as a team: Exploiting each other's nil-rate IHT band.

In October 2007, the Chancellor gave married and civil partners a major tax break. The IHT nil-rate band (the value of assets that can be passed on free of IHT) of the deceased spouse or civil partner now passes onto the surviving spouse or civil partner. In effect, this means that on the death of the second spouse or civil partner his or her nil-rate band is doubled. In the 2007/08 tax year the nil-rate band of a surviving spouse or civil partner is £600,000; by the 2010/11 tax year this will rise to £700,000.

The ideal situation is to write your will so that you leave your spouse or civil partner enough to live on but not so much that when he or she dies, the estate is worth more than the combined nil-rate band (£600,000 in the 2007/08 tax year rising to £700,000 in 2010/11). Anything above the combined nil-rate band should be left to an IHT-free *non-exempt beneficiary* (someone who would usually have to pay tax) such as your child.

The big no-no that you're trying to avoid is the *bunching of assets*, which is when one spouse or civil partner leaves the other spouse so many assets that when the second spouse dies, the estate attracts IHT. In other words, their estate at death is worth more than the combined nil-rate band.

Any money or assets that pass between spouses in life as a result of death are exempt from IHT.

Doing it the wrong way

Time for an enlightening example of bunching of assets. Here, Winston's estate is worth £400,000 while Jasmine's is worth £365,000. On his death, Winston leaves his wife Jasmine his share of the house, cash, and all his shares to a total value of £360,000. Winston leaves his son and daughter the rest between them: £20,000 each. As a result, Jasmine is now quite a wealthy woman, with total assets of £725,000. However, Jasmine dies a few years later, leaving her estate to her son and daughter. But before they can collect their gifts, the son and daughter face having to pay IHT.

Due to interest earned on savings and increases in share and property prices, Jasmine's estate increased to £800,000. The mortgage on the family home was paid off, so she didn't really need the big pot of money she had been left by Winston.

Jasmine left £600,000 free of IHT (the combined nil-rate band in the 2007/08 tax year), but on the rest of the estate – £200,000 – the son and daughter have to pay 40 per cent tax. The total tax bill is a whopping £80,000.

Jasmine's son and daughter are both making a start in the world and can't possibly afford to pay the IHT bill. Therefore, the executor of Jasmine's estate borrows the money to pay the IHT bill (remember the tax vampire must be fed first) and sells the family home to raise the money to pay back the debt.

Count me out

If you give money to an *exempt beneficiary*, through your will for example, that money is not included in your estate when IHT is calculated.

Exempt beneficiaries include: Your spouse, parliamentary political parties, museums, housing associations, sports clubs and community associations, and even your local authority. But by far the most popular exempt beneficiaries (not including your spouse, of course) are charitable organisations.

Only a charity registered in the UK qualifies as an exempt beneficiary. If you're in any doubt whether a charity qualifies as an exempt beneficiary, check to see if they have a UK charity number.

You can set up a charitable trust to drip-feed money into your chosen good cause and reduce your IHT liability – talk to a solicitor to find out how.

Make it crystal clear in your will which charity or other exempt beneficiary you're leaving a gift to. Note the charity's official registration number, which you can find on its Web site or in its literature.

But you can't just leave thousands to Battersea Dogs Home and leave poor Granny Gertrude out in the cold. Remember, if you gift a large part of your estate to an exempt beneficiary other than your spouse, then anyone who was financially dependant upon you could have the gift overturned on the grounds that it causes them hardship. Refer to Chapters 8 and 9 for who can and can't challenge your will.

Final result: HMRC scoops a cool £80,000 and the cherished family home has gone forever!

Doing it the right way

Now look at the same estate where Winston and Jasmine planned ahead a bit better and partly exploited their nil-rate bands.

On his death, Winston leaves his wife his share in the family home and a little cash, to a total value of £175,000. The rest of his estate, £225,000, is divided evenly between his son and daughter. No IHT is due at this point. Winston could have left less to Jasmine but he wanted to make sure that she had enough to live off; after all, he has to presume that she will outlive him for many years. Jasmine is now worth £540,000 (her assets of £365,000 combined with Winston's £175,000) – including the family home.

Sadly, after six years, Jasmine dies. Her estate has grown in value to £600,000 (she had to use some of the interest from savings accounts to live off so the wealth growth is smaller than the previous example) and this passes to her son and daughter.

Jasmine can leave £600,000 free of IHT, which is covered by the combined nil-rate band rules introduced in October 2007. As a result, there's no IHT to pay on Jasmine's estate. This example assumes that the combined IHT threshold in the 2007/2008 of £600,000 applies, although in reality the Chancellor has said that this threshold will rise to £700,000 in the 2010/2011 tax year.

The net result is of due to some estate jiggery-pokery in Winston's will, there is no IHT to pay on Jasmine's death and crucially, the son and daughter inherit the family home.

Doing even better

Even in the second example, Winston and Jasmine could have done a lot more to avoid IHT. In fact, with some extra smart moves, HMRC could have been cut out of the equation altogether – despite the fact that their combined estate was worth more than a cool half million pounds.

Throughout this chapter you'll see other ways in which Winston and Jasmine could have reduced their IHT bill further.

The key message is that exploiting two nil-rate IHT bands should be at the heart of combating IHT for a married couple.

Using Exempt Gifts to Save Tax

During your life you can make certain gifts that are exempt from IHT. Once these gifts are made, they disappear from your estate for good and become invisible to HMRC.

Gifts made for the maintenance of children or dependant relatives are also tax-free. You can make the following exempt gifts each year:

- ✔ Small gifts of up to £250 as many times as you like in any one tax year, but each gift must be to a different person. This is called the *small gifts exemption*.

- ✔ One big exempt gift of up to £3,000 a year. This is called the *annual exemption*.

You're not allowed to give the same person a small gift and a large £3,000 gift in the same tax year.

In addition, you can make the following gifts to mark a loved one's or even a friend's wedding:

> ✔ A gift of £5,000 on the wedding of a child. They could pay for the whole show with that or simply put it in the bank.
>
> ✔ A gift of £2,500 on the wedding of a grandchild. Should help them pay for that nice honeymoon.
>
> ✔ A gift of £1,000 to celebrate the wedding of other family or friends. Not a huge sum but better than a set of steak knives!

These exemptions apply no matter how many times the person gets married.

If you add the value of all these gifts together it's possible to move large amounts of money out of your estate in a relatively short period of time, and you get to see the beneficiary enjoying the gift.

As far as the tax-collector is concerned gifts larger than the tax exemption levels remain in your estate for a period of seven years, although the rate at which they're taxed falls over time. But the recipient of these gifts has to foot any tax bill in the event of your death.

Two gifts for the price of one

Anyone can use these tax exemptions but married couples have an advantage in that they have two sets of gift exemptions to use up. Also, because gifts between spouses are automatically exempt, married couples can give money to and fro to ensure that the exemptions are used to the maximum. This is particularly useful when one spouse or civil partner is richer than the other.

Back to Winston and Jasmine to show how this works: Remember, Winston's estate is worth £400,000 while Jasmine's is worth £365,000.

Winston uses his annual gift exemption to give his daughter £3,000 a year.

The son gets hitched. Winston makes a gift of £5,000 from his estate to mark the happy occasion. In addition, he gives £5,000 to Jasmine who in turn gifts the cash to her son to mark the big day.

By working together, the couple have managed to move lots of cash out of the estate. The tax inspector won't even get a sniff of this cash!

You can easily see how using exempt gifting, along with the nil-rate band, can ensure that large estates become small enough to slip through the tax net.

Don't go overboard with exempt gifting: Make sure that you can afford it. Remember, once the gift's gone, it's gone!

Exempt assets

Her Majesty's Revenue & Customs (HMRC) allows special exemptions for certain types of property. These types of property can be inherited free of IHT, at a discounted rate of IHT, or the payment of the IHT bill can be spread out over many years.

If you have any of the following assets in your estate, then you may be able to claim an IHT exemption:

- ✔ **Business assets.** Sole trader businesses, shares in a business partnership, land, buildings, and machinery can all attract an IHT tax break called *business property relief*.

- ✔ **Agricultural property.** Agricultural land, working farmhouses (not pretty piles in the Home Counties), and barns can attract IHT *agricultural property relief*.

- ✔ **Woodland.** You can postpone the payment of IHT on woodland until the timber on the land has been sold.

- ✔ **National Heritage property.** If you're lucky enough to own National Heritage property – including some listed homes but also some important works of art – this should be exempt from IHT. If you own one of these types of property, talk to an accountant to see how the exemptions work – just get your butler to fetch them!

Turn to Chapter 19 if you want more information on business exemptions.

Carrying an exempt gift forwards

If you don't use up your full exemption in one year, you can carry it forward to the next. This, ingeniously, is called a *carried-forward* exemption. The carried forward exemption only applies to the £3,000 annual exemption, and not to the small gifts exemption. Carried-forward exemptions are manna from heaven for hurry-up estate planning.

So if you don't make a £3,000 gift in one tax year, you can make a £6,000 gift the next. Likewise, if you only used part of your exemption in one tax year, you can use it the next. However, you're not allowed to carry forward to any subsequent year.

Gifts always use up the exemption for the tax year in which they are made before using up any exemption carried forwards from the previous tax year.

Gifting from Everyday Income

You're allowed to gift money from your income. If you can clearly show that a gift doesn't erode your capital or savings, then it is exempt.

Gifts from income are often used to slowly drain money from an estate to reduce its size and ultimately any IHT bill. The capital isn't touched; the interest earned on the capital is siphoned off into the pockets of your nearest and dearest.

Take the case of kind Aunt Jane, a spinster. Because Jane is single she has only her own nil-rate band to use up.

Back in January 2004, Jane's estate was worth £500,000, with some £240,000 held in building society accounts paying a fixed interest income of £18,000 a year. Jane doesn't need this much to live on so she gives her niece Margaret, her only surviving relative, £500 a month or £6,000 a year. This action doesn't eat into her gift exemptions because she is paying the money from income.

By the end of the 2007/08 tax year Jane has given Margaret £24,000 this way, but in order to keep it kosher she hasn't reduced the overall value of her estate in the process.

But clever Aunt Jane has gone a stage further and utilised her gift exemption in each of the previous four years by giving Margaret a total of £12,000 (£3,000 a year). These gifts are all above board and this time legitimately drawn from her estate assets. And as the icing on the cake – forgive the pun – Jane gives Margaret a further £1,000 to mark Margaret's wedding.

By April 2008, Jane will have managed to move £37,000 into Margaret's pocket and reduced her estate from £500,000 to £487,000.

If she had done nothing, Jane's estate would be worth £524,000.

All the time, the threshold for paying IHT had been on the increase, from £255,000 in 2003/04 to £300,000 in 2007/08 (increasing again to £312,000 in April 2008).

Even after four years of making gifts, Jane's estate is still big enough to be subject to IHT. However, through gifting she's reduced any eventual tax bill. Gifting isn't a magic one-hit solution, but a gradual way of beating the taxman.

Stick to the readies when making gifts of income. If you give anything else, say a car, you must prove that it was bought out of income rather than the capital. Tricky!

When making an exempt gift to someone, give them a signed note stating clearly which exemption – small gifts, wedding, or annual exemption – you are using. Doing so will make things easier for your executors when they sort out your paperwork.

Premiums on a life insurance policy written in trust for the benefit of some-one else are considered gifts out of regular income and therefore leave your estate for IHT purposes.

Maintaining the family – tax-free

Payments made for the *maintenance*, or upkeep, of a spouse, civil partner, children, or dependant relatives automatically leave your estate for IHT purposes and don't eat into your gift exemptions. This exemption is irrespective of whether you make these payments from income or by dipping into your savings or selling assets to meet the expense.

The definition of children is very wide and includes stepchildren, illegitimate, and adopted children.

If you're divorced, any maintenance payments to your former spouse are exempt from IHT.

Money that you pay to put your children through college can even be considered maintenance. Just think – next time your little treasure asks you for that £100 that she swears is for books, you can cross it off your estate for IHT purposes.

Revving-up Potentially Exempt Transfers

Exempt gifts disappear from your estate as soon as the cheque is cashed or the money handed over. However, you can transfer larger assets to someone else with the *potential* that one day they'll be deemed exempt from IHT. Funnily enough, these are called *Potentially Exempt Transfers* (PETs). Like most pets, they can be deeply rewarding but they can also bite.

With PETs, it's all about playing the waiting game. Seven years after you make the transfer it is considered outside of your estate and is exempt from IHT.

But what if you die six years and 364 days after making the PET? Well, the beneficiary of the PET is liable for IHT. However, even the tax-collector understands that it's not fair to treat a PET made so long ago as one made the day before death. So the IHT liability on the asset is *tapered* – which means it tails off over time, with nothing to pay after seven years. *Taper relief* sums work as follows:

Years between transfer and death	Rate of tax reduction
0–3	No reduction
3–4	20% reduction
4–5	40% reduction
5–6	60% reduction
6–7	80% reduction
7+	100% reduction

You can't make a PET to a spouse because transfers of assets to a spouse are automatically exempt from IHT.

The pros and cons of keeping a PET

You can adopt the simple PET strategy: Gift everything above the IHT threshold to your nearest and dearest in the hope that you'll live for another seven years and, hey presto, your estate is tax-free!

This strategy is fraught with danger for three simple reasons:

- ✔ **You could die within seven years.** If you die within three years of making the gift, the asset is still considered to be in your estate and any tax due has to be paid. After three years, the amount of IHT starts to reduce – refer to Chapter 15 for more on how this works.

- ✔ **The gift can owe Capital Gains Tax.** If you sign over property that has gained in value since you bought it, you may be liable for a CGT charge. Even if the person you transfer the asset to doesn't pay a penny for it, CGT could still be due on its market value. Chapter 14 has the news on CGT.

- ✔ **Once it's gone, it's gone.** By transferring an asset you're giving up all rights to it. You can't sell this asset if you need the money, and if it's your home you can't live in it unless you pay a market rent and pay income tax. Think hard before going ahead with a PET; you must be absolutely sure you can do without the asset you're giving away.

Don't let these dangers scare you off using PETs. PETs can play a crucial role in IHT planning, but only after you utilise your spouse's nil-rate band, and use exempt gifts and give gifts to exempt beneficiaries. A PET may ease your tax bill enormously, but just as easily – say, if you die soon after the transfer – not make a blind bit of difference!

If IHT does become payable on a PET it is usually levied on the asset's value at the time of the transfer rather than at the time of death. However, if the PET falls in value between the time of transfer and the date of death, it can be priced at the lower value for IHT purposes.

The person who has received the PET has to foot any IHT bill. However, if the recipient of the PET doesn't pay this bill within 12 months, then your executors are liable.

Don't Let the GROB Get You!

A GROB sounds like one of those papier-mâché monsters from the original Doctor Who! GROB, though, is an acronym and stands for *Gift with Reservation of Benefit* and if you fall foul of it then no amount of hiding behind the sofa can help you!

If you sign over an asset you can no longer *benefit* from it by using or enjoying it. With a house, that means you can no longer live there. If the asset is a work of art, then it can't hang in your home – otherwise it's a GROB.

A GROB means that your PET tax prize goes up in smoke regardless of whether you cross the seven-year finishing line or not.

You can bet your bottom dollar, pound, or euro that if you transfer a major asset (PET) in the years prior to your death, the tax inspector is going to examine it closely to see if you benefited from it. If you did benefit, the person you transferred the asset to could be in line for a major tax hit!

Gifts between spouses are not subject to GROB rules.

There are, however, perfectly legal ways in which you can still enjoy your asset:

- ✓ **Visitation rights.** If you give away your home to your child as a PET, naturally you're still entitled to visit them there. You can even stay with them for weekends or over Christmas, just as long as your main residence is somewhere else (perhaps that lovely Tuscan farmhouse).

- ✓ **Pay rent.** You can continue to use an asset as long as you pay the asset's new owner the going market rent for it. So if you give your home away to your child and continue to live there, you must pay them rent.

  Don't be tempted to fiddle the rent. HMRC is watching and if they deem that a fair market rent wasn't paid, then bang goes any IHT benefits.

  From April 2005, under the *pre-owned asset* rules, people continuing to live in property they have given away can be hit with an income tax bill. Take advice from a solicitor.

- ✓ **Your circumstances change.** If your circumstances take a turn for the worse, then you may be able to use the asset in a limited way once more without risking GROB. This situation most often applies when someone gives away their home to a relative and then falls seriously ill – they may be able to move back in without fear of GROB. If you encounter this situation, seek the advice of a solicitor.

No law exists against you giving away an asset as a PET and then continuing to use it as before. All that happens is that the clock doesn't start ticking on the PET transfer until you stop using the asset – only then does the PET start on its seven-year journey to becoming free of IHT. Bear in mind that HMRC values the asset from the date you stopped using it and committing GROB, not on the day of the transfer. Overall, no tax advantages exist in continuing to use an asset you've given away.

Strategies for Singletons

If you're single you may feel a little left out by all this talk of how great the spouse's nil-rate band is. But don't despair – you can also use lots of weapons in your fight against the tax-collector.

While it's true that only married couples can pass assets between each other regardless of size without fear of waking the IHT ogre from its slumber, you can also box clever and use other tools to avoid IHT. Keep your estate below the IHT threshold by using one or more of the following:

- ✓ **Give lifetime gifts.** Anyone is free to use exempt gifts and PETs to reduce the size of their estate.

- ✓ **Generation skip.** If you inherit a sizeable sum but already have enough money to live off, you can pass on the gift to your children to prevent your estate becoming so large that it attracts a whopping tax bill. Generation skipping is explained more fully in the next section.

- ✓ **Give to an exempt beneficiary.** You can leave money to charity and some other institutions free of IHT.

- ✓ **Use trusts.** Trusts take money out of your estate for the benefit of someone else. Trusts can be a very powerful tool in avoiding IHT (see Chapters 17 and 18 for more on trusts).

- ✓ **Have the right assets**. HMRC allows special IHT exemptions for some types of property such as business, woodland, and agriculture.

- ✓ **Use your own nil-rate band.** You may not have a spouse but you still have your own nil-rate band to exploit to the full.

Funeral expenses and debts are deducted from your estate before IHT is calculated.

The Generation Game: Reducing Tax by Generation Skipping

Generation skipping isn't some sort of competitive sport played by families, but instead a useful way of saving tax.

A swift look at quick succession relief

Sometimes IHT is due on two estates in quick succession. For example, suppose a parent dies and leaves lots of money to their child, who pays IHT, only for the child to die shortly after. Unless the estate passes to a spouse or another exempt beneficiary, then IHT is due again. The tragic circumstances are made even worse!

However, under such circumstances the beneficiary can claim *quick succession relief*. The closer the second death is to the first, the higher the percentage of relief from IHT can be claimed.

Years between first and second death	*Tax relief as a percentage*
Up to 1 year	100%
1–2	80% reduction
2–3	60% reduction
3–4	40% reduction
4–5	20% reduction
More than 5 years	No relief

What happens under *generation skipping* is that you give up the right to a gift in favour of your children. Ask a solicitor to draw up a *deed of variation* (a document whereby the beneficiaries agree to alter the gifts made in the deceased's will) to generation skip. Usually, this act involves you giving up the rights to a gift from your parent so that your son or daughter (the grandchild of the deceased) can inherit.

A beneficiary can choose not to take a gift left to them – this is called *disclaiming*. If a gift is disclaimed, it goes to the named alternative beneficiary; if there is no alternative beneficiary, it goes into the estate residue – what's left after taxes, creditors, and beneficiaries are paid.

Generation skipping can reduce the IHT liability on the original beneficiary's estate. Take the case of Frida, Miguel, and Gloria. Frida is Miguel's mother and Gloria's grandmother.

Frida leaves her entire estate, valued at £100,000, to Miguel. Miguel is wealthy and doesn't need the money, and also fears that the sudden injection of Frida's gift will push his estate above the IHT threshold. So, through a deed of variation, he changes the destination of Frida's estate and it goes to Gloria.

The key is that no IHT is due on the estate because the £100,000 is well below Frida's nil-rate band of £312,000. However, if Miguel had allowed the estate to pass to him, and increase his wealth above the IHT threshold, then when *he* dies IHT may be payable on his estate.

Reducing tax on collectibles

If you ever watch the BBC's *Antiques Roadshow* you know that having a set of collectibles or items of furniture is worth a lot more than having just one.

Owning a complete set of six Chippendale chairs is worth a lot more than owning one, two, three, four, or even five of the chairs.

If you own any valuable collectibles or furniture, take this unwritten law into account when making plans to avoid IHT. It may be a smart move to break the sets up, giving some items away as a PET to a child or relative.

If you gift some of the chairs to your spouse, then HMRC could treat all the chairs as *related property*. These are special rules that allow HMRC to value an asset as a proportion of an enhanced combined value.

The tactic to share out sets of collectibles and thereby reduce their worth for tax purposes can also be used when it comes to sharing out a majority shareholding in a business. After all, 60 per cent ownership of a firm is a controlling stake and worth a lot more than three 20 per cent stakes doled out to different family members.

With generation skipping, IHT is not saved immediately, but you avoid estate bunching and hopefully future IHT.

If you consider generation skipping, ask yourself some serious questions.

- ✔ **Can I afford it?** You're giving up a valuable inheritance. You have to be 100 per cent certain that you can live without the money.

- ✔ **Can my child handle the money?** You don't want a spendthrift teenager to inherit or the money could disappear in double-quick time. Remember, even the most responsible people can go a little wild when the financial shackles are off!

- ✔ **What is my state of health?** If you're suffering from ill health you may need long-term care, which can rapidly eat into your estate. You might need that money yourself in the future.

Quick succession relief is only available on the proportion of the estate inherited from the first death. The remainder of the second person's estate is subject to IHT as usual.

Protecting the Family Home . . . By Moving Out!

Making sure your family home passes to your children without an unpleasant tax bill attached is probably your number one objective! But a home is most people's biggest asset and as a result it's not easy to hide it from the tax-collector.

If your estate is worth more than the nil-rate band (or the combined nil-rate band if you have a spouse or civil partner) then you need to employ some or all of the following tactics to deal with your family home:

- ✔ **Use the nil-rate band.** Spread your assets about – make sure that your will is written so that other assets go to different beneficiaries. This uses the nil-rate band to the max and prevents bunching of assets.

- ✔ **Leave your home.** Alternatively, leave your home, or the share of your home, to someone other than your spouse or civil partner in your will. You're trusting that the beneficiary will continue to allow your spouse to live there; perhaps the beneficiary – a son or daughter – could move back in. Make sure your spouse or civil partner is happy with this arrangement, as they have the right to challenge the gift through the courts.

- ✔ **Put the home into trust.** You can arrange that on your death the home goes into a discretionary trust (explained in Chapter 17) for a beneficiary other than your spouse or civil partner, but the trustees allow the spouse to carry on living in the property. This arrangement uses your nil-rate band and your spouse is protected. You could even name your spouse as a trustee as well as a beneficiary. Importantly, when your spouse dies, the home is not in his or her estate for IHT purposes. See Chapter 18 for more on this tactic.

- ✔ **Give your home away**. You can simply sign your home over to a beneficiary as a potentially exempt transfer, and if you live for a further seven years no IHT is due. However, if you continue to live in the property, you fall foul of the GROB, explained earlier in this chapter.

- ✔ **Downsize.** If the children have gone you may not need your big old house. Why not sell up and move to somewhere smaller? For this action to be truly effective at reducing your estate, you have to move the money you make from the sale out of your estate fairly sharpish through using your annual gift exemption (explained earlier in this chapter).

- ✔ **Split the home.** If you have a big home, then you could split it into two or more residences. You can rattle about in one and your family take possession of the other. PET rules still apply but you don't have a problem with GROB. If you do go down this route, remember you need planning permission for the conversion.

Your main residence is exempt from Capital Gains Tax, so if you sell your own home, you're fine. However, if you pass on your home to someone who subsequently rents it out rather than living there, when they sell the property, the sale will be liable to CGT.

The nil-rate band of your spouse or civil partner automatically passes onto you at his or her death and vice versa. In effect, this doubles the nil-rate band of the surviving spouse or civil partner at their death. The upshot of this is that married couples and civil partners are going to be able to leave more money behind for non-exempt beneficiaries free of IHT. From now on fewer people are going to need to make tax saving plays (such as putting it into trust or downsizing) with the family home.

Fleeing the Country to Avoid IHT

Sounds very dramatic, doesn't it? More people than ever are now retiring abroad. Few up sticks with the sole intention of avoiding IHT; most people do it for the warmer weather and the hope of never again navigating the M25. Nevertheless, from an IHT avoidance point of view, you might find it pays to leave dear old Blighty!

If you live in the UK, IHT is levied on your *worldwide* assets, but if you live abroad, it's levied just on your *UK* assets. So if you have large assets abroad, you can move to sunnier climes later in life to protect those assets from the UK tax system!

By moving abroad permanently, you might be able to take advantage of two nil-rate bands: One in the UK on UK assets and one abroad on the foreign assets. If you have a spouse, you could exploit four nil-rate bands!

But IHT avoidance is never simple. If you've lived in the UK for at least 17 out of the 20 previous tax years, you're treated for IHT purposes as still living in the UK. As a consequence, IHT is still due on worldwide assets. If you leave the UK permanently, it's still a further three years before you escape the UK's IHT rules altogether. Bother! Nevertheless, if you move abroad you may find that the IHT bill on your estate is reduced. Seek out specialist tax advice before you go.

You're deemed to be living (the official word is *domiciled*) in the country in which you have a permanent home. You can only be domiciled in one country at a time. If you own a holiday home overseas and your main residence is in the UK, you're classed as living in the UK. However, if you sell or let out the UK residence and move permanently to the holiday home, that's classed as your main home.

IHT isn't just a British phenomenon; most major nations impose some form of tax on a deceased's estates. Make sure you don't jump from the frying pan and into the fire!

If you move abroad and die soon after, you could owe IHT in both countries. HMRC levies IHT on all worldwide assets, but any IHT bill arising in another country is deducted. If the UK tax bill on worldwide assets is £100,000 and the IHT bill from another country is £20,000, your estate pays £80,000 to the UK and £20,000 to the other country.

From one home to another

In England, you can only receive free local authority nursing home care if you have assets of less than £21,000. In Wales, the threshold is slightly higher. Care in Scotland is free regardless of personal assets. This rule forces many people to sell the family home in their twilight years, reducing the size of the inheritance pot. The way to counter this enforced sale is to get the asset out of your estate – through a PET, explained earlier in this chapter, or through a trust.

By putting an asset in trust you can ring-fence it from any calculations the local authority make about the size of your estate. (See Chapters 17 and 18 for more.)

However, local authorities and creditors can ask the court to set aside a trust. Putting your home in trust and then entering a nursing home soon after can lead to the court overturning the trust. This action is known in legal circles as *deliberate deprivation*.

If you live abroad but want your remains to be returned to the UK when you die, consider setting money aside in your will to cover the costs.

Dropping the Temperature: Estate Freezing

Wrap up warm, I'm about to take you on a tour of a frozen estate!

Estate freezing takes place if you decide that your estate is quite large enough, thank you. In this situation, you then ensure that all nil-rate bands, (your own and that of your spouse) exempt gifts, potentially exempt transfers, and gifts out of income are fully exploited – in short, the whole kit and caboodle of IHT avoidance is deployed to prevent your estate from getting any bigger.

Think about it: You don't even have to reduce the size of your estate because over time the IHT threshold will increase – if you can just keep your estate frozen, then you will find the tax liability shrinking.

But don't go on a mad splurge – giving away all you possess in order to get one over on the tax authorities. Remember, you have to keep enough in your estate to enjoy a comfortable and hopefully long old age.

Estate freezing takes a lot of effort as you have to be 100 per cent sure that you won't need the assets you're giving up. Over the long term, the results of estate freezing can be quite dramatic.

Chapter 17

Rolling Out the Big Guns: Understanding Trusts

*T*rusts can be like a magic potion for your estate, which makes it appear almost invisible to the tax-collector. You can use trusts to reduce tax, to protect your family's long-term finances, and to ensure that your beneficiaries get the full value of the gift you leave to them.

However, not all is rosy in the trust garden. Trusts require plenty of planning and if you use a solicitor to draw one up – which you should – plenty of cash. What's more, trusts aren't a completely sure-fire way of avoiding tax: You may replace one tax with another – drat!

In this chapter, I examine the different types of trust and how you can use them to shield your wealth from Her Majesty's Revenue & Customs (HMRC) and super-charge your estate plans.

Starting at the Beginning: A Quick Tour of Trusts

A trust is a legal arrangement where one group of people, the *trustees*, are made legally responsible for property for the benefit of another group of people called the *beneficiaries*. The property is held in trust, perhaps for a set period of time or until a particular event takes place, such as the beneficiary reaching adulthood.

Putting an asset into trust is like using one of those prize-grabbing machines in a seaside arcade. You pluck the asset out of your estate and deposit it somewhere else. The reasoning behind this action is that if an asset isn't in your estate when you die, then it can't be taxed.

Trusts usually involve a sum of money or a property being kept by the trustees, with the income from that property, such as rent or interest, passed on to the beneficiary or beneficiaries or, in some cases, paid back into the trust.

Trusts have their uses in the fight with the tax-collector but the popular myth that they are a quick fix to sort out your tax woes is wrong. Trusts are only one method in a wider strategy of tax saving – they should not be considered as a complete replacement for anything else you do to save tax such as using your exempt gift allowances (refer to Chapter 4) and making potentially exempt transfers.

Time for some legalese. A person setting up a trust is usually known as a *settlor* or occasionally a *grantor*. Any property put into trust is called *trust property* – easy one, that! The document setting out the terms of the trust is the *trust agreement*, *trust deeds*, or *settlement*. The act of putting an asset into trust is called *writing in trust*. Confused yet?

As I mention many times in this book, Scotland has a different legal system to England, Wales, and Northern Ireland. However, the laws governing trusts and trustees in Scotland are almost identical to those in the rest of the UK, so I won't make distinctions here.

So, putting this all together, you can use trusts for the following objectives:

- ✔ Protecting the family fortune over the long term
- ✔ Making sure that the beneficiary is looked after
- ✔ Avoiding tax

These objectives are explored in greater detail below and in Chapter 16.

Protecting the Family Fortune

Consider using a trust to protect the family fortune if you face one of the following scenarios:

✔ **The beneficiary is too young to inherit.** A beneficiary can't inherit until they're 18, so you can put the asset in trust until he or she comes of age. If you think that this legal age limit is not enough of a safeguard, then you can stipulate an older age. Just pop the asset into trust so that the beneficiary can profit from the interest on or income from the gift but is prevented from getting their hands on the asset itself. When the beneficiary finally inherits, he or she will be a little older and, hopefully, a little wiser.

✔ **The beneficiary is a spendthrift.** Not everyone is good with money. In fact, some of us are terrible with cash, and like to spend what we haven't got. If a loved one falls into this category you may consider putting any gift to them in trust. The asset helps them day-to-day, because the beneficiary receives income from the asset, but the asset is protected, to be passed onto someone else after a set period of time or when the beneficiary dies.

✔ **The beneficiary is bankrupt.** If your beneficiary is declared bankrupt, then his or her creditors can take whatever assets you leave them. However, if you put the asset into trust the worst that can happen is that the creditors get their hands on any income that the asset produces, such as interest.

✔ **The beneficiary is infirm.** Your beneficiary may need long-term residential nursing home care. Outside Scotland, the local authority can insist that people sell their assets to pay for care, which means a gift could end up being swallowed by the beneficiary's care home fees. However, if the gift is in trust the income from it helps the beneficiary and then the gift can be passed on to someone else.

The principal is the same whatever the scenario: You want the beneficiary to have some use of the asset but at the same time you want the asset protected from an unfortunate event or the beneficiary's poor judgement.

Protecting the Family

Trusts can be used for the benefit of a vulnerable or very special beneficiary while ensuring that on the death of the beneficiary the asset passes on to someone else.

✔ **Surviving spouse.** Perhaps your spouse is retired or you simply want to ensure that an asset is used by your spouse but passes on to someone else at their death. Your spouse may be very happy with the idea of a regular income from an investment or the use of a property.

Talking it through with your spouse before going ahead and setting up a trust is essential.

✔ **Mentally or physically disabled beneficiary.** Perhaps your beneficiary has some form of mental or physical disability that requires special care. Under such circumstances a trust is ideal. The trust ensures that your beneficiary is protected from having to look after an asset or even from being hoodwinked out of it by an unscrupulous person. The regular income from the asset could help meet medical and care costs or the use of the asset may mean that such costs are not required. Chapter 16 covers looking after vulnerable family members through trusts.

✔ **Charity.** You can set up a trust to pay money to a charity, providing it with a regular income stream. The charity doesn't own the asset outright so can't sell it, but you can make a difference over the long term.

Deciding Which Assets to Put into Trust

You can put anything you own into trust from the family home to your toothbrush. But remember: A trust is likely to cost a lot of money in solicitor's fees, so it's important to put the right property into trust with the aim of saving tax and looking after your loved ones.

Four different types of asset are usually put into trust:

✔ **Property.** This can include your main home, holiday home, investment property, or land. These types of property make up the bulk of most people's estates.

✔ **Life insurance.** The proceeds of a life insurance policy can be considerable and can be written into trust.

✔ **Money and shares.** Cash and shares that you don't intend to use for yourself (and that you don't think you need for an emergency) can be put in a trust.

✔ **Personal property.** This covers things like antiques and personal items of high value.

Don't bother with small items of personal property. Having lots of little items in trust costs more in solicitor's fees and proves a real pain for the trustees to administer.

Always ask yourself if the asset is large enough to be worth your while setting up the trust.

Matching the Asset to the Trust Beneficiary

One of the keys to a good trust is that the gift matches the needs of the beneficiary.

Think of your trust like an empty gift box that you're going to fill to make life easier for a loved one. Decide what the objective of your trust is, then fill the box with the asset that most closely meets this need.

If the beneficiary needs an income, leave them an *income-producing asset*, such as savings accounts, rental property, shares, and investment bonds. If the beneficiary needs a wad of cash in the future, leave them a *capital-enriching asset*, such as land, business interests, art, antiques, or the family home. When sold, these assets can provide a hefty lump sum.

You can leave a capital-rich asset and ask your trustees to sell it to provide an income for a loved one. However, the sale entails costs and hassle for the trustee.

Activating a Trust Before You Die

Most people think of trusts kicking in on death. But lots of trusts start when the person setting them up is still walking around right as rain. In fact, you can find big advantages to having a trust active while you're alive. The advantages include:

- ✓ You can see your trust in action, and make sure it – and the trustees – are up to the job.
- ✓ The earlier you remove property from your estate, the more inheritance tax (IHT) your estate may save.

Once you put an asset into trust it's no longer yours, but belongs to the beneficiary. You must be 100 per cent sure that you can do without the asset before putting it into trust.

A trust that goes into effect while you're still alive is called an *intervivos trust*.

A trust that takes effect when you're alive can be *revocable* or *irrevocable*. Once you put an asset into an irrevocable trust, it's gone forever. You have no future claim on the asset. Under a revocable trust, you're allowed to bring the trust to an end and take back control of the asset. A revocable trust is handy if you want the trust to fulfil a short-term goal while you're alive, such as looking after an elderly relative, or paying for your child's university education. Use a revocable trust if you want the safety net of being allowed to pull your money out of a trust if your circumstances change in some way. Revocable trusts can have a major downside, however. Assets held within a revocable trust are still considered part of your estate for IHT purposes. Under some types of irrevocable trust, though, the asset has left your estate as far as the tax authorities are concerned.

Table 17-1 sums up the pros and cons of each type of trust.

Table 17-1	Trusts: Advantages and Disadvantages
Revocable trust	
Advantages:	**Disadvantages:**
Short-term objectives can be easily achieved.	Pretty useless as far as tax savings is concerned.
You get your asset back if you need it.	
Irrevocable trust	
Advantages:	**Disadvantages:**
The asset is out of your estate and as a result there is the potential to save IHT.	You better be 100 per cent sure that you can do without the asset because once it's gone, it's gone!
The beneficiary has the security that the asset is, in effect, theirs and they can plan their future accordingly.	

Putting Your Trust in Solicitors

Trusts are complex beasts and it's a smart move to use a solicitor if you decide to have one set up.

You may only need a trust once in your life, but a solicitor will have set up hundreds of trusts during his or her career. Ask yourself – who is more likely to make a mistake?

Trusts don't come cheap

Setting up and running a trust costs money and sometimes lots of it. You need to pay for the advice of a solicitor and for him or her to draw up your trust deeds. The more bells and whistles attached, the costlier the trust. Budget for £1,000 and go from there!

If you set up the trust through a will, you'll have to fork out for the will costs, too. Other set-up costs might include valuing the asset to be put in trust, and the costs of transferring the ownership of the asset to the trust.

Once the trust has been set up there'll be occasional legal fees and the trustees' day-to-day expenses – from travel to stationery costs – to be met.

If you choose to put your faith in a solicitor it doesn't mean you should sit back passively. Ask any questions you need to, and check the solicitor's trust document. A properly drawn up trust should do the following:

✓ **Call a trust a trust.** The trust document should clearly state that a trust is being set up. This may seem an obvious point, but it's important that everyone involved in the process, from the trustees to the courts, is aware of what they're dealing with.

✓ **Set out the trustees' obligations.** The trust must give the trustees a clear job to do. Typical duties and obligations include how and when to make payments from the trust, and how to manage an asset put in trust.

✓ **Clearly identify assets and beneficiaries.** The solicitor should make crystal clear the assets that you want to put into trust, together with the full name of the beneficiary and your relationship to them. The solicitor shouldn't leave anything to chance; ambiguity may lead the courts to decide that the trust is void.

Chapter 6 goes into finding the right solicitor.

Adding the Magic Ingredient: Trustees

Without the right trustees your trust could fall flat as a pancake. The effort and common sense of your trustees combine to make the oil that keeps the wheels of your trust moving year in, year out.

Choosing the right trustees is explored in Chapter 6 but here, in brief, are some things to look for in a good trustee.

✓ **Competent and good with money.** Ideally, your trustee is a professional or someone with experience of handling money, property, or investment. If your trust includes business interests, then a background in running an enterprise would be a huge advantage.

✔ **The right age.** You want someone not so young that they are inexperienced, and not so old that they could soon pass away or become incapable.

✔ **Good relationship with the beneficiary.** A model trustee should know and care for the beneficiary but not so much that they could be tempted to break the terms of the trust if asked to by the beneficiary. The best choice is normally a family friend who is close to your loved ones but who holds you and your wishes in high regard.

You can appoint a solicitor, a bank, even, in some cases, a beneficiary to act as a trustee.

Name an alternative trustee who can take over if one of your original choices decides not to take up the job or stops performing their duties, perhaps due to ill health.

If the trustees you appoint can't act for whatever reason, then the court appoints someone else to act as trustee. If the trust kicks in when you're alive, you retain the right to appoint new trustees.

Show Me the Money: Trustees and Assets

The trustees have a *legal interest* in the trust. The beneficiaries have a *beneficial interest* in the trust. If the trustee is also a beneficiary, then they also have beneficial interest in the trust. To explain:

✔ *Legal interest* means that trustees have a duty of care to ensure that the asset within the trust is looked after properly. If the asset is a house, they should make sure that it's insured and secure. If the asset is cash, then the trustees should ensure the money is invested so that it's not at risk and that a reasonable income is obtained.

✔ *Beneficial interest* is when the beneficiaries have, for example, a right to income from an asset held in trust. If the trustee is a beneficiary, he or she has beneficial interest in the trust. However, if the trustee isn't a beneficiary of the trust, he or she is not allowed to help themself to money from the trust. The only exception to this non-profit rule is if a trustee is a professional such as a solicitor or accountant. They won't do it for love – they have to be paid their fees.

The trustee must deal with the trust's assets to ensure that the terms of the trust are fulfilled. For example, you may leave property in trust for the upkeep of your spouse after your death. The trustee may decide to sell the property to provide a cash sum to invest, from which the spouse is paid an income. The trustee must pass, in legal parlance, the brilliantly named *prudent man test* in every investment choice they make. Under the terms of this test, risk should be spread and investments reviewed regularly – so no blowing it all on the 3.30 at Kempton!

The trustee decides what investments he or she uses – unless the trust imposes limitations (see below) – and the beneficiary is not allowed to object. If the trustee invests the money in shares of tobacco firms and weapons' manufacturers the beneficiary can't object on ethical grounds. However, beneficiaries can ask the courts to step in if they feel the trustee is failing in his or her legal duty of care, such as letting a property in trust go to rack and ruin or investing the fortune in high-risk shares.

If the trustee, acting on his or her own behalf, purchases an asset from a trust, the beneficiary can step in and void the sale if they wish. This applies even if the price being paid for the asset by the trustee is a fair one.

A trustee is entitled to claim money from the trust to cover any expenses that arise from the execution of their duties. The trustee is duty bound to keep clear and accurate accounts, and give beneficiaries a copy.

Saving Tax Through a Trust

Some trusts have the power to reduce estate taxes. However, trusts really help save tax when they are drawn up using other tax-saving weapons such as the nil-rate band and gifting to a spouse free of IHT.

Trusts can achieve several objectives at once.

Take the example of Jackie and Paul. They're married with one grown-up son, Andrew. Jackie and Paul's estates are worth £200,000 each. Jackie and Paul own the family home – worth £500,000 – as *tenants in common*, which means they can dispose of their share of the home (each part worth £250,000) however they feel fit through their wills.

Jackie is 10 years older than Paul. She's retired and not in good health. Paul makes a will and in it he sets up a trust.

Under the terms of the trust, Paul puts his share of the family home and £50,000 in shares and cash into trust. The ultimate beneficiary is Andrew, but Paul sets up a discretionary trust (described below) and through a letter of wishes asks the trustees to allow Jackie to live in the family home during her lifetime. Paul also leaves Jackie £25,000 in the will (not written in trust).

Paul dies and a year later Jackie's medical condition worsens and she needs residential nursing care. Jackie uses her own assets to cover nursing costs, as well as the £25,000 Paul left her.

When Jackie dies two years later, Andrew inherits the £300,000 his father left for him in trust plus his mother's remaining assets – she had to pay for the nursing fees, but crucially Paul's share of the family home was kept intact – all of it free from inheritance tax.

Paul's trust achieved the following goals:

- ✔ Protected the family fortune from being hit too hard by Jackie's infirmity
- ✔ Ensured IHT wasn't due on Jackie's death
- ✔ Allowed Jackie to remain in the family home for as long as possible
- ✔ Provided for Andrew to use the income from Paul's investments held in trust to pay his way through college
- ✔ Enabled Andrew to acquire his substantial inheritance when he was older and hopefully wiser.

If Paul had left everything to Jackie, then her powered-up estate might have attracted IHT on her death and transferred to Andrew. If Jackie had carried on living in a residential nursing home, the family's main asset – the family home – could've ended up in the coffers of the local authority.

But the potential damage of Jackie's illness on the family's finances was ring-fenced, as was any IHT liability.

The inheritance tax nil-rate bands (the amount of money that can be bequeathed before it is liable to inheritance tax) of married couples and civil partners are now automatically combined. What this means in practice is that married couples and civil partners can leave up to £600,000 (2007/08 tax year) at the time of the second death without it incurring an IHT bill. This new joint threshold is set to rise to £700,000 by the 2010/11 tax year.

Checking Out Different Types of Trust

Plenty of trusts are out there, each doing their own thing. You must pick the right one to achieve your objectives, while all the time keeping one eye on any potential tax implications.

I explain the most common types of trust below, so that you can decide which one best fits the bill!

Bare trust

As its naughty name suggests, a bare trust is the simplest type of trust.

Under a bare trust, an asset belonging to a beneficiary is held in the name of the trustees. A bare trust is most often used when you want to give an asset to someone under the age of 18.

Bare trusts have tax advantages, too. Any income tax or Capital Gains Tax arising from the asset in the trust is usually paid by the beneficiary. So if the beneficiary is young, it's likely that he or she can use their full tax allowances to offset some of this tax bill. After all, if the beneficiary is under 18, it's unlikely that they have a job or own any major assets that could lead to a CGT bill.

Assets held in bare trusts for your child are taxed at your tax rate if that income is over £100 a year. This is to discourage people from shielding assets from income tax by merely putting them in a bare trust in their child's name.

Under a bare trust the beneficiary is the real owner and the trustees must do what the beneficiary tells them. The beneficiary is free to spend the money in the trust as he or she sees fit – holidays to Ibiza, racing cars, and so on – it's up to them!

Discretionary trust

In many ways a discretionary trust is the opposite of a bare trust. Under a bare trust, the beneficiary is king, with the trustees having to do his or her bidding. But under a discretionary trust, the trustees have the right to decide what the beneficiaries receive and when. This scenario means putting your faith 100 per cent in the 'discretion' of the trustees – are you ready for that? So, it is absolutely vital that you appoint the right trustees.

A discretionary trust has *potential beneficiaries* – meaning that none of the beneficiaries have the right to anything without the trustees' say-so.

At first glance, a discretionary trust looks like a power trip for the trustees, but such trusts can be very useful in beating the tax-collector and making sure that the real needs of the beneficiaries are met. Discretionary trusts are far and away the most flexible form of trust and are highly recommended by solicitors whose clients are looking to secure their family's financial future (Chapter 16 has more on using this kind of trust to help your family).

Knowing when to use a discretionary trust

The flexibility of a discretionary trust makes it ideal in any of the following scenarios:

✔ **A spendthrift beneficiary.** The trustees can judge when the beneficiary should and shouldn't receive money from the trust. This type of arrangement can help keep the beneficiary on the financial straight and narrow.

✔ **A disabled beneficiary.** The trustees have the power to help when a beneficiary needs a little extra help with life's expenses.

✔ **You're unsure who should get what.** Perhaps you don't know the financial circumstances of your potential beneficiaries. Giving the trustees the power to decide who should get what hopefully means that the trustees prioritise the beneficiary who is most in need.

Under such an arrangement your trustees have two years from your death to get their act together and decide who gets what. This two-year timescale gives your trustees real elbow-room to get their gifting in the best tax-saving shape!

✔ **Tax saving**. By granting your trustees carte blanche they can distribute your estate to take full advantage of your full IHT nil-rate band (the amount of money you can leave to a non-exempt beneficiary before IHT has to be paid). This is a great tactic often recommended by accountants for keeping the family home out of the clutches of the tax-collector. How to best use the nil-rate band discretionary trust to protect the family home and other assets is explained more fully in Chapter 16.

A spouse, civil partners, charities, and political parties are exempt beneficiaries. Exempt beneficiary status means that you can leave whatever you like without risking an immediate IHT bill.

A discretionary trust set up for the benefit of a mentally disabled beneficiary enjoys generous tax breaks (Chapter 16 has more).

You can name the beneficiary of a discretionary trust as a trustee. Doing so means that the beneficiary won't have to go cap in hand to the trustees every time they want a little cash from the trust because they're a trustee themselves.

Saving tax with a discretionary trust

First the downside: The income received by the trustees of a discretionary trust is liable to the top rate of income tax at 40 per cent. Income from share dividends is charged at 32.5 per cent.

As if that tax liability wasn't enough, if you transfer an asset into a discretionary trust when you're alive then the sale could be liable for Capital Gains Tax. Once the trustee sells the asset for a profit, or hands it over to a beneficiary, CGT may be owed.

A discretionary trust is the bee's knees when it comes to reducing inheritance tax. Any asset held in a discretionary trust attracts IHT at a reduced rate of 20 per cent: Half the normal rate of IHT. The tax advantages of putting a high value asset into a discretionary trust are plain to see.

Inheriting at 18 is crucial to reducing tax

Due to government tax changes, trusts have become less attractive from a saving point of view. When a trust is set up, a one-off 20 per cent charge applies on assets above the nil-rate inheritance tax threshold (£300,000 in the 2007/08 tax year rising to £312,000 in April 2008). In addition, a further one-off 6 per cent charge is levied on the trust's assets every ten years. In effect, what's happened is that the tax regime that already applied to discretionary trusts is now applied to the whole trust universe. However, accumulation and maintenance trusts that were set up before late 2006 where the child becomes entitled to the assets at age 18 (and no later) are not subject to the 20 per cent initial or ten-year anniversary tax charge. Accumulation and maintenance trusts set up at a later date are subject to the 20 per cent initial tax charge but not the ten-year levy, provided that the child inherits the trust's assets at 18.

Discretionary trusts are so good at helping to save tax that they often run for years and years. The tax-collector remembers each time the discretionary trust clocks up 10 years but instead of sending a birthday card he levies a one-off charge: 6 per cent on all assets worth more than the IHT nil-rate band. A further charge is levied when assets in a discretionary trust are distributed to beneficiaries or the trust comes to an end. The size of this charge depends on how near to the 10-year charge the disposal is made – the nearer to the 10-year date, the higher the charge. Happy birthday!

Accumulation and maintenance trust

An accumulation and maintenance trust is a type of discretionary trust with a twist. This trust is usually used for the maintenance and education costs of someone under 25 years of age and is designed primarily to ensure future financial provision for children and grandchildren.

You can set up an accumulation and maintenance trust for an unborn child.

Like a discretionary trust, the trustees decide who gets what and when.

The trustees' first job is to *maintain* the beneficiaries – to make sure they have enough money to live off. The trustees can also make one-off payments to a beneficiary to help them meet a challenge such as help with medical bills, or pay a deposit on their first home.

Once the trustees are satisfied that the beneficiaries are being maintained, the trustees can invest whatever money is left in the trust to increase its value. The beauty of an accumulation and maintenance trust is that the assets in the trust can actually grow over time.

An accumulation and maintenance trust is only allowed to accumulate for 21 years. After that time, all the money has to be used for maintenance.

Interest in possession trust

This type of trust gives the beneficiary the right to an income from the trust for the rest of their lives, or a specified period of time. However, the beneficiary does not have the right to the capital. When the beneficiary dies, or a specified period of time elapses, the asset in the trust passes to someone else. The idea of this trust is to keep the asset in the family by denying the beneficiary the right to sell it.

Using an interest in possession trust

You can use an interest in possession trust to let a beneficiary, usually a spouse, partner, parent, or sibling, live in the family home for the rest of their life but on death the property passes to someone else.

It is possible to grant your trustees a little discretion to allow them to hand out some or all of the capital from the interest in possession trust. This provision can prove useful if the beneficiary falls on hard times.

Interest in possession trusts help sidestep laws that force people to sell their homes if they enter a local authority care home. In England, people can only receive free local authority nursing home care if they have assets less than £21,500 (in Wales the threshold is £22,000). By putting a home into trust, you can ring-fence it from any calculations the local authority makes.

You can dispose of your main home without incurring CGT by selling it or transferring it into trust.

Interest in possession trusts versus tax

All in all, an interest in possession trust doesn't hold the same number of tax-saving options as the very flexible discretionary and accumulation and maintenance trusts. Crucially, when the beneficiary dies, the assets held in the trust are added to the beneficiary's estate for IHT purposes.

Income tax on the trust is either paid by the beneficiary or the trust.

If the income of the trust is paid directly to the beneficiary, then the trustees are said to have *mandated* the income. In short, the beneficiary is liable for any income and can offset their personal allowance for income tax against it.

Any income retained by the trust is charged at a rate of 20 per cent. In turn, if the beneficiary is a higher rate taxpayer – the top rate of tax in the UK is currently charged at 40 per cent – then he or she must pay more tax on their income from the trust.

Interest in possession trusts can create a nasty Capital Gains Tax bill. If you create an income in possession trust to start while you're still alive, then CGT may be due when you transfer an asset into the trust. If the trust kicks in after your death, then any CGT gain your asset made during your life is cancelled. However, the tax-collector may still try it on at a later date.

If the trustees subsequently sell the asset at a profit, or hand over the asset to the beneficiary, then it could be liable for CGT but only from the date of your death. An exception to this tax liability is if the asset is a share in an unquoted company – such as a small firm. The trustees are allowed to delay payment of CGT until they sell the asset. See Chapter 18 for more on how this tactic works.

Trustees have their very own annual CGT allowance, which they can use to minimise the tax bill. Sadly, the trustees' CGT allowance is only half that of an ordinary citizen. In the 2008/09 tax year, trustees are allowed to sell trust assets for a profit of £4,600 each year before CGT is due. CGT is charged at a flat rate of 18 per cent.

Protective trusts

If you think the beneficiary risks going bankrupt – perhaps they're not good with money or are struggling to get a business venture off the ground – you may consider using a protective trust.

A protective trust starts out just like a maintenance trust – paying the beneficiary a regular income – but if the beneficiary is declared bankrupt it morphs into a discretionary trust. Suddenly, the trustees have the whip hand and they can halt payments to the bankrupt beneficiary to stop them being gobbled up by hungry creditors. Protective trusts are designed to protect the beneficiary and, just as importantly, the assets of the trust.

In recent years, protective trusts have fallen out of favour because they don't offer the flexibility of discretionary trusts.

You can find simpler and cheaper alternatives to setting up a protective trust. For example, you may not trust the beneficiary with money, but perhaps you can trust their spouse? You can then leave the gift to the spouse, safe in the knowledge that they'll use it to help the beneficiary.

Revealing secret trusts

A secret trust involves leaving an asset or some money to a trusted person – such as the family solicitor – to pass on the asset to someone else. In effect, a trust is created.

But this trust is all very hush-hush, with the gift or asset not even appearing in the will. Secret trusts were often used in Victorian times to squirrel away money to an illegitimate child or a mistress. The idea of a secret trust is to keep the gift out of the public domain. After all, a will is a public document.

Secret trusts are rarely used these days, but talk to a solicitor if you want to set one up.

A Potent Combination: Trusts and Insurance

Strange things can occur when you combine insurance policies and trusts. Suddenly, a mundane run-of-the-mill trust can be imbued with special powers that can be of benefit to the trust's beneficiaries and even the person setting up the trust in the first place.

Loan trust

With a *loan trust* you make a loan to the trust (obvious, eh?). The loan is used to buy a life insurance bond. A loan trust offers two key benefits:

- ✔ You can ask for your loan back at any time.
- ✔ Any profits made from the bond are not liable to IHT.

Essentially, a loan trust is a revocable trust with a built-in tax advantage. A loan trust can help you have your cake and eat it!

Be careful. Any loan not repaid at the date of death – the second death in the case of a couple – is added back into the estate. This action rebuilds the estate you have just reduced. The exercise then becomes a bit pointless.

Split trust

A split trust sounds like a painful gymnastics accident but in fact it can help protect you and your family.

If you have an insurance policy that pays a death benefit and offers *critical illness cover* – which usually pays a lump sum if you have a life-threatening condition – you can split them up inside a trust. By splitting the two elements of the policy, your family receive the death benefits, free of IHT, when you die, while you get to hang onto the critical illness cover while you live, in case you need to call on it.

Write life insurance policies in trust to minimise your estate's IHT liability. Refer to Chapters 15 and 16 for more on life insurance and IHT.

Getting Ready for Trust Take-off

Astronauts at NASA have to go through a checklist before they take-off. If anything is missing they don't go to ignition. Likewise, you must check that you have everything in place before you embark on your trust journey.

Make sure that you:

- ✔ Identify any property that you are putting into trust.
- ✔ Decide who the beneficiary is and what objective you want to achieve through the trust.
- ✔ Secure trustees who are ready, willing, and able to oversee the trust.
- ✔ Work out what rules you want your trust to adhere to.

Now it's time to visit a solicitor to draw up your trust.

Be prepared for the solicitor to advise changes to your plans, and some of the rules you want the trust to follow may not be practical. Whatever the outcome, make sure you're clear in your mind as to what you want the trust to achieve and keep this at the centre of your thoughts.

Chapter 18

Using Trusts to Help Your Family

. . . .

In This Chapter

▶ Meeting your family needs through a trust

▶ Looking after your spouse and children

▶ Protecting the family home

▶ Changing a trust

▶ Remembering trust alternatives

. . . .

*Y*our old family photos tell lots of stories. From the joy of new arrivals, to the sadness of parting, your family is probably not the same as it was twenty, ten, or even five years ago.

Nothing in life remains the same, especially families. Who knows what will happen in the future? You need to be prepared. Cover all the bases and plan, plan, and plan again.

The big decision is whether or not it will be useful for your family if you incorporate a trust into your will – or even start one up when you're alive.

Family trusts are usually designed to meet one of the following objectives:

✔ Saving tax

✔ Looking after a loved one with special needs

✔ Passing assets on to children and grandchildren

✔ Making sure the spouse is looked after properly while the estate is kept intact

✔ Keeping the family home

We look at each situation in turn and show how a trust can help.

See a solicitor if you want to set up a trust. Chapter 6 covers choosing the right solicitor.

Saving Tax with Trusts for Your Family

With more estates than ever before falling into the inheritance tax (IHT) trap – some 3 per cent of estates paid IHT in 1994 and today the figure is close to 10 per cent – the tax-saving advantages of trusts are a real draw.

Turn to Chapter 17 if you need a refresher on the different types of trust.

Working a discretionary trust to the tax max

You want to reduce the IHT liability of your estate, but you still want to leave your spouse with enough to live on. What can you do?

Pay the maximum amount of money you can into a discretionary trust before IHT becomes due – your nil-rate band. Name your spouse and children as the potential beneficiaries of the trust. The trustees let your surviving spouse live off the trust and when your spouse dies your children inherit whatever is left free of tax.

If the surviving spouse is given all the income throughout his or her life, Her Majesty's Revenue & Customs (HMRC) might argue that it was in effect an interest in possession trust. Make payments to the children from time to time.

This type of arrangement is called a *nil-rate band discretionary trust*. This trust is a beautifully simple tax solution and a very popular way of beating HMRC – just remember that special one-off charge on the trust for each decade that it runs (refer to Chapter 17).

Discretionary trusts invest ultimate power in the trustees. Are you and your family comfortable with this situation? If the answer is 'no', then don't go there! A great solution is to name a beneficiary, perhaps your spouse, as trustee of the discretionary trust.

The naked truth of a bare trust

A bare trust offers a partial solution on the tax front. Any income tax or Capital Gains Tax arising from the asset in a bare trust is paid by the beneficiary. So if the beneficiary is young, it's likely that he or she can use their full tax allowances to offset some of the tax bill.

Helping a Needy Beneficiary

Trusts can help members of your family who are infirm due to age or because of mental or physical disability.

You probably have two goals in mind when looking at setting up a trust to help a vulnerable family member:

- ✔ Making sure the vulnerable person is provided for
- ✔ Ensuring the asset passes safely onto another family member when the beneficiary passes away

 When setting up a trust for a vulnerable family member, it's vital to get your choice of trustees right. The wellbeing of your loved one rests on a combination of the trustees' diligence and thoughtfulness. What's more, don't scrimp! A trust of this nature has got to be perfect, so consider naming a solicitor as a trustee to work alongside a trusted family friend.

 If your beneficiary has a mental disability and no one's ready, willing, and able to act as trustee, don't panic. The Mencap Trust may be able to act as trustee. However, the Mencap Trust can't act as executor and only agrees to be a trustee of a trust they have approved. For more information, contact Mencap National Centre, 123 Golden Lane, London EC1Y 0RT, Tel: 020 7454 0454, or visit their Web site at www.mencap.org.uk.

Calling on a discretionary trust

A discretionary trust is probably your best option. Firstly, the vulnerable family member can benefit from a regular income from the trust. Secondly, the trustees have the power to make any necessary payments from the trust for one-offs such as tailor-made holidays or special equipment.

 If the vulnerable person is just one of many potential beneficiaries, write to the trustees stating that you want the infirm beneficiary's needs to be put first – this is called a *letter of wishes*.

Using a disabled person's trust

A *disabled person's trust* allows you to put large amounts of money – above and beyond the normal IHT nil-rate band of £312,000 from April 2008 – into a trust free from any IHT liability. These trusts are often used when someone has become disabled due to personal injury and has received a large compensation cheque.

One proviso with a disabled person trust is that more than half the assets in it must be for the benefit of the disabled person.

Using the interest in possession option

An interest in possession trust grants the beneficiary the right to use an asset while still alive but states that the asset should pass to someone else on the death of the beneficiary. This type of trust offers more security for a vulnerable beneficiary than is the case with a discretionary trust, as the trustees are given a strict set of rules they are bound to follow.

The idea of an interest in possession trust is that the vulnerable person – perhaps an aged spouse – gets to live in a degree of comfort, but their circumstances cannot erode the capital of the asset, which ultimately is kept in the family.

Interest in possession trusts have far fewer tax advantages than discretionary trusts.

Using Trusts for Your Little Rascals

You may want to pass on an asset to your children and grandchildren, but what if they're too young to inherit in their own right? The answer could be to place the asset into trust. Here are some scenarios where trusts can help:

- **Having lots of little ones.** If you have lots of children or grandchildren, then you might consider putting a pot of money into a discretionary trust and naming them as beneficiaries. Some of your children or grandchildren may turn out to be real bright sparks and a trust could enable them to go to a good university. Whatever the challenge, under a discretionary trust the trustees are free to dish out the dosh to whichever child or grandchild needs it most.

- **Paying for school fees.** Gifts to children and grandchildren are often made with a particular purpose in mind, such as helping them meet the costs of university. For instance, you can put the asset into a discretionary trust, asking the trustee to make payment if the child studies at university. Alternatively, you can put the asset into a bare trust, specifying that the child should inherit at a certain age – say, 21. Just remember that under a bare trust the beneficiary is the absolute owner of the asset and the trustees must do what they're told.

If you're married with children, it's a racing certainty that you and your spouse ultimately want your children to inherit your estate. However, gifts between parents and children are liable to IHT. Draw up your will so that when the first parent dies, a substantial part of the wealth passes to the children, making proper use of the nil-rate band. Refer to Chapters 15 and 16 for more on using the nil-rate band.

An accumulation and maintenance trust (described in Chapter 17) can be the right choice for gifting to your little monsters. Under this type of trust, the trustees use the assets to provide an income for the beneficiaries while investing whatever is left over with the aim of increasing the value of the trust. This type of trust allows the children or grandchildren to benefit when they are growing up – trustees can make payments to cover school fees, living costs, and even put a deposit on their first home – while all the time getting the asset to work as hard as possible. The idea of an accumulation and maintenance trust is that when the children or grandchildren reach a specified age, they take on the still-intact trust assets.

Trusting to Look After Your Spouse

Providing for your spouse while ensuring as many assets as possible pass to your children or other beneficiaries is the holy grail of most people's trust plans. But it's not as hard as you might think to square this particular circle!

Using a discretionary trust is probably the best route – see the section on 'Saving Tax with Trusts for Your Family' earlier in this chapter.

You can use an interest in possession trust again. You give your spouse the right to use an asset or enjoy an income from it for life, but it passes to someone else on the death of your spouse.

This type of trust doesn't save on IHT because when the first beneficiary (say, a spouse) dies, the assets of the trust are added to their estate for IHT purposes. This can lead to estate bunching – where the assets of a married couple end up in the estate of the one surviving spouse at their death – which is a big tax no-no!

Looking after your spouse through a trust and saving tax are two sides of the same coin. For example, a nil-rate band discretionary trust achieves a double whammy of providing for your spouse and ensuring what's left passes to another beneficiary tax-free.

The inheritance tax nil-rate bands (the amount of money that can be bequeathed before it's liable to inheritance tax) of married couples and civil partners are now automatically combined. What this means in practice is that married couples and civil partners can leave up to £600,000 (2007/08 tax year) at the time of the second death without it incurring an IHT bill. This new joint threshold is set to rise to £700,000 by the 2010/11 tax year.

Home Free: Putting the Family Home Into Trust

Your natural instinct is probably to ensure the family home remains just that, the family home, after you've gone. A home is such a large asset that it's worth special consideration.

The family home can come under threat from many directions when you die – many of which you can't plan for and are purely bad luck – but here are a couple that you can prepare against:

- ✔ **The attack of the tax-collector.** An IHT bill can be so high that the house must be sold to pay it. Ways to reduce IHT liability to prevent this are explored in Chapters 15 and 16, but you can make doubly sure by putting your home into trust.

   If you do put your home into trust, consider using a nil-rate band discretionary trust, to use your nil-rate band to the max.

   Assets above the nil-rate band are still liable to IHT, but at a reduced rate (refer to Chapter 17 for more).

   Whether your surviving spouse or civil partner continues to live in the home is entirely up to the trustees. However, you can avoid this problem by naming your surviving spouse or civil partner as a trustee.

- ✔ **The surviving spouse or civil partner goes into residential care.** The family home may be sold to pay the local authority for care. Put your share of the family home into trust and you can protect it from being sold in this way.

   Your spouse or civil partner can put their share of the home into the trust, too – if it is owned on a tenants-in-common basis. Chapter 5 goes into more detail.

Putting a home into a bare trust is risky as the property can be considered to belong to the beneficiary and sold to pay for residential care.

Beware of accidental trusts

In your keenness to protect an asset such as the family home, be careful not to create an *accidental trust.* For example, stating in your will that you want your spouse to have the family home but that it should pass to your son on the death of your spouse accidentally creates an *interest in possession trust.* Your spouse or civil partner may not be able to sell the home if they have money worries or need to move somewhere smaller. But you were only expressing a heartfelt desire that the family home should pass between your loved ones.

If you think you're inadvertently entering trust territory with your will, seek immediate legal advice.

Boo, Hiss! Closing Tax Loopholes

Ever since IHT was introduced, people have been using trusts to sidestep it. HMRC is a bit of a lumbering beast but it's cottoned on to trust tactics.

HMRC has closed some trust loopholes. The closed loopholes apply to situations where the trust kicks in when the person setting it up is still alive. Some key loopholes that have been closed include:

✔ **Gift with reservation of benefit (GROB).** Don't get grobbled! If you sign over an asset, you can no longer use or enjoy it otherwise you're deemed to still be deriving a benefit. With a house, the GROB means you can no longer live there without paying fair market rent to whoever now owns the asset. An asset in trust from which you're still deriving an income is not considered a PET (refer to Chapter 16), which means it's liable for IHT no matter how long the trust has been up and running. See Chapter 16 for more on the dreaded GROB.

✔ **Pre-owned assets.** So you gift your home to try and sidestep IHT, but you pay rent to the beneficiary. Be very careful – HMRC is clamping down on this type of arrangement. In certain circumstances, HMRC could impose an income tax charge for the asset on you, the trust donor.

It may still be worthwhile paying the pre-owned asset charge, but always seek independent financial and legal advice before mixing the family home and trusts.

✔ **Designer trusts.** Some of the best minds in the country are engaged drawing up ever more complex forms of trusts catering for the super-rich. But HMRC imported an American idea to nip some of these plans in the bud. In future, those clever trust designers have to tell HMRC in advance of any new trust tax dodges they plan to sell to super-rich clients. This scenario puts the trust designers in a catch-22 situation and should stop nifty tax-saving schemes in their tracks!

Changing trust beneficiaries

One of the most common reasons for changing a trust is to alter beneficiaries. You can make this change quite easily under most well drawn-up discretionary trusts. You can specify beneficiary *classes* as opposed to individual names – and so leave a trust to grandchildren rather than an individual grandchild, for example. Armed with this flexibility, the trustees should be free to help the family member most in need.

To specify your wishes, write to the trustees saying which particular beneficiary you want to help.

Ringing in Changes to Your Trust

Family circumstances change – divorce, death, and illness occur, and that's just looking on the bright side. As a result of a change, perhaps a trust you set up a couple of years ago is no longer relevant.

How you go about changing a trust depends firstly on whether it is set up through a will or kicks in while you're alive.

Altering a trust in a will

A trust set up through a will is not active until the testator – the person whose will it is – has died.

If you want to make alterations to a trust in a will, you simply go about it in the same way you would change any other aspect of your will.

Two ways to change a will and therefore a trust within it are:

- ✔ **Writing a codicil.** This is a legal document used to make additions and changes to a will. Chapter 9 covers properly wording a codicil.
- ✔ **Revoking and writing a new will.** When it comes to major changes to your will – and remember trusts are complex and can easily count as a major change – it's often best to start from scratch by revoking your old will and drawing up a new one. Chapter 9 has more on revoking a will.

Changing a non-will trust

Whether you're allowed to change a trust that's active while you're alive depends on whether it's a revocable or irrevocable trust (Chapter 17 has more on these types of trusts).

If the trust is an irrevocable one, tough! You can't change this trust because you no longer have any legal claim over the assets held within it. However, your trustees may have the right to do so.

Under a revocable trust, you can change it by bringing it to an end and taking back your asset. Then you can start up a new trust.

Considering the Downsides of Trusts

Not all is hunky-dory with trusts. Trusts can be tricky to change, expensive to set up, and they aren't necessarily the tax-saving panacea of popular imagination.

Before putting pen to paper and drawing up a trust with a solicitor, ask yourself:

✔ Do my beneficiaries agree with my plans?

✔ Am I up to speed with the tax implications of the trust?

✔ Am I prepared to give up the ownership and use of the asset going into trust?

✔ Is the trust flexible enough to take account of the challenges that my family may face in future?

✔ Can I achieve the same objective cheaper, faster, or better by using a trust alternative? (See below.)

Ensure that your beneficiaries are happy with your choice of trustees. If the beneficiaries and the trustees don't get on, this can lead to serious tension and claims of bias.

Picking Easier Options: Alternatives to Trusts

Setting up a trust can be a lot of hassle and expense. You need to consider whether there are alternatives out there that you can act on today.

Take an example. You may want to ensure that your child has his or her university fees paid for, and has enough to live off while studying (aka beer money). The trust solution would see an asset put into trust to meet studying costs, while the alternatives are:

✔ **Simply gift the child the cash.** The advantage of this action is that the gift may reduce your estate's liability for IHT. However, consider how trustworthy your child is with money.

✔ **Have money ready to pay the fees.** Simply keep the money in a savings account and meet the costs of putting your child through university as they crop up. Remember, you're allowed to make a single £3,000 large gift from your estate each year, which isn't liable for IHT. In addition, any payments for the maintenance of loved ones, and out of income, instantly leave your estate for IHT purposes (refer to Chapter 16 for more on gifts which are exempt from IHT).

✔ **Leave an age-dependent gift in your will.** Most people go to university in their late teens or early twenties. You can specify that your child should inherit at 21 so there's a pretty good chance (assuming that your child goes to university) that the gift is used to meet university costs, from the start or to pay back the student loan.

Any variant of these trust alternatives can apply to any situation you and your would-be beneficiary find yourselves in.

Chapter 19

Taking Care of Business: Inheritance Tax and Your Firm

In This Chapter

▶ Defeating the tax-collector with business property relief

▶ Reducing business inheritance tax through gifts and trusts

▶ Transferring your business to a successor

*F*or all intents and purposes a business is a living thing: Neglect it and it dies. If you were to die suddenly, then the months that it could take for your nearest and dearest to sort out your financial affairs could spell the end for your business – depriving those closest to you of your biggest asset.

Once a business shuts its doors, it rarely reopens them. Have a proper strategy in place for what should happen to your business when you're no longer around.

What's more, keep one eye focused on the tax-collector when drawing up your plan. Otherwise, you risk Her Majesty's Revenue & Customs (HMRC) taking a great big bite out of your estate through inheritance tax (IHT).

In this chapter, I look at how to leave your business (or share of a business) in a tax-efficient way, helping your loved ones to inherit the reward of all your hard work.

Winning the Tax War with Business Property Relief

When you die, your estate is assessed to see if inheritance tax is due on it. Any assets over £300,000 (2007/08 tax year) rising to £312,000 in April 2008 attract IHT at 40 per cent. If you own a business, or share of a business, then these assets can be included in your estate for IHT pur don't plan and those closest to you have to find the money to pay an IHT bill on your death, they may have to sell the business or some other asset – even the family home – to raise the money needed to meet the tax bill.

However, you can use a major weapon available for business people. Drum roll, please: Business property relief (BPR).

Business property relief allows you to pass on some – but not all – of the assets of a business free of IHT. This relief means that business assets enjoy a much better deal from HMRC than everyday assets like a house, car, or cash in a savings account.

The reason for the relief is pretty obvious. HMRC recognise that, unlike other assets, a successful business plays an important role in the economy and the community – it keeps people employed, who pay taxes, as does the business itself. HMRC doesn't want to kill the goose that lays the golden egg by imposing a stiff IHT charge on business assets when the owner dies.

One hundred per cent BPR is available on:

- ✔ A 100 per cent-owned business or share of a partnership
- ✔ Shares in an *unquoted* trading company – this means a company that is incorporated but isn't large enough to be listed on the London Stock Exchange

One hundred per cent does exactly what it says on the tin and means that the asset is completely free from IHT.

One hundred per cent BPR is not available on shares in quoted companies. Shares in quoted companies – the BPs, Tescos, and ICIs of this world – are treated in a very similar way to cash or property. However, relief is available on business property held overseas.

Fifty per cent BPR is available on land, buildings, plant, and machinery owned by an individual but used for business purposes by a company in which the individual has full control or a partnership interest in.

Fifty per cent BPR means that half the value of the asset can be passed on free from IHT.

The deceased must have owned the business for at least two years prior to death for it to attract relief.

Using Business Property Relief to the Max

Business property relief allows you to move substantial assets to non-exempt beneficiaries (beneficiaries who would usually be subject to IHT) on your death without incurring an IHT bill. You can gift £312,000 from your estate to non-exempt beneficiaries.

Take the example of business owner Sanjit, his sister Jayshree, and her grown-up daughter Meera.

Sanjit dies and leaves Jayshree a home and cash worth £500,000 and a business worth £150,000. As the total value of Sanjit's estate is not worth more than the IHT threshold there is no IHT to pay. Soon after inheriting, Jayshree, who is quite elderly and not up to running the enterprise, sells the business and pockets the money. A year later she dies and Meera inherits everything. IHT is due because Jayshree's estate is worth more than the IHT threshold as she not only had Sanjit's money but her own, around £75,000 to be precise. Crucially, no business assets exist any more for which business property relief would help offset the IHT pain.

What should Sanjit have done? Tax could have been saved if Sanjit had left his cash and home to Jayshree, while leaving those business assets that enjoy 100 per cent BPR to Meera. Meera could sell the business assets she inherited and pocket the cash without fear that the tax-collector would come knocking.

When Jayshree dies, Meera will not have to pay IHT on her estate as Sanjit's business assets had aleady passed to her on his death.

If Jayshree had held onto the business assets, then BPR would still have applied. Selling of the assets helped create the IHT problem.

All in all, leaving business assets to your spouse may not be the smartest tax-saving ploy. Gifts to your spouse are automatically exempt from IHT. By gifting your spouse assets that enjoy BPR, you're squandering a major tax-saving opportunity. Where possible, leave exempt assets to non-exempt beneficiaries (in other words, not a spouse, charity, or political party).

Knowing Business Property Relief Limits

Now for the catch . . .

Business property relief is a very handy tax-saving weapon but it isn't the be-all and end-all. Unfortunately, some business assets do not enjoy property relief – these are called *excepted assets*.

Under the following circumstances, no relief is available for the business:

- ✔ It hasn't been used for wholly or mainly business purposes for the past two years.
- ✔ The asset is not required for future use in the business.
- ✔ The land or building is let out.
- ✔ Large cash balances are held by the firm.
- ✔ The asset is subject to a contract of sale.

Many business partnerships are caught out by the fact that assets that are subject to a contract of sale do not attract business property relief. Business partners often enter into a legal agreement that when one of them dies, their share of the business is sold to the survivor – as a result, no BPR is available.

Reducing Tax on Excepted Assets

If you own business assets that don't enjoy relief, you may need to take action to minimise any IHT bill.

The two chief tactics you can adopt are:

- ✔ Gift the asset to a beneficiary.
- ✔ Put the asset into trust.

Gifting business assets to reduce tax

Like everyone else, business owners are allowed to make gifts to reduce the size of their estate for IHT purposes. These gifts are completely exempt – which means they pass out of the estate for IHT purposes from the moment they are handed over – or are *potentially* exempt. Potentially exempt transfers (PETs) completely disappear from your estate for IHT purposes after seven years. Refer to Chapters 15 and 16 for more on exempt and potentially exempt gifts and how to use them in your great IHT-avoidance scheme.

Gifting BPR-rich assets

The good news is that you can gift business assets that enjoy business property relief (BPR) without putting that relief at risk.

But you have to follow strict rules; ignore these and the valuable BPR can go up in smoke! The rules are:

✔ The person being given the asset has to retain ownership of it until the person giving them the asset dies. However, the person receiving the business asset can replace it without losing valuable business property

relief. So if machinery is gifted, it can be replaced without losing relief.

✔ At the time of the transfer, the asset must already be in a position to enjoy business property relief. This means, for example, that a gift of business property must not be let out at the time of the transfer.

When making a gift of a business asset, specify what category the gift falls into. Is it an exempt gift or a potentially exempt transfer? Being specific about the gift makes the executor's job easier.

Over many years, gifting can substantially cut down on the cash that passes to HMRC. Business owners often use gifting to give a family member a substantial share in the business tax-efficiently.

Exempt gifts include lots of small gifts and one big gift of up to £3,000 in any one tax year. In addition, you can make exempt gifts on the occasion of the marriage of a child, grandchild, close relative, and even friend.

Focus on assets that are not due business property relief if you decide to dish out some of your business assets in the hope of making use of the exempt gift rules.

Putting your business into trust

Your business assets need more careful handling than the average Joe's, so take specific legal advice before drawing up a will, or incorporating a trust in your will. Contact your local Chamber of Commerce who may be able to recommend a qualified solicitor with expertise in dealing with business people.

You would put business assets or shares in a business into trust for one of two reasons.

✔ To avoid paying taxes, particularly IHT.

✔ To transfer assets to a beneficiary under controlled conditions.

Business assets are the same as any other asset: If they're put in trust, IHT is reduced or avoided altogether. The ways in which trusts help save tax are explained in Chapters 17 and 18.

Get good legal advice if you're considering putting business assets into trust. Trusts are complex, and businesses are complex, so when you put the two together you get double complexity!

If you put business assets into trust, try to appoint a trustee with experience of running a business.

If the value of the asset you're putting into trust is above the IHT threshold then it may be subject to an initial tax charge of 20 per cent. Check out Chapters 17 and 18 for more.

Taking it Easy When You Pay Inheritance Tax

Even those schooled in the dark arts of tax avoidance recognise that it's often impossible to completely sidestep the IHT tax grab. The good news is that any IHT payments on business, agricultural, and woodland assets can be spread out over 10 years.

The thinking behind this payment plan is that to demand tax payment in one go could damage the business, farm, or woodland enterprise. What's more, these types of asset are *illiquid* – not easily sold – and to force a sale to pay a tax bill is unlikely to lead to achieving the best price.

Instalments are interest-free provided they are made on time. Spreading the payments over 10 years effectively reduces the tax bill, as inflation erodes its value over time.

Taking a Bow: Exiting the Business Stage

You may love being in business and can't imagine giving it up. But few business people die in the saddle. At some point in the future, you'll probably find that you're ready to exit stage left. Illness or injury may stop you from working, or you may just want to retire.

If you don't have an exit strategy, the people who inherit may have to sell or wind up your business. After all, the main beneficiary of your will may not have the skills or inclination to run your business. One way around this situation is to leave your business through your will to someone who is up to the job of running it. However, if your business is a major part of your estate, then your spouse or dependants may have an automatic legal right to it. (Refer to Chapters 4 and 8 for more details.)

Get off my land!

Farms get their own special tax break, called *agricultural property relief*.

Farmland, farm buildings, and farm cottages usually qualify for 100 per cent agricultural property relief. Farm animals and equipment don't qualify for relief.

The deceased must have owned the farm for two years prior to death for relief to be due. If the farm property has been let out, the deceased must have owned the property for seven years to qualify for the relief, which might be 100 or 50 per cent according to the terms of the tenancy.

Woodland relief exists too. With woodland, the payment of IHT can be postponed until the timber on the land is sold. However, to qualify for a tax nugget, the deceased must have bought the woodland at least five years prior to death or received it as a gift.

Sometimes you can mix and match IHT exemptions. For example, if you use woodland for business purposes such as a campsite, you can claim business property *and* woodland relief.

For more information on exemption and relief, download leaflet IHT17: Businesses, Farms and Woodlands, from HMRC's Web site: www. hmrc.gov.uk.

If you decide to hand over the business to a family member, you'll be helping to secure your loved one's future and saving on IHT.

Three clear early-exit strategies you can adopt are:

- ✔ Sell your business.
- ✔ Wind up your business.
- ✔ Transfer the business to a family member.

I look at each of these steps and their tax implications below.

 Web sites specifically designed for business owners include the Government's Business Link, at www.businesslink.gov.uk and the Federation of Small Businesses at www.fsb.co.uk. Both sites have info on selling or passing on your business to others.

Selling the business

Businesses are not simply machinery and premises. In fact, much of the plant is often hired. Instead, a business is a bank of loyal customers and a reputation. A business sold as a *going concern* (still running) is usually worth more money than one that's been broken up.

You have the choice of selling to a rival, to someone who wants to enter the market, or through a trade sale.

Selling to a rival or to a new entrant into the market usually ensures the best price, although, naturally, this depends on the strength of the business. Alternatively, you could sell your business by advertising in a trade magazine such as *Daltons Weekly*. Check out www.daltonsbusiness.com, too.

From a tax and estate planning perspective, selling up offers both an advantage and a pitfall.

The key advantage is that you convert an illiquid asset, which can vary in value quite wildly, into cash: A liquid asset with a rock solid value. This situation can make it easier to plan for your future and that of your family.

However, from a tax perspective, the downside of selling up is that some business assets come with IHT relief. By selling up, you convert an asset with tax breaks to one with none – cash. Remember, as far as reducing any IHT bill is concerned, cash is not king! Spend the money wisely by using exempt transfers and making gifts.

If you're in a business partnership, your partner probably has first refusal on your share of the business.

Winding up the business

You might think that winding up a business is a sign of failure. While this is sometimes true, at other times the assets of a business can be worth an awful lot, particularly if you have lots of unsold stock. A thriving market exists in buying and selling business assets. When a wind-up occurs, the business assets are sold off individually to raise money.

From a tax and estate planning perspective, winding up a business can have the same advantage as selling the business as a going concern. Through wind-up, you raise cash that can be used to see through your estate plans. Likewise, the pitfall is the same as when you sell up – you're exchanging an asset with tax breaks (a business) for one with none (cash).

If you sell business assets for a profit, Capital Gains Tax (CGT) may be due. CGT is charged at a flat rate of 18 per cent.

Transferring the business

Many small business owners want to pass on their business to a family member, often a son or daughter. This action can help secure the family's long-term financial future while retaining business property relief intact, as long as the family member keeps running the business.

If you want to transfer your business interests to a family member or successor, a gradual approach can work best. You can use your exempt gifts and potentially exempt transfers to build up the holding of your relative or successor. Likewise, get your successor involved in the day-to-day running of the business several years before you anticipate him or her taking over.

If your business is *incorporated* – has shares and shareholders – then all you have to do is transfer the shares in the business from your name to that of your successor. However, if the business is run as a sole trader or a partnership, all of the individual assets of the firm will have to be transferred. Doing so can be both time-consuming and costly.

Part V
The Part of Tens

'Isn't it time we stopped all this family bickering over the financial implications of dad's demise & informed the solicitors & the undertakers?'

In this part . . .

This wouldn't be a *For Dummies* book without the Part of Tens. Here you find mini-explosions of useful information on making sure your will plans hit the spot and sidestepping inheritance tax.

Chapter 20

Ten Items to Keep with Your Will

In This Chapter

▶ Leaving the details of your major assets
▶ Making known your funeral wishes

*M*aking sure your wishes are followed from beyond the grave doesn't end with signing your will. The people you entrust with making sure your wishes make it off the page and into reality need a little extra help from you.

Keep relevant documents and extra information with your will to ensure that your executors hit the ground running. Save them the time and stress of hunting through your personal possessions and they'll thank you for your forethought and remember you even more fondly!

Importantly, being thorough and keeping the right information with your will can stop your executors missing a trick – perhaps not locating a beneficiary's gift, an insurance policy, or some money which can be used for creditors.

Bank and Building Society Accounts

Make sure your executors know where you keep recent statements from the banks and building societies you have accounts with.

Your current account statement shows the details of any firms receiving direct debits from your account. Your executors can then cancel these debits to make sure that no money leaves your estate. What's more, the statement can give a clue to any debts you may have.

Most building societies may allow your executor to dip into the funds you hold with them to pay inheritance tax or meet funeral bills.

Keep a list of all your bank accounts with your will, no matter how small the account, or how long ago it was opened. An estimated whopping £10bn is held in *dormant accounts* in the UK. An account is deemed dormant if no withdrawals or deposits have been made for seven years. More often than not, this is because the account holder has died and forgotten to let their executors know the account exists.

Once the executors gain *grant of probate* – the official legal seal of approval allowing the executors to gather in and distribute the deceased's estate – from the courts, the money from bank and building society accounts is transferred into their account to pay creditors, expenses, and beneficiaries. Head to Chapter 12 for a description of the probate process.

Insurance Policies

Leave a copy of all current insurance policies with your will, particularly your life insurance policy.

A copy of the death certificate may be all that's needed to trigger a life insurance policy payment, if the payment is to someone other than the executor. The beneficiary of the policy can usually get their hands on the money quickly.

If you haven't named a beneficiary for your life insurance policies, the money is considered part of your estate for inheritance tax purposes. This can mean a hefty tax bill. Chapter 14 has more on the tax implications of life insurance.

Leave copies of any other insurance policies – such as home, car, and travel – with your will. Some of these policies may need to be cancelled after your death, or renewed, or transferred to someone else.

National Savings Accounts

If you're one of the legions of National Savers, leave a list of your holding and account numbers with your will for your executors to find.

National Savings investments, which are backed by the Treasury, can be used to meet any inheritance tax due prior to grant of probate.

Your executors can ask for a cheque from your National Savings account to be written out to the Inland Revenue – it's getting one branch of the Government to pay another!

Your executors can arrange for any Premium Bonds (bonds with National Savings) to remain entered into prize draws, while the estate goes through probate. You never know, your nearest and dearest may scoop a jackpot from beyond the grave, for up to a year after death.

Details of Stocks and Shares

Whether you just dabble in the stock market or are a wannabe Warren Buffett – the legendary US investor – leave the details of any holdings with your will.

If your shares are wholly in your name leave the share certificates with your will, or a note making clear where to find them.

If you own your shares through a *nominee account* – an account held with a stockbroker – you won't have the original share certificates, so instead leave your latest share account statement with your will.

If the shares you own are in your own company, you may want to keep the official documentation in a safe deposit box or with your solicitor.

Most nominee account statements put a valuation on any shares held. This valuation is very useful for your executors when they tot up the value of your estate to see if inheritance tax is due.

Keys to Your Property

If you have a home, car, garage, business, or safe deposit box, you're bound to own lots of sets of keys. One of your executors' key responsibilities – excuse the terrible pun – is to secure your property after your death. If you own an unoccupied buy-to-let property or holiday home, your executors should ensure it is secure and not at risk from intruders and thieves. Your executors will find it pretty tough without the right keys.

Think about the property your executors will need to secure on your death. Have the appropriate keys cut and leave them with your will so your executors can get on with the job at hand.

If you keep your will in a bank safe deposit box, then leave a note for your executors telling them where the key or pin number for the box can be found on your death.

A List of Small Items of Personal Property

The golden rule with a will is to keep it simple! No one is going to thank you for turning your will into a long litany of who gets each and every small item of your personal property.

Writing in your will 'I leave to my son Ian my toothbrush, electric sander, seven pairs of grey socks, and signed copy of *Wills, Probate & Inheritance Tax For Dummies,* 2nd Edition, is a no-no.

Write a list of small gifts and their intended recipients in a letter and keep it with your will. Make reference to the letter in your will if you want a binding direction as to who gets what and you're unlikely to change your mind. Use a precatory trust if you are more relaxed about it, are prepared to rely upon the 'moral obligation' to carry out your wishes, and want the flexibility to change those wishes as to who gets what from time to time *after* the will has been executed.

Wend your way to Chapter 4 for more on leaving small, sentimental items to the right people.

Your Prepaid Funeral Plan

Many people buy them, but few tell their relatives about them!

No, it's not a riddle. It's a pretty good description of what happens with many prepaid funeral plans.

For a one-off or regular payment, a company promises to pay for your burial or cremation. But if you don't tell your loved ones that the financial side of your funeral is taken care of, they may pay again for your send-off. Don't be caught out like this: If you buy a prepaid funeral, let your loved ones and executors know, and leave a copy of the policy with your will.

Don't physically attach any document to your will. For example, if you staple a letter to your will and the staple falls off, the executor may presume that pages are missing from your main will.

Your Funeral Wishes

Many people take an active role in planning what should happen at their funeral. From what music will be played, to who will carry the coffin, planning a funeral can be comforting and even fun. After all, a funeral is a celebration of a life led and a deep expression of feeling for those left behind.

However, even the best-laid plans will come to nothing if you don't make sure that the wider world knows about them.

You may choose to tell your loved ones what you would like to happen at your funeral, but this may be tough for them to deal with. Draw up a letter setting out your funeral wishes and leave it with your will. Just remember to tell your executors and nearest and dearest where the letter and the will are kept.

It is a mistake to set out what you want to happen at your funeral in the will document itself. Your will may not be read for several days or even weeks after your death, and by then your funeral may already have taken place.

Turn to Chapter 10 if you want more information on expressing your funeral wishes.

Instructions on Donating Your Body

As well as leaving money and property to your loved ones, you can leave a different kind of legacy to perfect strangers, such as a new lease of life to someone needing an organ transplant.

If you choose to leave your body to medical science, tell your loved ones and keep a written record of your wishes with your will.

Carry a donor card if you want your organs to be donated after your death, as speed is of the essence when it comes to transplants. Don't just leave instructions with your will, otherwise by the time they are discovered it's likely that your organs will no longer be of any use.

If you want your entire body to be used to help trainee doctors, contact your local medical school. Keep a copy of any correspondence with your will. For starters, the medical school sends you a form to fill out authorising them to take your body when you die. Keep a copy of this with your will. Don't forget to instruct your executor to contact the medical school in the event of your death so that they can take your body.

Organ, tissue, and body donation are explained in Chapter 10.

A List of People Who Need to Know

From long-lost friends to creditors, your executors have the hard task of telling people of your demise. Just going through your address book should locate most people, but what about your solicitor, accountant, or mortgage lender?

It is important that creditors get to know of your death because legally they have a right to be paid before your beneficiaries get their hands on your loot. If your executors don't track down your creditors early on, they can emerge late in the probate process to claim what's theirs. Creditors' late appearance can throw all your executor's hard work into chaos.

Write a list of who you owe money to and keep it with your will. Most creditors are far from shy when it comes to keeping in touch – credit card firms bill you monthly, while mortgage lenders provide annual statements – but it's worth making a list so that your executors know who they are dealing with.

Likewise, write the names and most recent contact details of those from your past who you wish to be told of your demise on a piece of paper. Keep this paper with your will and ask your executor to contact them.

Your executors are legally bound to be fair to all your creditors. Putting adverts in newspapers alerting the wider world to your death is one action that may need to be taken. If executors fail to act fairly they can be sued. See Chapter 14 for more on tracking down creditors.

Chapter 21

Ten Problem Wills to Avoid

In This Chapter

▶ Taking proper care of will formalities

▶ Getting married or divorced and wills

▶ Conditional gifts and altered wills

*Q*uestion: What's worse than dying without a will?

Answer: Dying with a problem will.

Problems come in all shapes and sizes. A badly drawn-up will can lead to family disputes and years of expensive legal wrangling. Under certain circumstances a problem will can be deemed invalid – not worth the paper it's written on!

At the very least, a problem will can hold up the probate process, creating a headache for your executors.

Here's a quick look at ten problem wills – take heed and make sure that yours is up to scratch.

An Unsigned Will

A will is a legal document and must be signed by the *testator* (the official name for the person making the will).

Everyone may know that the will's yours; you may have discussed its contents with your nearest and dearest and you may even have written it in your own hand. Nevertheless, your will has all the legal weight of a shopping list until you sign it.

You can put your signature anywhere on the will document – start, middle, or end. However, it's best to sign the will at the end to keep things simple.

Don't forget to put the date on the will when you sign it. Your executors can more easily decide whether it is likely that you have made a new will since.

If you want to be really thorough, sign and number each page of your will. This action stops anyone inserting a fraudulent page into the document.

If you're unable to sign your own will, someone must read it to you and you have to indicate that you understand and agree with its contents. Do this in front of witnesses and add an *attestation* clause (more in Chapter 7).

An Unwitnessed Will

Signing your will isn't enough: You must also have your signature witnessed. You need two witnesses and they must be present when you sign your will. Your witnesses must be over 18 and be of sound mind. Refer to Chapter 6 for details on who can and can't witness a will.

If your will is not witnessed it is deemed invalid and any previous (witnessed) will replaces it. If you didn't make a prior will, you are deemed to have died *intestate* (without making a will at all). Head to Chapter 6 for the low-down on witnesses.

Don't have a beneficiary or the spouse of a beneficiary witness your will. Beneficiaries who witness a will are automatically disinherited.

Your will should contain an *attestation clause*. This clause explains the process of signing and witnessing. If your will doesn't have an attestation clause, then your witnesses may be required at a later date to make a sworn statement that they witnessed your will.

Get your witnesses to put their full name and address below their signature. These details help your executors trace the witnesses if they need to.

In Scotland you only need one witness to your will and they don't need to be present when you sign.

Getting Married = New Will

Your old will is automatically revoked when you get hitched (unless you live in Scotland). That great will document with all those smart tax-saving plans and painstaking allocation of gifts might as well never have existed.

What do you do? Draw up a new will as soon as possible after marriage.

You can make a will in *expectation of marriage*, which names your betrothed. This type of will won't be revoked by marriage. (Chapter 9 has more on this type of will.)

There are two of you now and if you share the same ideas on who is to inherit you might consider making a joint, mirror, or mutual will. Turn to Chapter 2 for more on these types of wills.

If you die without a valid will your property is distributed under *intestacy*. This situation almost always means that your spouse – if you have one – gets the lion's share of your estate. Intestacy works for some people but it's a very blunt instrument and can ultimately leave large estates wide open to an inheritance tax bill. Refer to Chapter 2 for how intestacy works.

Getting Divorced = New Will

If you get divorced your former spouse is automatically cut out of your will. The rest of the will still takes effect. This situation can create a real headache because the spouse is usually the main beneficiary. If your ex-spouse is cut out, then what money was supposed to go to them ends up in the *estate residue*.

The estate residue is what's left in your estate after creditors and beneficiaries have been paid. In cases where the spouse is disinherited by divorce, the estate residue can be worth a lot of money and unless you've distributed that money in your will it will be distributed under intestacy.

Divorce should nearly always prompt you to make a new will.

If you want your former spouse to get anything when you die, make a will and name them as a beneficiary.

Despite all I've just said, your former spouse may still have a claim to your estate (see the next section).

A Will Leaving Dependants Out in the Cold

Laws are in place to stop you cutting your spouse or dependants out of your will – so just squash that mean streak. Under the Inheritance (Provision for Family and Dependants) Act 1975, your spouse and those people deemed dependant on you at your death can ask the court for money from your estate. Refer to Chapter 4 for a list of who qualifies as a dependant.

In reality, not all dependants are equal in the eyes of the court. The key is to make sure your spouse and children are looked after. The court will understand if there isn't enough to go around all your dependants just as long as you do your best by your spouse and children.

If you plan to do something out of the ordinary like leaving the family home to a local animal sanctuary, it's vital to talk it through with your spouse and dependants. Only take such a radical step if your spouse and dependants are completely behind what you're doing and so won't make a claim against your estate.

If you plan to leave nothing to someone who might have a claim on your estate, put your reasons in a letter and give your executors a copy. If your will is challenged by the unhappy dependant after your death, the executor can show this letter to the court and the court may honour it.

A Will with Strings Attached

Tacking a condition onto a gift left in a will may have its appeal, but it's highly dangerous and can lead to your will being called into question. The courts don't look kindly on wills that try to exert undue influence from beyond the grave. For example, you can't make a gift conditional on a beneficiary not marrying a particular person, not having sex, or even not breaking the law. In fact, your beneficiaries have the right to ask the court for permission to collect their inheritance without having to meet any condition you set. If the court deems that the condition is unreasonable they will void it. Likewise, if the court decides that the condition is open to interpretation (not clearly defined), they may still void it.

Using conditional gifts to play God is a recipe for trouble!

You're allowed to make a gift to a spouse conditional on them not remarrying.

If your will is challenged, your executors have to fund court costs from your estate.

A Will That Creates an Accidental Life Interest

You have the choice of leaving your beneficiaries a gift outright or the *life interest* in a gift. By giving outright you hand over the asset to your beneficiary lock, stock, and barrel. By creating a life interest gift you allow your beneficiary to have an income from the asset but they are barred from selling it outright. Chapter 7 explains this in more detail.

Be careful that you don't create a life interest unintentionally. Writing in your will that your spouse should get everything and on their death it should pass on to your children automatically creates a life interest. However, you might have been merely trying to say what you want your spouse to do with the gift. Keep your intentions clear.

Be specific about any gift you make in your will. If you leave money to charity, state the charity's full name and charity number. If you're not crystal clear, the gift may fail. If that happens, the gift simply goes into the estate residue and won't find its way to the intended beneficiary.

An Altered Will

Making changes to a will can be tricky. You can change a will in two ways. You can use a *codicil* or write a completely new will. A codicil is a separate document drawn up after the original will that adds to or alters the will.

Codicils are normally used to change an executor, trustee, or guardian, or to alter gifts to a beneficiary. Codicils can be complex and have to be precisely worded. Jump to Chapter 9 for more.

Draw up a new will if you have lots of changes to make.

Don't attempt to make alterations to your will after it's been signed and witnessed. Merely crossing out names of beneficiaries or executors won't do. Your will could soon become a bit of a mess and difficult for your executors to decipher.

A Will Appointing Elderly Executors

Age is supposed to bring with it wisdom (it's funny how the older I get, the more I agree with that idea). It might feel right to name an executor who is older than you are or perhaps quite a bit older – after all, an executor has to be organised, literate, numerate, trustworthy, good at handling money, and not afraid of a bit of hard work. However, if you live to a ripe old age – fingers crossed – then your executor might die before you.

If the executor you appoint in your will dies, then someone else, usually a beneficiary, must step into the breach and ask the court for permission to administer your estate.

Appointing more than one executor to share the work of distributing your estate and to ensure that a second pair of eyes sees everything that is done is a good idea. Ideally, aim to appoint two or three executors.

Appointing too many executors, or executors who live far away, can lead to delays in administrating your estate. Remember, your executors will have to meet at least a couple of times to carry out the wishes in your will.

You can call in the professionals and appoint a solicitor or a bank to act as executor, but they charge for their services.

An Elderly Will

A will made many moons ago can have as unsatisfactory an outcome as one not being made at all!

Life moves on, and with it you become richer or poorer, you move home, your children are born and grow up, and beneficiaries, executors, guardians, or trustees may die. Your will needs to reflect these changing circumstances. If your will doesn't move with the times, then your loved ones may not be properly provided for or HMRC may take a large bite out of your estate. Chapter 9 covers the circumstances that may prompt you to look again at your will.

Review your will every year to make sure its terms are up-to-date. Think of your will as a new car: If you don't maintain it, over time it may not get you to where you want to go.

Chapter 22

Ten Tips for Getting Your Estate into Tax-Saving Shape

In This Chapter

▶ Reducing the likelihood of paying inheritance tax

▶ Inheriting money the right way

▶ Making use of everyday tax breaks

*G*etting your estate into tax-saving shape takes time and thought. But once you've taken tax-saving steps you can rest easy knowing that your loved ones will enjoy as much of your money as possible after you've gone.

In this chapter, I look at some of the simple steps you can take to get your estate fit for the fight with the tax-collector!

Use the Nil-Rate Band to the Max

The first £312,000 of your estate can be gifted free of inheritance tax (IHT). This amount is called the *IHT threshold* and anything below this is your *nil-rate band*. Anything over £312,000 is taxed at 40 per cent.

Your nil-rate band, combined with the fact that whatever you leave to your spouse, same-sex civil partner, or charity is IHT free, provides you with a powerful tax avoidance weapon.

However, if you leave your entire estate to your spouse, when your spouse dies the combined estates can get hit with a hefty IHT bill. This potential problem situation has eased a little of late as the IHT nil-rate band of a deceased spouse or civil partner automatically passes to the surviving spouse or civil partner. In effect, this means that the surviving spouse or civil partner has their IHT nil-rate band doubled. Couples with large combined estates (say, over £600,000, which maybe subject to IHT on the death of the second spouse or civil partner) still have to tread carefully and take tax saving steps to reduce IHT.

The best way around this future scenario is to leave enough money for your spouse to live off, with whatever's left going to other beneficiaries, perhaps to your children. You can give away up to £312,000 to anyone free of IHT, but that's your limit!

Go to Chapter 16 for more on using your nil-rate band.

Own Your Home on a 'Tenants-in-Common' Basis

What happens to your home when you die depends very much on what basis you own it. If you own your home with someone else, you're either *beneficial tenants in common* or *joint tenants*. If you're joint tenants, then when you die your share of the property automatically passes to the person who owns it with you. If you share property ownership on a beneficial-tenants-in-common basis, each tenant is free to dispose of their share of the property as they see fit through their own will.

Owning your home on a beneficial-tenants-in-common basis gives you far more estate planning options. Dividing your property between your spouse and grown-up children can be a very smart tax ploy. Such a move can reduce the size of the taxable estate on the death of your surviving spouse, because half the house has already been passed to the adult child. You can't use this tactic if you own a property on a joint tenancy basis with your spouse, because they automatically inherit on your death.

When the first beneficial tenant in common dies, a beneficiary inherits their half share of the house. The beneficiary might then try to force the property to be sold to realise their half share (in other words, get their hands on the money). This leaves the second tenant in common in a sticky situation.

Chapter 5 tells you all about how to leave your home in a will.

The share of one beneficial tenant in common never passes automatically on death to the other beneficial tenant or tenants in common. You must state in your will who you wish to inherit, or your part of the property will be divided up under the laws of intestacy (refer to Chapter 2 for more on intestacy).

Make Use of Annual Gift Exemptions

Each year you're allowed to make gifts, which, once made, leave your estate forever as far as the tax-collector is concerned. These *exempt gifts* give you an opportunity to siphon off part of your estate so that any ultimate IHT liability is avoided or reduced.

You're allowed to make large gifts of up to £3,000 each year to one person and any number of small £250 gifts – but every small gift has to go to a separate individual. Over time, you can use exempt gifts to move substantial sums out of your estate and thereby reduce its IHT liability.

Any gifts you make for the ongoing upkeep of a dependant don't count as part of your estate for IHT purposes.

If the value of the gifts you make exceeds your annual limit, then the gifts are no longer exempt. As a result, if you die within seven years of making the gift, it is included in your estate for IHT purposes.

You're allowed to carry over the unused balance of the £3,000 gift exemption from one tax year to the next, but no further.

Give Away High-Value,
Low-Income Assets

In later life many people give away their major assets, even their own home. They do so not because they are struck with an altruistic urge to forsake their worldly goods – not a bit of it – but to reduce the eventual tax bill on their estate.

Any assets you give away cease to be a part of your estate for IHT purposes after seven years from the date of transfer. This gifting is called a *potentially exempt transfer* (or PET for short). The downside of gifting an asset is that once it's gone, it's gone. You're not allowed to gift an asset and still derive an income from it or the tax-collector will deem that the asset is still part of your estate. If you gift your home (perhaps to your children), you're not allowed to live in it without paying the proper market rent. The key is to gift assets that you can afford to do without – usually, this means high-value, low-income assets, such as your car.

After three years from the date of the transfer the amount of tax potentially due on a PET worth more than the IHT threshold of £312,000 from April 2008 starts to fall.

Head to Chapters 14 and 15 for more on gifting to reduce IHT.

Deep-Freeze Your Estate

If you think you have quite enough money to live on – lucky you! – you can *freeze* your estate. Estate freezing is when you bring all the tools of IHT avoidance to bear, such as exempt gifts, gifting out of income, and potentially exempt transfers – all to make sure your estate doesn't grow any bigger. In short, as the money comes into your estate through the front door it goes out through the back door! The big idea is that while your estate is frozen, the IHT threshold is increased by the Government and as a result the amount of tax – if any – your estate is liable for falls over time.

Freezing your estate isn't foolproof and involves a lot of very careful planning. All your carefully laid plans may be undermined by a bumper injection of wealth into your estate such as through a large inheritance, rapidly increasing house prices, or even a mammoth win on the horses!

Get independent financial advice if you want to play the estate freezing game.

Be 100 per cent sure you can comfortably do without any asset that you give away.

Set Up a Trust

Using a trust can really help to get your estate into tax-saving shape.

An asset is *held in trust* for a set period of time or until a particular event takes place. *Trustees* take care of the asset in the best interests of the *beneficiary*, the person who will benefit from it. For example, trustees might keep an amount of money in trust until a child reaches the age of 18.

Trusts work by plucking an asset out of your estate – and if it's not in your estate when you die, then it can't be taxed. Trusts can be set up when you're still alive or through a will.

Head to Chapters 17 and 18 for loads more on trusts.

Build Up Exempt Assets

Certain types of assets can be passed on free of IHT or at a reduced rate. These assets are called *exempt assets* and the more you have of them in your estate, the less the tax-collector can take. Keep exempt assets in your estate and gift the non-exempt ones, like cash.

Exempt assets include business assets, woodland, farmland, and even National Heritage property.

If you're married and have children, you can reduce IHT by giving non-exempt assets such as your home and savings accounts to your spouse while leaving your exempt assets to your children. Your non-exempt assets become exempt because assets gifted to your spouse are IHT-free.

If your exempt asset is a profitable business, bear in mind that any money taken out of the business loses its exempt status and just becomes part of your ordinary non-exempt estate. So plough back those profits!

Hold on to any exempt assets in your estate: If you sell up, the proceeds are considered part of your estate and are potentially liable for IHT.

Write a Joint, Mirror, or Mutual Will

If you're married, you and your spouse may choose to make your wills at the same time. If you agree over who should benefit when you have both gone, then using a joint, mirror, or mutual will can make sense.

A *joint will* is a single document stating the wishes of two people. *Mirror wills* are two wills made in identical terms, although the people making the will can revoke these at any time. A *mutual will* is very similar to a mirror will, but each party agrees that the wills can't be revoked. Chapter 2 explains these wills in more detail.

These types of wills allow you to link up your estate plans with your husband or wife. Using a joint, mirror, or mutual will can be a good way of ensuring that nil-rate bands (the amount of money you can leave free of IHT) are used and exempt assets are left to non-exempt beneficiaries.

Inherit Money Tax-Efficiently

Inheriting money or property can help your finances but it can also create problems. The inheritance may be large enough to push the value of your estate beyond the IHT threshold. You have two options to avoid the snapping jaws of the tax system:

- ✔ Distribute the inheritance to your likely beneficiaries through exempt gifts and potentially exempt transfers. Hopefully, over time, your estate plans will absorb the inheritance nicely.

- ✔ Instead of inheriting yourself, sign the loot over to your children. This action is called *generation skipping* and it's a good option if you don't really need the inheritance. With generation skipping you avoid future IHT due on your death. The aim of generation skipping is to stop a bumper inheritance from taking your estate above the threshold for IHT.

If a beneficiary dies soon after inheriting from an estate that has already been subject to IHT, then *quick succession relief* may be available, meaning that you don't pay as much IHT. The closer the second death is to the first, the more relief from IHT can be claimed. Refer to Chapter 16 for the relief available.

Take Advantage of Your Tax Breaks

Take steps to reduce the amount of tax you pay during your life to pass on more to your loved ones when you die. The tax-collector isn't generous by nature so when you see a tax break, grab it with both hands.

Some key tax breaks to consider include:

- ✔ **Buying a pension.** Contributions you make into a personal or company pension scheme have generous tax relief. In effect, every 80p you pay into your private or company pension, the Government tops up to £1, or more for higher-rate taxpayers. What's more, some pension schemes are structured so you get a large lump sum on retirement and your loved ones get a cash pile if you die before retirement.

- ✔ **Saving in an ISA.** Normally, your savings are taxed at 20p in the pound – more if you're a higher rate taxpayer – but you're allowed to shelter up to £3,000 a year in a mini-cash Individual Savings Account (ISA). Over time, you can save a lot of tax this way and leave a larger savings pot behind for your loved ones. You can pop up to £7,000 worth of shares into a stocks and shares ISA each year. Any money you make on the shares is free of Capital Gains Tax (CGT). However, the more money you leave to loved ones, the more IHT may be due.

✔ **Buying tax-free investments.** Some National Savings investments and index-linked gilts (bonds issued by the Government) – in effect, loans to the Government – are allowed to grow in value free of tax. The more of these investments you have, the less the tax-collector eats into your estate.

Just because an investment is tax-efficient doesn't make it right for you. National Savings and gilts are tax-efficient and very safe, but they are unlikely to grow as fast as some other investments. Consult an independent financial adviser (IFA) if you want more advice on investing.

Tax breaks are available for people willing to invest their money in small- and medium-size businesses through Venture Capital Trusts and Enterprise Investment Schemes. *Paying Less Tax For Dummies* by Tony Levene (Wiley) is crammed with tax-reducing tips. If you want to know about these specialist investments go to www.taxefficientreview.com.

Appendix

Sample Wills

*T*hese three sample wills give you an idea of how your last will and testament might look and what phrases and parts you need to include. See Chapters 7 and 8 for how to write your own will.

You can copy these wills, simply substituting the personal details for your own.

The three sample wills are a *standard will* where gifts are left to a spouse and children, a *simple will* where everything is left to a spouse, and a will setting up a *discretionary trust* – the most commonly used and most flexible type of trust.

Get your will read over by a third party to check that everything's in order. Consult a solicitor if you need professional legal advice.

Standard Will

This last will and testament is made by me, Andrea Hubbard, of 11 Acacia Avenue, Anytown, Anyshire, being of sound mind, on 1 July 2008.

I revoke all previous wills and codicils.

I appoint Paul Hubbard of 11 Acacia Avenue, Anytown, Anyshire, and Graham Stuart of Stuart and Sons Solicitors of 4 High Street, Anytown, Anyshire as executors of this will.

And should one of them fail or be unable to act I appoint to fill any vacancy Anna Day of 19 Acacia Avenue, Anytown, Anyshire.

The decision of my executors whether to sell or to retain my property is a matter for them alone and they will not be liable for any loss caused as a result of the exercise of their discretion. My executors may invest and change any investments freely.

I give all my real and personal property of any kind which is not disposed of in my will to my executors. My executors must hold this property upon trust to sell the whole or any part of it or keep the whole or any part of it in the same form as it was at the date of my death for as long as my executors decide.

My executors must pay out of the money arising from such sale: My funeral expenses, any testamentary expenses, any debts, any legacies, and taxation payable by reason of my death.

I give all of my jewellery to my daughter Cassandra Hubbard.

I give £5,000 cash and my car to my son Thomas Hubbard.

I give my house at 11 Acacia Avenue, Anytown, Anyshire to my husband Paul Hubbard.

To Paul Hubbard of 11 Acacia Avenue, Anytown, Anyshire I give the residue of my estate.

If any of the above persons does not survive me by 28 days they will be treated as having died before me; in such circumstances all gifts to them should go into the residue of my estate.

Signed by Andrea Hubbard in our presence and then by us in hers.

Signature, name and address of first witness.

Signature, name and address of second witness.

Simple Will

In this will, Andrea leaves all her property to her spouse, Paul, while including a survivorship clause.

This last will and testament is made by me, Andrea Hubbard, of 11 Acacia Avenue, Anytown, Anyshire, being of sound mind, on 1 July 2008.

I revoke all previous wills and codicils.

I appoint Paul Hubbard of 11 Acacia Avenue, Anytown, Anyshire as executor of this will.

And should Paul Hubbard fail or be unable to act I appoint Anna Day of 19 Acacia Avenue, Anytown, Anyshire to fill the vacancy.

The decision of my executor whether to sell or to retain my property is a matter for him alone and he will not be liable for any loss caused as a result of the exercise of his discretion. My executor may invest and change any investments freely.

I give all my real and personal property of any kind which is not disposed of in my will to my executor. My executor must hold this property upon trust to sell the whole or any part of it or keep the whole or any part of it in the same form as it was at the date of my death for as long as my executor decides.

My executor must pay out of the money arising from such sale: My funeral expenses, any testamentary expenses, any debts, any legacies, and taxation payable by reason of my death.

I give all my property of every kind to Paul Hubbard of 11 Acacia Avenue, Anytown, Anyshire.

If Paul Hubbard does not survive me by 28 days then he will be treated as having died before me. In such circumstances all gifts to him should go to my mother Pauline Cooper of 10 No Name Road, Anontown, Wherevershire.

Signed by Andrea Hubbard in our presence and then by us in hers.

Signature, name and address of first witness.

Signature, name and address of second witness.

Will with a Discretionary Trust

In this will, Andrea Hubbard sets up a nil-rate band discretionary trust naming her son and daughter as beneficiaries.

A discretionary trust is very popular because it gives the trustees real elbow room to distribute an estate so to make the most of the nil-rate tax band each of us has – the amount of money (£312,000 in the 2008/09 tax year) that everyone is free to gift without IHT being due. Be aware that from April 2008, the nil rate bands of spouses and civil partners can be joined together to allow the surviving spouse or civil partner to leave double the nil-rate band amount free of IHT. Jump to Chapters 17 and 18 for more information on trusts and how to best use a discretionary trust.

This example is for guidance only – to give you a taster for what a will with a trust looks like. If you want to power up your will with a trust, consult a solic-itor; see Chapter 6 for how to find a good one.

This last will and testament is made by me, Andrea Hubbard, of 11 Acacia Avenue, Anytown, Anyshire, being of sound mind, on 1 July 2008.

I revoke all previous wills and codicils.

I appoint Paul Hubbard of 11 Acacia Avenue, Anytown, Anyshire, and Graham Stuart of Stuart and Sons Solicitors of 4 High Street, Anytown, Anyshire as executors of this will.

And should one of them fail or be unable to act, I appoint to fill any vacancy Anna Day of 19 Acacia Avenue, Anytown, Anyshire.

The decision of my executors whether to sell or to retain my property is a matter for them alone and they will not be liable for any loss caused as a result of the exercise of their discretion. My executors may invest and change any investments freely.

I give all my real and personal property of any kind which is not disposed of in my will to my executors. My executors must hold this property upon trust to sell the whole or any part of it or keep the whole or any part of it in the same form as it was at the date of my death for as long as my executors decide.

My executors must pay out of the money arising from such sale: My funeral expenses, any testamentary expenses, any debts, any legacies, and taxation payable by reason of my death.

Discretionary trust

I appoint as my trustee my daughter Cassandra Hubbard, son Thomas Hubbard, and Graham Stuart of Stuart and Sons Solicitors of 4 High Street, Anytown, Anyshire.

The trust gift is the maximum amount which I can gift to my trustees without inheritance tax becoming payable.

My trust beneficiaries are:

My daughter Cassandra Hubbard and son Thomas Hubbard.

The fund means the assets held by my trustees upon trust.

My trustees are to:

Use the capital of the fund for the benefit of my beneficiaries as my trustees think fit.

My trustees may exercise their discretionary powers when and how they think fit, and need not make any payments to or for the benefit of the beneficiaries, nor ensure equality among those.

My trustees may wind up the trust before the last day of the trust's distribution period by distributing the fund among such of my beneficiaries as my trustees think fit.

The distribution period of the trust should start not earlier than three months after my death and end not later than 50 years after my death.

I give the residue of my estate to my husband Paul Hubbard.

If Paul Hubbard does not survive me by 28 days he will be treated as having died before me. In such circumstances all gifts should be given in equal shares to my daughter Cassandra Hubbard and son Thomas Hubbard.

Signed by Andrea Hubbard in our presence and then by us in hers.

Signature, name and address of first witness.

Signature, name and address of second witness.

Index

• *D* •

• **G** •

• Q •

quick succession relief, 218–219, 280

• R •

reading of wills, 106
reasonable time, right to inheritance within, 173
receiver, 115
rectifying a will, 130
reducing inheritance tax (IHT)
  agricultural property relief, 212
  business property relief, 212
  charity, leaving a gift to, 209
  with estate freezing, 222
  exempt assets, 212
  with exempt gifts, 210–212
  family home, protecting from tax, 219–221
  with generation skipping, 217–219
  with Gift wit Reservation of Benefit (GROB),
    216–217
  gifting from everyday income, 212–213
  by moving abroad, 221–222
  National Heritage property as exempt asset,
    212
  nil-rate band, exploiting the combined,
    207–210
  with Potentially Exempt Transfers (PETs),
    214–215
  quick succession relief, 218–219
  singles, strategies for, 217
  woodland as exempt asset, 212
re-evaluating the estate, 180
reference number, 177
registering a death
  coroner, deaths involving the, 147–148
  death certificate, 147
  disposal certificate, 147
  documents for, 146–147
  informant, who can act as, 146
  overview, 145–146
  in Scotland, 148
  who is eligible for, 146
regular income left to beneficiaries, 54
relatives. See family
remains, arrangements for your, 30
renounces, when an executor, 80
rental yield, 38
repossession of house, 63–64
residential care, avoiding having family home
  sold to pay for, 246

residuary estate
  distribution of the estate, 194
  overview, 58, 59
  writing in will how to handle, 98–99
residuary gifts, 98
retired, changing your will when you've
  become, 126
revocable trusts
  changing, 249
  overview, 228
revocation clause, 95
revoking and writing a new will, 248
richer, changing your will when you've
  become, 125
rules for writing your will, 95–97

• S •

safekeeping of your will, 91
SAIF (Society of Allied and Independent Funeral
  Directors), 150
same-sex civil partner
  dying at same time as your, 108
  intestacy and, 29
sample wills
  simple will, 284–285
  standard will, 283–284
  will with a discretionary trust, 285–286
savings, calculating the value of your, 42
Scotland
  beneficiaries, when you die at the same time
    as your, 109
  changing a will, 121
  children as beneficiaries, 32
  common property, 67
  confirmation, 171–173
  disputing your will, 52
  Form of Docket, 189
  grandchildren as beneficiaries, 32
  intestacy in, 30–33
  laws governing creation of wills in, 11
  legal rights to estate, 31
  moveable assets, 31
  no spouse, who inherits when there is, 32–33
  nursing homes in, 73
  plenishings, spouse having right to, 31
  power of attorney, 116
  prior rights, 30–31
  property, transferring, 189
  registering a death, 148
  spouse as beneficiary when there
    is no will, 30–31

• *T* •

Notes

FOR DUMMIES®

Do Anything. Just Add Dummies

UK editions

978-0-470-51291-3

978-0-470-03135-3

978-0-470-51501-3

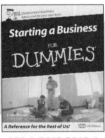
978-0-7645-7018-6

978-0-7645-7056-8

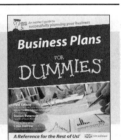
978-0-7645-7026-1

978-0-7645-7023-0

978-0-470-51510-5

978-0-470-05815-2

Answering Tough Interview
Questions For Dummies
(978-0-470-01903-0)

Being the Best Man
For Dummies
(978-0-470-02657-1)

British History
For Dummies
(978-0-470-03536-8)

Buying a Home on a Budget
For Dummies
(978-0-7645-7035-3)

Buying a Property in Spain
For Dummies
(978-0-470-51235-77)

Buying & Selling a Home For
Dummies
(978-0-7645-7027-8)

Buying a Property in Eastern
Europe For Dummies
(978-0-7645-7047-6)

Cognitive Behavioural Therapy
For Dummies
(978-0-470-01838-5)

Cricket For Dummies
(978-0-470-03454-5)

CVs For Dummies
(978-0-7645-7017-9)

Detox For Dummies
(978-0-470-01908-5)

Diabetes For Dummies
(978-0-470-05810-7)

Divorce For Dummies
(978-0-7645-7030-8)

DJing For Dummies
(978-0-470-03275-6)

eBay.co.uk For Dummies
(978-0-7645-7059-9)

Economics For Dummies
(978-0-470-05795-7)

English Grammar For Dummies
(978-0-470-05752-0)

Gardening For Dummies
(978-0-470-01843-9)

Genealogy Online
For Dummies
(978-0-7645-7061-2)

Green Living For Dummies
(978-0-470-06038-4)

Hypnotherapy For Dummies
(978-0-470-01930-6)

Neuro-linguistic Programming
For Dummies
(978-0-7645-7028-5)

Parenting For Dummies
(978-0-470-02714-1)

Pregnancy For Dummies
(978-0-7645-7042-1)

Renting out your Property
For Dummies
(978-0-470-02921-3)

Retiring Wealthy For Dummies
(978-0-470-02632-8)

Self Build and Renovation
For Dummies
(978-0-470-02586-4)

Selling For Dummies
(978-0-470-51259-3)

Sorting Out Your Finances
For Dummies
(978-0-7645-7039-1)

Starting a Business on
eBay.co.uk For Dummies
(978-0-470-02666-3)

Starting and Running an Online
Business For Dummies
(978-0-470-05768-1)

The Romans For Dummies
(978-0-470-03077-6)

UK Law and Your Rights
For Dummies
(978-0-470-02796-7)

Writing a Novel & Getting
Published For Dummies
(978-0-470-05910-4)

FOR DUMMIES®

Do Anything. Just Add Dummies

HOBBIES

Poker
978-0-7645-5232-8

Knitting
978-0-7645-5395-0

Drawing
978-0-7645-5476-6

Also available:

Art For Dummies
(978-0-7645-5104-8)

Aromatherapy For Dummies
(978-0-7645-5171-0)

Bridge For Dummies
(978-0-471-92426-5)

Card Games For Dummies
(978-0-7645-9910-1)

Chess For Dummies
(978-0-7645-8404-6)

Improving Your Memory
For Dummies
(978-0-7645-5435-3)

Massage For Dummies
(978-0-7645-5172-7)

Meditation For Dummies
(978-0-471-77774-8)

Photography For Dummies
(978-0-7645-4116-2)

Quilting For Dummies
(978-0-7645-9799-2)

EDUCATION

Psychology
978-0-7645-5434-6

The Koran
978-0-7645-5581-7

Anatomy & Physiology
978-0-7645-5422-3

Also available:

Algebra For Dummies
(978-0-7645-5325-7)

Astronomy For Dummies
(978-0-7645-8465-7)

Buddhism For Dummies
(978-0-7645-5359-2)

Calculus For Dummies
(978-0-7645-2498-1)

Cooking Basics For Dummies
(978-0-7645-7206-7)

Forensics For Dummies
(978-0-7645-5580-0)

Islam For Dummies
(978-0-7645-5503-9)

Philosophy For Dummies
(978-0-7645-5153-6)

Religion For Dummies
(978-0-7645-5264-9)

Trigonometry For Dummies
(978-0-7645-6903-6)

PETS

Puppies
978-0-470-03717-1

Dog Training
978-0-7645-8418-3

Cats
978-0-7645-5275-5

Also available:

Aquariums For Dummies
(978-0-7645-5156-7)

Birds For Dummies
(978-0-7645-5139-0)

Dogs For Dummies
(978-0-7645-5274-8)

Ferrets For Dummies
(978-0-7645-5259-5)

Golden Retrievers
For Dummies
(978-0-7645-5267-0)

Horses For Dummies
(978-0-7645-9797-8)

Jack Russell Terriers
For Dummies
(978-0-7645-5268-7)

Labrador Retrievers
For Dummies
(978-0-7645-5281-6)

Puppies Raising & Training
Diary For Dummies
(978-0-7645-0876-9)

Available wherever books are sold. For more information or to order direct go to www.wiley.com or call 0800 243407 (Non UK call +44 1243 843296)

FOR DUMMIES®

The easy way to get more done and have more fun

LANGUAGES

Speak Spanish — the fun and easy way!

Spanish FOR DUMMIES

A Reference for the Rest of Us!

978-0-7645-5193-2

Speak French — the fun and easy way!

French FOR DUMMIES

A Reference for the Rest of Us!

978-0-7645-5193-2

Start speaking Italian

Italian FOR DUMMIES

A Reference for the Rest of Us!

978-0-7645-5196-3

Also available:

Chinese For Dummies
(978-0-471-78897-3)
Chinese Phrases
For Dummies
(978-0-7645-8477-0)
French Phrases For Dummies
(978-0-7645-7202-9)
German For Dummies
(978-0-7645-5195-6)
Hebrew For Dummies
(978-0-7645-5489-6)

Italian Phrases For Dummies
(978-0-7645-7203-6)
Japanese For Dummies
(978-0-7645-5429-2)
Latin For Dummies
(978-0-7645-5431-5)
Spanish Phrases
For Dummies
(978-0-7645-7204-3)
Spanish Verbs For Dummies
(978-0-471-76872-2)

MUSIC AND FILM

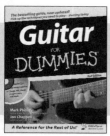

Guitar FOR DUMMIES

2nd Edition

Mark Phillips
Jon Chappell

A Reference for the Rest of Us!

978-0-7645-9904-0

Filmmaking FOR DUMMIES

A Reference for the Rest of Us!

978-0-7645-2476-9

Play-along audio CD included!

Piano FOR DUMMIES

A Reference for the Rest of Us!

978-0-7645-5105-5

Also available:

Bass Guitar For Dummies
(978-0-7645-2487-5)
Blues For Dummies
(978-0-7645-5080-5)
Classical Music For Dummies
(978-0-7645-5009-6)
Drums For Dummies
(978-0-471-79411-0)
Jazz For Dummies
(978-0-471-76844-9)

Opera For Dummies
(978-0-7645-5010-2)
Rock Guitar For Dummies
(978-0-7645-5356-1)
Screenwriting For Dummies
(978-0-7645-5486-5)
Singing For Dummies
(978-0-7645-2475-2)
Songwriting For Dummies
(978-0-7645-5404-9)

HEALTH, SPORTS & FITNESS

Fitness FOR DUMMIES

3rd Edition

A Reference for the Rest of Us!

978-0-7645-7851-9

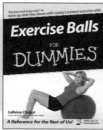

Exercise Balls FOR DUMMIES

LaReine Chabut

A Reference for the Rest of Us!

978-0-7645-5623-4

Asthma FOR DUMMIES

William E. Berger, MD, MBA

A Reference for the Rest of Us!

978-0-7645-4233-6

Also available:

Controlling Cholesterol
For Dummies
(978-0-7645-5440-7)
Diabetes For Dummies
(978-0-470-05810-7)
High Blood Pressure
For Dummies
(978-0-7645-5424-7)
Martial Arts For Dummies
(978-0-7645-5358-5)

Menopause FD
(978-0-470-061008)
Pilates For Dummies
(978-0-7645-5397-4)
Weight Training
For Dummies
(978-0-471-76845-6)
Yoga For Dummies
(978-0-7645-5117-8)

FOR
DUMMIES®

Helping you expand your horizons and achieve your potential

INTERNET

978-0-470-12174-0

978-0-471-97998-2

978-0-470-08030-6

Also available:

Blogging For Dummies
For Dummies, 2nd Edition
(978-0-470-23017-6)

Building a Web Site For
Dummies, 3rd Edition
(978-0-470-14928-7)

Creating Web Pages
All-in-One Desk Reference
For Dummies, 3rd Edition
(978-0-470-09629-1)

eBay.co.uk
For Dummies
(978-0-7645-7059-9)

Video Blogging FD
(978-0-471-97177-1)

Web Analysis For Dummies
(978-0-470-09824-0)

Web Design For Dummies,
2nd Edition
(978-0-471-78117-2)

DIGITAL MEDIA

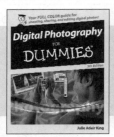

978-0-7645-9802-9

978-0-470-17474-6

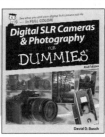

978-0-470-14927-0

Also available:

BlackBerry For Dummies,
2nd Edition
(978-0-470-18079-2)

Digital Photography
All-in-One Desk Reference
For Dummies, 3rd Edition
(978-0-470-03743-0)

Digital Photo Projects
For Dummies
(978-0-470-12101-6)

iPhone For Dummies
(978-0-470-17469-2)

Photoshop CS3 For Dummies
(978-0-470-11193-2)

Podcasting For Dummies
(978-0-471-74898-4)

COMPUTER BASICS

978-0-470-13728-4

978-0-470-05432-1

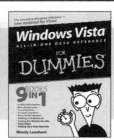

978-0-471-74941-7

Also available:

Macs For Dummies,
9th Edition
(978-0-470-04849-8)

Office 2007 All-in-One Desk
Reference For Dummies
(978-0-471-78279-7)

PCs All-in-One Desk
Reference For Dummies,
4th Edition
(978-0-470-22338-3)

Upgrading & Fixing PCs
For Dummies, 7th Edition
(978-0-470-12102-3)

Windows XP For Dummies,
2nd Edition
(978-0-7645-7326-2)